Refractory Men,
Fanatical Women

Refractory Men, Fanatical Women

Fidelity to conscience during the French Revolution

Edwin Bannon

First published in 1992
Gracewing
Fowler Wright Books
Southern Ave, Leominster
Herefordshire HR6 0QF

Gracewing Books are distributed

In New Zealand by
Catholic Supplies Ltd
80 Adelaide Rd
Wellington
New Zealand

In Australia by
Charles Paine Pty
8 Ferris Street
North Parramatta
NSW 2151 Australia

In Canada by
Novalis
P.O. Box 900
Outremont H2V 457
Canada

In USA by
Morehouse Publishing
P.O. Box 1321
Harrisburg
PA 17105
U. S. A.

© Edwin Bannon

Typesetting by Action Typesetting Ltd, Gloucester.

Printed and bound in Great Britain by Cromwell Press Ltd, Melksham

ISBN 0 85244 226 2

CONTENTS

PREFACE vii
PRELUDE: The Lighted Fuse (1789-1792)
  1789 1
  1790 8
  1791 20
  1792 24

PART I.
THE SEPTEMBER MASSACRES (1792)

1. The Round-up of the Refractories 29
2. At the Abbaye 43
3. At the Carmes 53
4. At Saint-Firmin and La Force 66

INTERLUDE: A Context of Terror (1792-1794) 77

PART II.
THE VIRGIN MARTYRS (1793-1794)

5. The Rue de Grenelle Contemplatives 85
6. Monsieur Vincent's Daughters of Charity 105
7. The Martyrs of Orange 119
8. Carmelite Dialogues 135

PART III
DROWNINGS AND DEPORTATIONS (1793-1795)

9. The Calotins' Drink 163
10. The Convict Ships 177

POSTLUDE: The Roll of Honour 199

CODA: 207

To the countless Lasallian confreres, living and dead, whom I have had the privilege of knowing during many years of happy religious life.

PREFACE

September 2nd 1992 will inaugurate a series of bicentenaries of the martyrdoms of priests and members of religious congregations, killed in hatred of the Catholic faith during the French Revolution. Their stories have been abundantly recorded in French publications: never in my experience has the expression 'l'embarras du choix' been more apt to the purpose. But in English there is next to nothing, even in translation from the French. An occasional but extremely rare monograph (I have found only one, but that may be because it concerns a member of my own congregation - it will be mentioned in the course of my account), a paragraph, or a sentence, in one or other English study of the Revolution, but nothing more.

A bicentenary seemed an appropriate occasion for an attempt to fill the gap, for these were men and women whose fidelity to their conscience and to their vocation has potent inspiration for the Church today. All the sources listed in my bibliography (and many others) are on the shelves of the library, or in the archives, of the Rome generalate where I work, and their immediate accessibility was a hardly resistible encouragement to attempt the task. But although the research has been painstaking my account is offered to a general readership, not as an original contribution to the historiography of the Revolution. Specialists, and even general students of modern French history, will be already more than familiar with the limited information about the Revolution which I have needed to include in order to provide the backdrop for the drama which is the principal concern of these pages. Any originality that may be claimed is to have made known to English- speaking readers for the first time an episode of Church history which can hardly fail to stir our admiration for the priestly and religious way of life. The de-Christianisers of the French Revolution knew that to achieve their objective they must either win the priests and religious to their side or destroy them. I have aimed in the following pages to give an objective account, not judgmental of the persecutors, non-adulatory of the persecuted, of how they went about their impossible task.

E.B.

PRELUDE: THE LIGHTED FUSE

1789

The influences and events which led to the assembling of the States General on May 5, 1789, were harbingers of the Revolution which a shrewd observer of the world about him, Restif de la Bretonne, had predicted a decade before. The ever-widening gap between the aristocracy and the working-classes, the diffusion of the rationalist philosophy of the Encyclopedists, and the industrial and financial crises, exacerbated by the shady dealings of the latter-day tax-gatherers known as the *fermiers généraux*, all left the indecisive monarch, Louis XVI, no option but to issue the summons of August 8, 1788.

The convoking of elected members of the three social orders of the nation, the Clergy, the Nobles and the "Rest", known as the Third Estate, as a consultative body, was a device instituted by Philip IV in 1302. The intention was that the measure be used only in cases of extraordinary emergency, and it had not in fact been invoked since 1614, when Louis XVI, urged by his advisers, now had recourse to it 174 years later. But by then Rousseau's *The Social Contract* had made the institution an anachronism, and when the delegates finally assembled, with due pomp and circumstance, at Versailles on Tuesday, May 5, it was (as not a few of them must have realised) to prepare for death. It was also (but rather fewer would have opined or, certainly, intended this) to ignite the fuse which led to the explosion of violence, three years later, against the Catholic Church and its most visible representatives.

1

The agenda, stated in simplistic terms, was to redress the wrongs outlined in the lists of grievances which the electors of the various regions had been authorised, or rather invited, to present to their delegates. Some 60,000 of these *cahiers de doléances* have survived and are an invaluable source of information about the social condition of France on the eve of the Revolution. They highlighted the urgently-felt need for reform in many areas, including the privileges enjoyed by the clergy and the absolutism of the monarchy; but, says André Latreille, "almost unanimously the people paid homage (in the lists) to the Catholic, Apostolic and Roman religion and, far from being critical of its dominance, recognised the unity of faith and worship as one of the unchallengeable traditions of the kingdom". Likewise, according to another more recent authority, Michel Vovelle, the lists manifest a universal reaffirmation of loyalty to the monarchy as such. But the agenda placed before any deciding assembly becomes a hostage to the fortune of the personalities of those who will debate it, and the 1139 delegates elected to the 1789 States General included men of intellect, eloquence and will-power capable of changing the course of history.

Tensions emerged from the start. Of the elected deputies 291 belonged to the first order, the clergy, 270 to the nobility and 578 to the *tiers état*, the commoners. The last-named, therefore, were slightly stronger numerically than the clergy and nobility combined; but their votes were worth only half of those of the two upper classes. The *tiers état* proposed that the votes be counted by heads, and when this was refused by the other two orders they declared themselves unilaterally a national assembly. The king sent the master of ceremonies, the Marquis de Dreux-Brézé, to order them to return to the room that had been allocated to them so that matters could proceed in the proper manner. Honoré-Gabriel Mirabeau, an aristocrat by birth but elected by Aix-Marseilles as a third estate delegate, answered the summons in terms which manifested an early challenge to royal authority: "Go back and tell your master," he said, "that we are here by the will of the people, and only bayonets will remove us!"

The argumentation which led to this unilateral declaration had lasted into the beginning of June and throughout it was evident that no mere compromise solution would be forthcoming. Moreover of the 291 elected clergy 208 were of "inferior" (non-prelatial) rank — parish priests and curates largely from rural areas — and many of these were in sympathy with the commoners who represented the interests of their own parish flocks. It was one of the clergy delegates, the Abbé Sieyès ("the mole of the Revolution" Robespierre was to call him, thereby exemplifying an early use of a term which has become household in our own time) who had prepared the way for the amalgamation of the three orders with a pamphlet entitled *What is the Third Estate? Nothing. What should it be? Everything*! Just over half of the lower clergy, in fact, now declared themselves in solidarity with the *Tiers*. Accepting the inevitable, and concerned to defend their rights from within, a group of 47 nobles, led by Stanislas Clermont-Tonnerre, also joined the self-constituted national assembly. The king, yielding to a current of history he could not stem, asked the rest of the clergy and nobles to unite with the breakaway group. "Ah," said J.S.Bailly, the group's elected president, when the reluctant remnant arrived, "now the family is complete!" A few days later, July 9, a new title, the Constituent Assembly, was adopted, with the implicit assumption of responsibility for providing the country with a new Constitution.

While all this was taking place in Versailles the people of Paris, twenty kilometres away (but also throughout the country as a whole), were growing increasingly restless with the economic conditions and on July 14 occurred the storming of the Bastille prison, an event which historians have interpreted in multiple ways but which symbolises more than any other the passing of the Ancien Régime. "Is it a riot?" said Louis XVI when he was awakened by a courtier to be told the news. "No, Sire," was the reply, "it's a revolution."

During the week of August 4-11 the clergy and nobles offered, under the prompting of the Duke de Noailles, to make a sacrifice of their privileges for the good of the nation and, specifically, for the alleviation of the financial crisis. In the case of the clergy this meant the abolition of the tithes and their diversion to the public treasury — a measure which the clergy deputies accepted in a spirit of solidarity with the revolutionary aspirations.

The decree of August 11 which ratified the abolition, to become operable as from January 1, 1791, included the clause that the government would assume responsibility for "providing the means for divine worship, for the subsistence of its ministers, for the charitable assistance of the poor, and for the repair and maintenance of the properties", all of these being the purposes to which the tithes had been put. The decree signalled the demise of feudalism, and the mood of the moment was expressed in the proposal of the Archbishop of Paris, Mgr. de Juigne, that a Te Deum be sung in the royal chapel in the presence of the King and of the entire national assembly. But when the exuberance had subsided there was a dawning realisation that the pastoral clergy would suffer a metamorphosis which would cancel the traditional relationship between priests and people developed over centuries. From being a territorial proprietor with an assured income for the works of corporal and spiritual mercy exercised in proportion to his personal holiness and apostolic zeal, the parish priest would become a transitory civil servant, a functionary in receipt of a state subsistence allowance.

The new Constitution, for the formulation of which the Constituent Assembly had, by definition, assumed responsibility, was not to be unveiled until mid-September 1791, but already influential voices were being raised in favour of a declaration of human rights as a foundation document. The text of such a declaration was the subject of debate in the Assembly for five weeks, from July 11 to August 17. An excellent guide to this debate and its end-product is provided by Pierre Pierrard and it is his discussion mainly that we follow here. Seven different drafts, varying from 71 articles to 13, were successively considered and wholly or partially rejected. On August 20th the deputies (almost 1200 of them) growing more and more impatient with the failure of commissions and individuals to produce a result, decided to seek a formulation in plenary assembly, and within six days, by what a senior historian of the Revolution, Alphonse Aulard, calls a kind of "miracle", produced the elegantly worded text in 17 articles which was promulgated on August 26, 1789. It bore the marks of Rousseau's influence, and also that of Montesquieu's *L'Esprit des Lois*, and although historians have praised its self-evident positive values there is a substantial recognition also that it was a flawed document, containing no balance of the duties alongside the rights of man and conceding nothing to the rights of man's Creator. The sentence that concludes the preamble, "The National Assembly acknowledges and declares, in the presence and under the auspices of the Supreme Being, the following rights of man and of the citizen ..." was added to the original text only after an intervention of the Abbé Henri Baptiste Grégoire, supported by a sufficient number of other delegates. And even so, the word "God", which was embedded in the corporate consciousness of the French people almost from the beginnings of Christianity, was studiously avoided in favour of the term "Supreme Being", the pagan cult of which was to be later, on June 8, 1794, translated into a bogus, face-saving liturgy by Maximilien Robespierre.

But the Declaration promised more than the Constitution to which it was to be the preamble would deliver. As Louis Madelin has expressed it: "All men are born equal and must have equal rights – that is the Declaration; but they won't – that is the Constitution. It would have been wiser to heed Malouet (a royalist member of the Assembly) and not lead people to the top of the mountain and show them the Promised Land and then deny it to them ..." The debate on August 23 which led to the formulation of article 10 ("No one may be harassed because of his opinions, even his religious ones") was naturally, as Pierre Pierrard points out, of special interest to the clergy deputies who had been generally reticent, if acquiescent, during the previous deliberations. Religious liberty, yes, but ought there not to be an amendment naming the Catholic religion as that of the State? But Mirabeau argued against any allusion in the text to an adherence to a particular cult, and his eloquence won the day.

Article 11 also aroused concern among the clergy: "The free communication of thoughts and opinions is one of the most precious rights of man; every citizen may therefore say, write and publish freely whatever he chooses, subject to having to answer for any abuse of this liberty in cases determined by the law ... " The main protagonist this time was Robespierre who declared: "You must not waver in making a frank declaration of the freedom of the press. It is only despotic government that has invented restrictions and thereby succeeded in diminishing all other rights." The anxiety voiced by the Bishop of Amiens about "the danger that unlimited freedom of the press represents for religion and morality, religion having already suffered much from published attacks" was supported by several priests, but the opposition in general, even among the clerical deputies, was low-key. The qualifying clause of the article was, it seemed, a sufficient safeguard against the abuse of what, in itself, was a self-evident desideratum.

A net effect of the Declaration was to abrogate the privileged status which the Gallican Church had hitherto enjoyed. But a reflection of the doyen-historian of the Revolution's impact on the Church, Pierre de La Gorce, is apposite at this point:

> Need we lament the loss of those honours which time had heaped on the religion of Christ? The accumulation of perishable dignities was often no more than a dead weight encumbering souls in their journey to God. We shall see the clergy of France deprived of their patrimony, the religious congregations mutilated, ecclesiastical discipline undermined, and even the essentials of faith attacked. But in the wake of a Church unprivileged and deprived came the suffering, militant and persecuted Church which would redeem the lukewarmness and weaknesses of the past and deserve by expiation to live anew.

What La Gorce calls the process of secularisation now began in earnest. On September 28, almost exactly a month after the vote approving the Declaration, the clergy, still concerned to maintain solidarity with the national well-being, consented to the surrender of ecclesiastical gold and silverware "superfluous to the needs of divine worship", so that this could be converted by the Mint into currency. It was a substantial contribution to the Treasury (estimated at eighty million livres) but far from sufficient to transform the massive national deficit into assets. However, there were still other resources held by the Church which might be able to perform that particular miracle, and it fell to a Catholic prelate to focus the Assembly's attention on this way out of the dilemma. On October 10, Charles Maurice de Talleyrand-Périgord, Bishop of Autun, proposed the motion that all ecclesiastical benefices and real estate be placed "at the disposal of the Nation". He argued that the clergy were not proprietors in the same sense as were individual landlords. The properties at their disposal had been bequeathed or donated, not for the personal benefit of the recipients but for the fulfilment of services to be rendered by these. Provided therefore that the State (as already agreed with regard to the tithes) guaranteed to each titular the due means of subsistence and assumed responsibility for the services for which the benefices and donations had been instituted, the intentions of the benefactors would be respected and the clergy concerned could have no grounds for complaint. The case was persuasively argued, and if it was far from being self-evidently convincing, the prelate's clinching statement that the sale of the properties thus taken over could well realise three thousand million livres made the prospect irresistible, and a sizeable majority of the deputies (568 out of the 954 present on November 2) voted the measure through.

It was confiscation despite the rhetoric and pseudo-logic of Talleyrand and his seconders (notably Mirabeau and Joseph Barnave), and the decree of November 13, applying the vote of the Assembly, was unapologetic and peremptory. Georges Rigault cites a passage from the text conserved in the National Archives:

> All holders of benefices of any kind, and all superiors of ecclesiastical residences and establishments, without exception, are required, within two months at the latest of the publication of this decree, to appear before the royal magistrates and present a detailed declaration, written on plain paper, of all holdings, moveable and immoveable, appertaining to the said

benefices, residences and establishments, together with their revenues, and to furnish within the same period a detailed statement of such services as are entailed by them.

The process thus launched of inventorying "the nationalised ecclesiastical possessions" was the least complex of the operations needed to put the resources at the service of the Revolution, a topic which at this point engages the attention of the historians. Michel Vovelle offers a particularly concise and lucid analysis of the problems caused by "a succession of unforeseen circumstances" But the economics of the situation, with the ambivalent role of the paper money which gave a new word — "assignat" — to the French language, need not concern us here. It is Professor Vovelle's conclusion that belongs to our outline survey, namely that in the religious sphere the nationalisation of the Church's holdings "was a turning-point in the history of the Revolution, which involved a complete reconsideration of the place of the clergy in French society."

The surprising thing (surprising, at any rate, with hindsight) is that the clergy remained generally acquiescent. The Assembly, in fact, was careful at this stage to avoid seeming anti-religious. Courtesy, and even deference, was the characteristic mark of the non-clerical members' attitude to their reverend colleagues. The Archbishop of Aix, Jean de Dieu de Boisgelin, who in the debate on the ecclesiastical holdings had propounded the view that nationalisation was here only a polite word for plunder, and who had given warning about the immense difficulties the spoliation would entail, was nevertheless elected president of the Assembly on November 23.

1790

But the new year had not advanced very far when bolder measures, without the excuse of national needs, began to show that the de-Christianisation of French society was the object in view for a powerful element in the Assembly. Already on December 17, Jean Baptiste Treilhard, a lawyer who had been elected to the States General by the city of

Paris and had been a prime mover for the amalgamation of the three orders into a single Assembly, presented a report which purported to "rectify" (as befitted an assembly holding the responsibility for a new Constitution) "an ancient abuse" – the recognition by the civil power of vows pronounced in religious monasteries and convents. Such interference by lay authority in matters of religion was not acceptable, argued Treilhard with an impressive command of weasel-words. Every member of a religious congregation, male or female, must henceforth be free to renounce the engagements taken and leave his or her community. Moreover it should henceforth be illegal to pronounce religious vows, such things being incompatible with liberty. Hence, also, there should be no further admission of postulants. Male religious already with vows, who opted to remain so bound, would be allowed to continue, but if their reduced numbers warranted it, they would be grouped together in fewer houses. Nuns would be allowed (even with reduced numbers) to continue where they were, and those who were engaged in education or other charitable works, would be exempted from the new regulations until further notice.

Treilhard's colleagues on the Assembly's committee for matters relating to the Church thought that these measures were too drastic to introduce in December – so soon after the nationalisation of the Church property – but their spokesman, "a lawyer of wide erudition and a tireless worker", as Pierre de La Gorce calls him, returned to the question in February of the new year. His proposals, slightly modified, became law on the 13th of that month. Mgr. La Fare, Bishop of Nancy, understood what was happening and his bold observations to the Assembly have been much quoted:

> Far be it from me to believe that your intention is to bring about the destruction of religion, but you must agree that what you have done here today is the right way to go about such a purpose. I appeal to the Assembly to take heed of the grievance lists and to implement the corporate wish expressed therein that the Catholic, Apostolic and Roman religion remain, and be declared to remain, the religion of the State.

But the intervention was brushed aside, a speaker of the left asking La Fare if he wanted "to arm fanaticism in order to protect its abuses". It was specified that municipal officials would visit monasteries and convents to ascertain the individual choice of each member of the community. Those who opted to leave would receive a pension; for those who remained the community would receive a subsistence allowance.

Archive records show that the application of this decree was less provocative than might have been expected. The ordinary people were not directly disadvantaged by it: they still had their parish clergy for their spiritual needs and the hospitals and schools conducted by religious remained, so far, at their service. The officials entrusted with the visitation of the communities were generally courteous in their procedures, and even recorded, in some cases, their admiration for the religious who opted to remain faithful to their vows. The majority of these were nuns; men withdrew in greater numbers and when the "amalgamation" clause was implemented for these (with more regard for the mutual proximity of buildings than for the identity of rules) the exodus was accelerated.

Two months after Mgr. La Fare's courageous but ineffective intervention another voice was raised in the Assembly in a bid to check the developing movement. This time it was a member of the ecclesiastical committee itself which, in the person of J.B. Treilhard, had gained the vote of February 13. This was Dom Christopher Gerle, a Carthusian monk, at one time held in high esteem in his Order but turning eventually into a politician. He was, says La Gorce, "a man of piety bordering on mysticism, but one easily taken in by fine words who had been drawn to the Revolution as to a glittering dream". At a meeting of the Assembly in April 1790 a speaker on the right, François de Montesquiou-Fezensac, had pointed out the absurdity of an ecclesiastical committee self-evidently hostile to religion. It was Dom Gerle who stood up to defend the committee of which he was a member. "No," he said, "there is no prejudice in this committee; it is a slander to say that we are opposed to religion." And then, as if to prove his point, he called upon his fellow-members to move a decree, there and then, that the Catholic, Apostolic and Roman religion was, and would ever remain, the religion of the nation.

The proposal took both sides of the chamber by surprise, but the clergy deputies were the first to react. The debates on the nationalisation of the Church properties and on the suppression of religious vows had left them more or less wordless, the first because they might have seemed to be fighting their own financial corner, the second because the religious life as such, especially the "non-active" forms of it (reputedly less than fervent in many places) failed to arouse their corporate wrath. But a proposal favouring the inviolability of the Catholic religion, coming from within the powerful ecclesiastical committee itself, was an unexpected call to action. Dom Gerle's challenge was greeted with loud acclamations intended to carry the motion under the impact of surprise. But the left had already sufficiently recovered to propose and obtain an adjournment. During this interval discussion went on in the cafés and so-called clubs, and when the proposal came up for voting on April 13, a liberal-minded aristocrat, of the La Rochefoucauld family, pre-empted discussion by proposing a change of agenda, formulating the motion in these terms:

> The National Assembly, considering that it neither has, nor can have, any power to encroach on conscience and religious opinion, that the majesty of religion and the respect which is due to it do not allow of its becoming a subject of deliberation, that the attachment of the National Assembly to Catholic, Apostolic and Roman worship cannot be called into doubt at the very moment when this cult is about to be given priority in public spending, hereby decrees that it neither can, nor should, debate the motion proposed.

Consternation on the right! "Just so," shouted Jean Jacques Duval d'Eprémesnil, a dyed-in-the-wool conservative, noted for his verbal shots aimed at the extremists across the chamber, "just so did those who were going to crucify Jesus Christ begin by paying Him homage!" "A national apostasy!" said the Bishop of Uzès, Mgr. Béthisy de Mézières, who forthwith drew up a protest for which he gained the signatures of 295 deputies. But it was not enough, and at 4.00 p.m. La Rochefoucauld's motion was carried. "It may be said," observes André Latreille, "that on this day the division between the self-styled 'patriots' and the representatives of the Gallican Church became public and also manifestly wider."

But the breaking-point – the schism – was still to come. The ecclesiastical committee, still pursuing its purpose as the body responsible for reforming specified abuses listed in the *cahiers de doléance*, now addressed the task of providing for the future status of the Church in the Constitution in process of being formulated. Already, the previous November, one of its members (and its future historian) Durand de Maillane, had submitted a project which, says La Gorce, envisaged nothing less than a total reorganisation of the French Church. The committee included two prelates, the bishops of Clermont and of Luçon, and these had rallied the support of seven of the other thirteen members to block De Maillane's project and a stalemate lasted throughout December and January. The way-out was a hardly disguised subterfuge. The ever-busy Treilhard presented to the meeting of February 5 a complaint that the work of the ecclesiastical committee had become too onerous for a membership of only fifteen. His proposal that the number be doubled was accepted by a majority and the appropriate candidates were duly elected. Durand de Maillane comments in his history of the proceedings of the ecclesiastical committee: "Henceforth the Committee was in a position to get on with its work." It did so to such effect that, although the debate was hard-fought and a few amendments were gained, a decree establishing the Civil Constitution of the Clergy, by and large as conceived by De Maillane but introduced by another member called Martineau, was voted on July 12, 1790.

The lengthy bill detailing the Civil Constitution was divided into four sections. The first of these envisaged the limitation of ecclesiastical offices. Only those of clerics having a direct responsibility for the care of souls were to be retained. Cathedral and collegiate chapters were to be abolished and only bishops, parish priests and curates were to be eligible for stipendiary office. But these three categories would be re-distributed: the existing 135 episcopal sees, with widely diverse numerical populations, would be reduced to 85, these corresponding to the geographical departments. The 18 existing archdioceses were to be replaced by 10 metropolitan sees. Towns having fewer than 6000 inhabitants would have only one parish; those having more than that total, and also country districts, would have their parishes re-grouped according to strict need.

The second section dealt with appointments to the recognised offices. Bishops would be elected by the citizens of a *département* who were eligible to vote, that is tax-payers of a certain category, regardless of whether they were Catholics or not. The corresponding citizens ("active" as they were called) of a parochial district would elect the parish priest. Bishops would choose their Vicars, parish priests their curates. But the bishop would be unable to remove a vicar from office without the majority assent of the body of vicars forming the episcopal council; nor would the parish priest be free to dismiss a curate except for a reason judged valid by the bishop with the approval of his council. The parish priest would be canonically instituted by his bishop, and the bishop by his metropolitan. But a newly consecrated bishop was not to apply to the Pope for the ratification of his appointment; he would merely inform the Holy See by letter "in testimony of the unity of faith and communion that must be maintained with it".

The bill next dealt with the annual payments to be made to the incumbents of the three categories of pastoral office. Metropolitan bishops would receive 20,000 livres and other bishops 12,000; episcopal vicars would receive from 2000 to 8000 according to the population of their administrative areas; parish priests qualified for 1,200 and curates for 700. Payments would be made quarterly in silver. And henceforth all services would be rendered gratuitously by the incumbents: collections and stole fees were to be abolished and any offerings the faithful insisted on giving would be deposited in a box for subsequent distribution to the poor.

Finally the decree, responding here to repeated complaints

in the *cahiers*, legislated for the duty of residence: pastors of whatever rank who absented themselves from their place of residence without good reason would be penalised by loss of pay.

Such, in outline, was the new charter for the Church — One, Apostolic and Roman — in France, and the most conspicuous feature of it was the absence of any recognition of the authority of the visible head of that Church. The powerful orators who pushed the bill through to the majority vote of July 12 claimed that the guiding motive of all that was proposed was to purify the Church, not to change it. The leading spokesman for the opponents of the decree, Archbishop Boisgelin, whose tendency throughout this and other debates of the Assembly was to conciliate rather than to precipitate the schism he feared and foresaw, argued that the envisaged purification was a matter for the Church itself: let an ecclesiastical council be convoked, he said, which would propose the needed reforms and obtain their sanction from the Pope. But to this idea Armand-Gaston Camus, a diehard Jansenist (who, says Louis Madelin, harboured a smouldering resentment against the papacy because of Clement XI's bull "Unigenitus") replied: "What is the Pope? He is a bishop, a minister of Jesus Christ like other bishops, and his authority is for the diocese of Rome." But, says the same historian, this was only scoring points. Camus and his colleagues were well aware that it would take more than the stroke of a pen to separate the Eldest Daughter of the Church from the visible representative of the Church's Founder. That was probably why (in the view of an earlier historian, Albert Mathiez, and other commentators) the final draft of the bill concluded with the sentence, "The King will be requested to take all measures deemed necessary to ensure the full and complete execution of this decree" — code language inviting Louis to negotiate the approval of Pius VI for the Constitution. It was a vain hope, if ever there was one, and not only because this clause was forthwith voted out by the Assembly.

For one thing, the king's own profoundly Catholic conscience resisted the implications of the decree. In theory his power of veto could have blocked its implementation and, no doubt, his instinct was to react thus. But even he was aware that his power of veto was gradually becoming a relic of the past and that an attempt to use it at this conjuncture would have been disastrous. Moreover his closest counsellors — among them two bishops, of Bordeaux and Vienne — advised against confronting the Assembly. Louis gave his approval to the Constitution on July 22. "His Majesty has done what his religion inspired him to do," commented Count Montmorin, Louis' minister for foreign affairs, in a letter to the French ambassador in Rome, meaning that the royal approval was an ineluctable choice against schism. But the king's conscience told him to the contrary and a sense of guilt was to haunt him until the day of his death by guillotine, two and a half years later.

Pope Pius VI did not pronounce on the Civil Constitution of the Clergy until eight months later — "eight interminable months", says André Latreille, though this French historian offsets the disapproving tone of his "interminable" by analysing the motivation for the delay (as does, even more persuasively, the British historian E.E.Y. Hales). One reason for the prolonged silence of Rome was the reluctance of the Pontiff to pronounce before the French hierarchy did so. It was, in fact, the episcopal members of the Constituent Assembly who, on October 30, 1790, published an *Exposition of the Principles concerning the Civil Constitution of the Clergy*. Jean Leflon cites Dom Henri Leclercq's assessment of this document:

> Under the obligation to protect their faith and that of the whole Church, the bishops assumed a combat role and, standing shoulder to shoulder, unerringly and unflinchingly defended the position, pending a decision of the Pope. Their inspiration was a dictum of Bossuet: "The bishops pronounce and then refer their judgment to Peter".

But the conciliatory influence of Mgr. de Boisgelin is present also in the Exposition, for it affirms the willingness of the bishops to re-establish the needed accord between the civil and ecclesiastical powers and thus ensure the peace of consciences and public calm. The overriding concern was to forestall "a deplorable rift".

Camus and Treilhard and their supporters were not impressed. The bishops' stance was answered a fortnight later (November 15) by a decree voted in the Assembly, the effect of which was to bring the appointment of bishops under the direct control of the civil authority. If the metropolitan refused to consecrate a candidate voted by the people, the candidate could apply successively to the other bishops of the metropolitan area. If all of these declined, the voted nominee could appeal for justice to the local magistrates' court which would give him right of possession and would appoint a consecrating prelate from anywhere.

Such drastic (and, it seems in retrospect, absurd) measures showed that the application of the Civil Constitution was running into trouble in the provinces and, compounding the messy situation, the Assembly produced, just twelve days after the decree of the 15th, what it intended to be the decisive measure. Every prelate, parish priest and other ecclesiastical functionary was to swear an oath "to be faithful to the Nation and to the King and to maintain with all their power the Constitution decreed by the National Assembly and accepted by the King". Any who refused to pronounce this oath would be deposed and, if they continued to exercise their functions they would be "prosecuted as disturbers of the public order".

A much-quoted elder historian of the Revolution's encounter with the Church, Albert Mathiez, succinctly assesses the effect of this new decree. The Constituent Assembly, he says, had wanted to create a national Church and use religion to consolidate the new order. What it did now was to shatter not only religious unity but also the unity of France which, like the Church, found itself split down the middle; so far from consolidating the new order, it put it at grave risk. "The result," he concludes, "was that a great number of priests who, up to that point, had been good servants of the Revolution, now perceived an obligation of conscience to set themselves in an opposition to it which they had not previously felt or foreseen. And this, in turn, meant that the aristocratic party had its ranks swelled by a formidable reinforcement of persons of troubled conscience. Instead of founding a State Church, the Constituent Assembly had only established a Church of a faction, but of a faction now in power, a church henceforth at grips with the old Church, that of the party provisionally in defeat."

As E.E.Y. Hales notes in another connection, Mathiez was capable of overstating a case, and the above assessment could be misleading if it were read to mean that the clergy now allied themselves with the aristocrats in an anti-revolutionary conspiracy. The clergy were not hostile to the Revolution but to what the de-Christianising powers were making of it, and their hostility took the form of passive resistance rather than of the plotting of which those same powers eventually and universally accused them and made an excuse for the persecution we are to read about. It was the clergy who had initiated the amalgamation of the three orders in the meeting of the States General, and their evident sympathy with the reforms the Revolution was capable of achieving had led to an attested saying that went the rounds in royalist circles during the early days of the upheaval: "It's the confounded clergy who started the Revolution!"

But Mathiez's judgment is on target in its assessment of what can happen when people's consciences are put at stake, and even historians who dwell on the positive aspects of the work of the Constituent Assembly concede that the Civil Constitution of the Clergy, compounded by the obligation of the oath, was its major blunder. But, comments Leflon, so far from attempting to repair the blunder, the Assembly let itself be drawn by it into a path which had to lead to legal and bloody persecution.

Once again, "the mediocre monarch" (Vovelle's expression), Louis XVI, pressurized not only by the Assembly but also by the ever-growing restlessness of the people, sanctioned the latest decree on December 26, and the terms of the decree required that forthwith the clergy members of the Assembly themselves should pronounce the oath within eight days of the royal approval. The first to do so, on the 26th itself, was the Abbé Henri Grégoire, a brilliant and complex character whose name recurs in all accounts of the Revolution. A tailor's son, born in 1750, he was a pupil of the Jesuit College at Nancy from the age of thirteen to eighteen, and retained to the end of his chequered career a deep sense of gratitude for his old teachers. His fierce antipathy to ultramontanism was matched by his dislike of Voltaire and Rousseau and the Philosophers, and this in turn was commensurate with his enthusiasm for Pascal, Bossuet and the Benedictine scripture scholar Augustine Calmet. Grégoire was elected to the States General by the clergy of Nancy and was active in most of the debates of the Assembly, often taking an independent and seemingly inconsistent stance (for example, he supported the abolition of clerical privileges and the tradition of the stole fees though he had argued strongly, but in vain, for the maintenance of the tithe; he likewise spoke out against the suppression of the monastic orders but was a participant, if a defensive one, in the elaboration of the Civil Constitution of the Clergy of which, however, he disapproved the final form). His lead in pronouncing the Constitutional oath on the day of its ratification was followed two months later by his acceptance of election as bishop of the *département* of Loir-et-Cher. He died on May 28, 1831, refusing to the end to retract his oath of 1790 but insisting on receiving the last sacraments from a fellow-constitutional bishop.

Gregoire prefaced his swearing of the oath with a carefully worded speech of which the keynote was struck in the sentence: "After the most mature and most serious reflection, we declare that we discern in the Constitution nothing that can wound the sacred truths which we must believe and teach." His speech was listened to with close attention and, at its conclusion, other clerical delegates — sixty-two according to the records — lined up to take the oath there and then; they included such notabilities as the Abbé Gouttes who, shortly before, had had his turn as President of the Assembly, the Abbé Dumonchel, Rector of the University of Paris, the Abbé Expilly who had just been named for the see of Quimper, and the Abbé Jallet who had led the way in rallying the clergy to join the Third Estate in the opening conflicts of the States General.

None of the episcopal delegates pronounced the oath on the first day but on the morrow a lead was given, predictably, by Talleyrand. His appearance at the Assembly chamber early in the morning of the 27th, well before the place began to fill up, is quotably described by Pierre de La Gorce:

> There were hardly a hundred people present in all. The bishop had seemingly chosen such a moment deliberately, being a man of refined taste who would have felt embarrassed by the vulgar cheers of the public gallery. He was a little paler than usual and wore his habitual mysterious smile which could mean anything. Contrary to his custom he was dressed in his episcopal robes, and even wore his pectoral cross. He mounted the dais, walking less slowly than usual, as if in haste to accomplish an important duty. The scattered hearers awaited a speech, but the bishop studiously avoided giving one. It was not his moment for an oratorical harangue or else, believing as he still did a little less in the constitutional Church than in the other, he deemed it unworthy of a gentleman to indulge in hypocritical sentiment. Having sworn, he slipped away almost on tip-toe before the audience filled up, a touch ashamed of his renegade act, but at the same time feeling a sense of relief. New Church, old Church, he would have readily escaped from either; he believed that both were under sentence of death, and he had no taste for agonies.

Talleyrand's gesture proved less catalytic than had been the Abbé Grégoire's. Only one prelate of the Assembly followed his example, Jean-Baptiste Gobel, Bishop of Lydda who, along with Talleyrand, had declined to sign their colleagues' *Exposition des Principes*. He pronounced the oath on January 3, but he did preface the act with a speech, insisting on the claims of spiritual jurisdiction and expressing his conviction that the Assembly had not intended anything that would jeopardise the salvation of souls; he added then, however, a firm protestation of his attachment to the Civil Constitution. His reward was to be elected Bishop of Paris ten weeks later, on March 13.

The tally of oath-takers (the *assermentés* as they came

to be called) within the Assembly itself amounted to 62 abbés (just under a third of the total of priest-delegates) and 2 bishops out of 44 prelate members. "A great day for the clergy of France," said the renowned Superior of the Seminary of Saint Sulpice, the Abbé Emery, whose name we shall meet again, "They have written one of the most magnificent pages in their history!" – an assessment which may seem to us, from our safe distance, a shade exaggerated.

As for the acceptance or refusal of the oath throughout the country as a whole, an admirable analysis (headed "Une Géographie des Serments") is provided by Pierre Pierrard. For example, in 83% of the parishes of Rennes (Brittany) the refusal both of parish priests and of curates was total. A similar pattern emerges for the neighbouring areas, the Vendée, Maine, Anjou; all forty-three parish priests and forty-six out of the fifty-one curates of the Cholet district refused to swear. In Normandy the example was set by a total refusal on the part of the clergy attached to the Cathedral of Rouen. But even in this area there were pockets of "patriots" (the term used for outright supporters of the Revolution) and in the area of Saumur 89% of the clergy pronounced the oath. M. Pierrard's analysis is fascinating to study with a map of France to hand, especially conjointly with his discussion of the implications of the geographical spread, implications on which he and a fellow-historian, Bernard Plongeron, have spread much light in recent years.

1791

The long-awaited verdict from Rome came in the March of 1791. Pius VI's 2000-word brief *Quod aliquantum* made it clear from the start that there could be no expectation of a compromise. Saying that he had already many months previously summoned a special meeting of the Cardinals to consider the situation in France, the Pontiff continued:

And while we were still preoccupied with the question we

learned that the National Assembly had, about mid-July, published a decree which, under the pretext of establishing a merely civil constitution for the clergy (as its title implied) overturned the most sacred traditions and most solemn discipline of the Church. It swept aside the claims of this primary Apostolic See, the rights of bishops, priests and religious orders of both sexes, the rights indeed of the whole Catholic community. It abolished certain most sacred ceremonies, took possession of ecclesiastical properties and revenues, and prepared the way for calamities which only experience would make believable.

A number of appeals to precedent are included and historical parallels are drawn − among them the stance of Thomas Becket when Henry II sought to impose "a constitution of the clergy somewhat similar to that of the National Assembly but with fewer articles", and the contrast in the behaviour of "the bishop of Autun". A second, but much shorter, letter, beginning with the word "Charitas", followed a month later, April 13. In it the five bishops who had taken the oath are named and an appeal is directed to them and to all other clergy who had done the same to retract under pain of suspension and ultimately of excommunication.

The two papal documents left no doubt about what was at stake: to pronounce the oath was to place oneself outside the fold of the Catholic Church. The effect was to polarise the clergy and faithful into two groups: the Constitutional Church, now the only legal one, and what was called the "Refractory Church" − the only orthodox one, maintaining union with the Pope. The minority of clergy who opted for the former were often (as recent historians have been at pains to show) prompted by a deep-seated sense of patriotism and also by an abiding conviction that the Revolution's ecclesiology was nearer to the gospel than that of the Ancien Regime, and perhaps most of all by their concern for their parish flocks. But the rest − almost all the bishops and two thirds of the parish clergy − chose, come what might, to remain true in conscience to the Church of their baptism and sacerdotal ordination.

A kind of civil strife emerged, at first at parochial level.

Non-juring priests were evicted from their parishes and replaced by *assermentés*, but their parishioners, in large numbers, refused to accept the ministrations of the latter (whom they called "intruders") and followed their expelled pastors wherever they could, often at great personal sacrifice, to hear Mass and receive the sacraments. Sometimes fighting broke out between such parishioners and those who had accepted the imposed clergy. Often the unsophisticated staunchness of the former was expressed in ways that were provocative of fisticuffs, like the recorded case of the "intruder" brought in from Paris to take over a country parish and, on his official inaugural entry into the church, being followed by devout ladies sweeping the aisle as he passed in order to decontaminate the sacred place – a comic spectacle if the implications were not tragic.

A practical problem requiring solution before the Constitutional Church could be well and truly launched was to find consecrating bishops for the eighty sees needing to be filled. The only five prelates who had taken the oath themselves had declined to undertake the daunting task: as a current witticism put it, "they were prepared to swear ('jurer') but not to curse ('sacrer', the primary meaning of which is 'to consecrate')". Eventually the malleable Talleyrand had accepted the role and, on February 24, 1791, had consecrated Louis Alexandre Expilly who had been elected to the see (*département*) of Finistère, and Claude Marolles, elected to Aisne. The ceremonial followed the traditional form with, needless to say, the glaring omission of the reading of the papal mandates and the oath of fidelity to the Pope. Thenceforward the consecrations proliferated rapidly.

On the political front the flight, in June 1791, of Louis XVI with his family from what had become a prison-like existence at the Tuileries palace, and his arrest at Varennes and ignominious return to the capital spelt the effective end of royal power. Soon he was being referred to by the "patriots" as plain "Louis Capet" or, more contemptuously still, as "Monsieur Veto". A demonstration in the Champ-de-Mars in mid-July, calling for the end of the monarchy, was checked by a proclamation of martial law, the Assembly itself becoming alarmed by the rapid escalation of people-power. The order to fire on the crowd, resulting in the death of some fifty people and the wounding of many, dispersed the gathering but served only to intensify the demagogic groundswell it was meant to quell.

The Constituent Assembly, having formulated the Constitution it had set out to produce, reached the end of its mandate on September 30, 1791. That same evening the haut-monde of Vienna, homeland of Louis' unpopular queen, Marie-Antoinette, was enjoying the premiere of the pauper Mozart's *Die Zauberflöte* − an irony which the constituents would have grimly appreciated were they aware of it. It is doubtful whether even they were quite satisfied with the charter they had produced. The American ambassador in Paris at the time, Gouverneur Morris, confided to his diary that it was "a Constitution that the Almighty Himself could not make to work except by creating a new species of human beings" − nor was he thinking only of the clauses which directly concerned the Church. "The Constitution of 1791 presupposed a stability which was simply not established," writes Michel Vovelle, the translation of whose *La Chute de la monarchie 1787-1792* provides the best available examination in English of the Constitution.

The Legislative Assembly (for membership of which the Constituents had, on a machiavellian proposal of Robespierre, decreed themselves ineligible) assumed office on October 1 with the responsibility for implementing the Constitution. Its term of office was destined to last only until August 10 of the following year, but those ten months brought the burning fuse of anti-clericalism and anti-Catholicism to the point of detonation.

The new Assembly of 745 members, representative of the rival ideologies of the so-called Clubs, inherited, among others, two major problems, one religious, the other political. On the one hand there was the schism and its attendant troubles; on the other, there was the refusal of the new order (disorder, as they saw it) by the aristocrats, many of whom had emigrated and were assumed to be plotting the overthrow of the Revolution by foreign invasion. Almost inevitably a tendency to merge the two issues developed within the new Assembly and in the minds of the "patriots" as a whole. The priests and religious – the "refractories" and the "fanatics" – became identified as counter-revolutionaries, a fifth column to be eliminated. The escalating outbreaks of civil strife in various parts of the country were attributed by the propaganda to the machinations of the non-jurors, and the new Assembly voted a decree on November 29, requiring every member of the clergy to swear the Civil Constitution oath within eight days under pain of being "suspected of revolt against the law and of harmful intentions against the Nation", the penalty being deprivation of any stipend and expulsion from the area where they lived. "By what kind of right," protested Archbishop Boisgelin, "do legislators make laws, not to punish crimes but to invent them?"

The king, already burdened in conscience with having sanctioned the decrees of the Civil Constitution and the oath, now imposed the veto, which was still his, on that of November 29. But in many parts of the country the local authorities, influenced by the Jacobin propaganda, applied the decree anyway, forcibly closing the churches and presbyteries of the non-juring parish clergy; many of these emigrated (mostly to England) but many also chose to make their way to Paris, hoping to divert attention from themselves pending better times.

1792

On the political front the major event, one which was to have repercussions for the clergy and faithful whose allegiance to papal authority remained unshaken, was the Legislative Assembly's declaration of war, on April 20, 1792, on "the King of Bohemia and Hungary" (a title of the Austrian Emperor). It was intended as a pre-emptive strike against the anti-Revolution coalition developing among the European powers. "Tant mieux!" – "So much the better!" – was the reported exclamation of Queen Marie-Antoinette on hearing the news. She was the sister of the lately-deceased emperor, Leopold II (her French subjects referred to her, with a spit, as "L'Autrichienne") and she was confident that the coalition would restore the *status quo* in France.

Early defeats of the French forces at Tournai and Quiévrain suggested that the Queen's confidence was well-placed. But events now, in fact, precipitated, not the restoration of monarchical authority, but its definitive obliteration. A new decree, voted May 27, 1792, specified that any priest delated as a non-juror by any twenty "active" citizens must leave French territory immediately, but the King refused to sanction it and thereby gave excuse to the rabble-rousers for proclaiming that the *réfractaires* and their supporters — the *fanatiques* — had royal authority for their anti-revolutionary scheming.

Three days later the now trigger-happy Legislative Assembly decreed the disbandment of the 6000 troops constituting the royal bodyguard, and a week after that (June 8) the levying of a body of 20,000 "national guards" to be recruited from the provinces and encamped around Paris. Louis accepted the first but refused the second: his power of veto was rapidly approaching vanishing-point, but it was in the Constitution which the Legislative Assembly was mandated to implement. On June 20 a mob invaded the Tuileries palace and demanded the sanction of the decrees for the exiling of non-juring clergy and for the levying of the national guards. Despite being called a traitor to his face by one of the leaders of the break-in, called Legendre, Louis held out.

But the show of firmness came too late to matter. At the beginning of July Prussia entered the enemy coalition and her troops, under the command of the Duke of Brunswick, made rapid advances. On July 25 Brunswick issued an insultingly worded ultimatum to the French nation: all who dared to take up arms against the invading troops would be deemed rebels against royal authority and would be punished by immediate death. An invitation to rebel against royal authority could not have been worded better, and exactly a week later, August 10, the royal palace was invaded again, this time by force of arms, and the King and his family were carried off to imprisonment in the looming gothic pile known as the Temple.

One immediate effect of this "official" abolition of royal authority was to render inapplicable the existing oath of loyalty "to the Nation, to the Law and to the King ..." and only four days after the imprisonment of the royal family a new formula was imposed by the Assembly, to be sworn by all persons in receipt of State remuneration. It was worded thus:

> I swear to be faithful to the Nation and to maintain Liberty and Equality or to die in defence of them.

This came to be known as the Liberty-Equality oath and its role in the story of the martyrs of the Revolution will be referred to in the appropriate places. But we are now in mid-August 1792 and already the rounding-up of the non-juring clergy has begun, especially in Paris, the scene of what all the historians refer to as the September Massacres.

PART 1

THE
SEPTEMBER MASSACRES

1

THE ROUND-UP OF THE REFRACTORIES

The Paris electoral ward known as the Luxembourg had within its confines the parish church and presbytery of Saint Sulpice as well as the famous seminary conducted by the Sulpician Fathers. Priests schooled in the spirituality of the founder, Jean-Jacques Olier, were, almost by definition, non-jurors to a man and, by the same token, commanded the loyalty of their huge parish. The constitutional parish priest's sermons were echoing around almost empty pews in the vast edifice. The ousted curé, Mayneaud de Pancemont, was in hiding, but very much at the heart of the parish, safe from betrayal by his flock and ministering to them and to his Sulpician confreres as well as to numerous other clergy who had come to the capital from the provinces and had found lodgings in the Luxembourg area. The authorities were aware of Pancemont's activities but could not put their hands on him.

Another cleric, equally untraceable but even more active in pursuing his priestly ministry, was Picot de Clorivière, a Jesuit (or "ex-Jesuit", as the term was at the time, since the Society had been suppressed by Pope Clement XIV twenty years before) who was a living legend. Like Pancemont he was at the beck and call of the many priests and faithful who sought his ministry, but he found time to establish the bases for an order of men to replace the suppressed Society, as well as a congregation of Sisters. The *Bibliothèque de la Compagnie de Jésus* lists over a score of works from his pen, varying in length from eighty pages to six hundred. Henri Daniel-Rops summarises Clorivière's spiritual teaching thus: the mystical life is simply sanctifying grace seeking to fill the

29

heart which does not refuse it; the soul diminishes in order to allow God's light to illumine its darkness; unless that sense of the divine is present, asceticism of itself achieves nothing; what matters is the will to encounter God and lose oneself in Him.

The authorities of the Luxembourg Section had good reason then, from their point of view, to hunt down such men as Pancemont and Clorivière and the clergy whom they directed. The roundup began on August ll and targeted immediately a prelate known to be in the area, the Archbishop of Arles, Jean Marie d'Allemand Dulau. Mgr. Dulau had occupied the see of Arles since 1775 and had left a reputation there which ranks him with St. Charles Borromeo. M. Prevost, Archivist of the Bibliothèque Nationale of Paris, writes of him in the article he contributed to the new *Dictionnaire de la Biographie Française:*

> He conducted his episcopal residence as a religious community characterised by perfect order and discipline. He gave new life to his seminary and developed missions within the diocese, generously making available the funds at his disposal ... His annual income (including his personal fortune) amounted to 100,000 francs of which he used only what was necessary for maintaining the work of his curia, giving away the rest for charitable purposes. As a member of the hierarchy's committee for the relief of the famine of 1789 (which had helped to bring about the summoning of the States General) he excelled in generosity and in fund-raising for poor relief ...

Elected to the States General, Dulau was one of the speakers in favour of merging the three orders. In accordance with the terms of the Civil Constitution of the Clergy his diocese was suppressed and, because he refused the oath of adherence, he was replaced in the reorganisation by the Abbé Roux who was elected to the role of metropolitan of the coastal region of the Mediterranean. Dulau protested and declared his intention to continue his episcopal ministry, forthwith addressing a circular letter to his priests urging them to stand firm in their loyalty to the Church. The

54-year old archbishop was the first arrested quarry of the Luxembourg search parties.

Two other prelates known to be living in the same area were brothers, François Joseph and Pierre Louis de La Rochefoucauld, bishops respectively of Beauvais and Saintes. Both had been delegates to the States General and François Joseph had been a particularly outspoken critic of the tabled motions of the ecclesiastical committee of the Constituent Assembly. Both lived in the same lodging and although as yet there was no warrant for the arrest of Pierre Louis he requested to be taken along with his brother when the latter was marched off to the Section headquarters. François Joseph's will, cited by Joseph Grente, reveals something of this prelate's faith, humility and charity; it is also probably representative of the moral stance, in their diverse circumstances, of the majority of the non-juring clergy:

In the name of the Father and of the Son and of the Holy Spirit. The circumstances in which the clergy find themselves who have refused to swear the oath demanded of them by the Constituent Assembly, give reason to fear the fury of the populace who are being turned against them. I therefore believe it appropriate to express my wishes in writing in the event that God will permit that I be a victim of this animosity.

I declare that I have nothing to reproach myself with on the score of what is called the counter-revolution. I have never, directly or indirectly, done anything against the new government. I would presume to claim myself the best of all patriots, since nobody is more disposed to render willingly the service all owe their country. So much for what concerns temporal authority.

I further declare that I am a bishop of the Catholic, Apostolic and Roman Church; that I believe all the truths that my religion has taught me and bids me practise and teach; that, by the grace of God, which I humbly beg, I shall die within the fold of the Catholic, Apostolic and Roman Church.

I ask God's pardon for the faults and negligences I have committed in the discharge of the awesome ministry confided to me by the Church, as well as for all I have done wrong throughout my life. I hope in God's mercy for the remission of my sins and for the blessed life of the elect.

> I name the Bureau of the Poor of Beauvais heir to all I possess. And I request, and order, that I be buried as a poor man.

The character of Pierre Louis is sufficiently manifested by his insistence on being taken into custody with his brother, even though the searchers had not yet his name on their list. The latter detail is, in fact, surprising. From the point of view of the anti-clerical forces he had done plenty to make him an object of their hostility. His diocese of Saintes was one of those suppressed under the rearrangement imposed by the Civil Constitution, but he did not cease to act as bishop, especially urging his priests not to waver in refusing the oath when it was demanded of them. A pastoral letter to them contains this passage:

> To do our duty, in obedience to God, must be the sole object of our concern. We must not despair of His Providence, but be sure that, after putting our faith to the test, He will know how to help us in the ills that may befall us. And if He ordains that we die for such a noble cause, let us rejoice to have been judged worthy to suffer for Him.

When a constitutional bishop was imposed on the *département* embracing the suppressed diocese, Pierre Louis issued an ordonnance declaring the installation null and void and forbidding the clergy and faithful to have anything to do with the "intruder". The mayor of Paris burned a copy of the ordonnance in a public square.

Another notable quarry for the hunters of the "calotins" (a term of contempt derived from the use, by many clergy, of the calotte or skull-cap) was Père Hébert, superior of the Paris community of the congregation founded by St. Jean Eudes. His house in the Rue des Fossoyeurs was known to harbour non-juring priests who had sought the anonymity of the capital. On a first visit Père Hébert and two other prime suspects, Canon Berton and the Abbé Rose, were arrested. The residence of the Saint-Sulpice parish clergy was also visited. By midnight of the 11th a haul of fifty priests had made it a good day's work for the Luxembourg, and the chosen place for their confinement was the monastery of the Discalced Carmelites in the Rue Vaugirard.

The Section committee was aware also that the Sulpician community had an annexe seminary and also a retirement home in the rural district of Issy, a few kilometres to the south-west of the city. A visit of a search-party there on the feast of the Assumption, a few days hence, seemed likely to be fruitful. The mission was entrusted to a committee-member by the name of Claude Lazowsky; he was known to have property in Issy and therefore to be familiar with the district. A detachment of fifty men was allocated to him and the search began as soon as they arrived in the township. By 3.30 p.m. some thirty priests and seminarians were assembled in front of Lazowsky who harangued them, expressing his satisfaction at having collected such a fine bunch "of accursed scoundrels who pay the Swiss [the King's bodyguard] to cut our throats and who manufacture daggers in secret to slay our wives and children". None of the clerics lined up in front of him was, in the strict meaning of the term, "refractory", since the obligation of the oath applied only to state "functionaries" and these were either not yet, or no longer, such. But the prevailing mood in Paris after the arrest of the royal family made light of such legal niceties.

At this moment the mayor of Issy arrived on the scene to protest against the bellicose intrusion of the search-party made without any reference to him. A document in the Paris national archives relates his intervention in some detail. It is, in fact, a report subsequently drawn up by the mayor himself and it is worth quoting because it offers a much better impression than any reconstruction could do of the spirit and manner in which the priest-hunts were conducted:

> 1792, the fourth year of liberty, Wednesday August 15, at 4.00 in the afternoon, I, J.B.Gogue, Mayor of the township of Issy, received information that a company of some fifty armed persons had entered various houses and communities situated in Issy, and that these people were at present in the house occupied by the Abbé Du Bourg. I immediately made my way to the said house and found there a crowd of armed men together with a large number of priests and seminarians who had been arrested by the guards and assembled in this place.

I straightway made known that the officer in charge must show me his warrant for this. Whereupon an individual dressed in blue trousers and a tunic with a high collar, without giving his name or rank, showed me two pieces of paper from one of which he read a few words but offered no further information. I therefore asked him on what grounds he had taken such action without first presenting himself to the municipal authorities, and to this he replied that he had no need of authorisation from us, that he had come with his brothers-in-arms and that there was no need for further formalities; there was no law, he said, that could stop him, that the Nation was now sovereign and absolute, and that if we had done our duty in the first place there would have been no need for him to take these measures.

Such language took me by surprise, since the municipality had received no notification of any law authorising the removal of persons by force; what he said seemed even to be at variance with the decree which declared that for the eviction of priests a delation of twenty active citizens was required as well as the completion of formalities following such a delation. I did not, however, think it prudent in the present circumstances to invoke the full authority of the law against the violent intrusion, since I saw that the tempers of the men were very heated and that they were prepared to confront our municipal gendarmerie. In fact they said they would deal with any oppostion with their firearms. Hence I thought it better not to insist nor to press the law in face of force which seemed to me dangerous.

I deemed it my duty, using all the prudence permitted by the circumstances, to have a report drawn up of the search which the party's spokesman had claimed he had the right to make. I expressed the wish to instruct our municipal clerk to compile such a report, detailing the persons and articles removed from the domiciles which had been entered by force. But immediately the leader objected to this and wrote a minute of the affair himself, obliging me to sign it, something I deemed it better not to refuse though expressing my protest and reserve. The same individual, still acting on his own authority, next lined up the priests and the students, thirty-one in all, whom he had removed from different religious houses of the town, namely the retirement home of St François de Sales and the Saint-Sulpice annexe.

The procession moved off to the sound of drums, led by

Lazowsky on horseback; the prisoners, regardless of the age of the retired men, made the journey on foot, flanked by their fifty captors. Their destination was the Carmelite monastery, the designated prison for the Luxembourg Section, and an eye-witness account, to be quoted later, tells of the exhausted state in which the group from Issy arrived. The final tally of priests confined in the Carmes (the monastery's local name) included the three bishops already named, seven vicars general, thirteen college or seminary staff, twelve hospital or convent chaplains, eleven other diocesan priests or seminarians, thirteen Jesuits (but not including Pere Clorivière), twelve Sulpicians, three Benedictines, two Capuchins, two Brothers of the Christian Schools, two Eudists, one Franciscan Friar Minor, and one member of the Paris Foreign Missions.

While the Luxembourg was thus filling up the Carmes, the neighbouring Section, called the Jardin des Plantes because it included the botanical gardens of the city, was equally busy. The improvised prison this time was the seminary of Saint Firmin, and on August 13 the first arrests were made in the building itself − the staff of the establishment with eighteen priests from the provinces who had found lodging there. The seminary was under the direction of the Vincentian Fathers and the rector was Louis Joseph François, a marked man from the patriots' point of view because of pamphlets he had written in criticism of the abuse of power. The transformation of the seminary into a prison was effected by the simple procedure of placing armed guards at every exit with instructions to allow no one to leave but to let anyone who arrived enter.

In the evening of the same day a squad was despatched to another seminary within the Section confines, that of Saint Nicolas du Chardonnet, to inform the rector, René Marie Andrieux, a Jesuit, that he and his staff were under arrest and were to be removed to Saint Firmin. An eye-witness account of the transfer has survived, written by the bursar of Saint Firmin, Père Boullangier. Père Andrieux led the way amid the jeers and threats of a crowd of people who (says Boullangier) had received many kindnesses from the seminary staff now walking calmly before them into captivity.

Another group was added later, four members of the staff of the Cardinal Lemoine College next door to Saint Firmin. Then it was the turn of some of the clergy who directed the residence of the Recent Converts; the superior of this establishment was another Jesuit, Pierre Guerin du Rocher, whose writings, directed against the influence of the Encyclopedists, had won him the commendation and a stipend from Louis XVI, while Marie Antoinette had chosen him as her confessor. There was still room in the improvised prison and the Hospital de la Pitié was duly visited and the superintendent, the Abbé Pierre de Saint-James (*sic*) and two chaplains, together with three laymen employees of the hospital, were arrested.

In hardly more than twenty-four hours the Jardin des Plantes section had confined some eighty prisoners in the Saint Firmin seminary and these included two canons, thirteen parish priests, nine curates, nineteen seminary staff, six hospital staff, fourteen other diocesan clergy, six Jesuits, three Canons Regular, two Fathers of Christian Doctrine, two Vincentians, one Capuchin and one Eudist.

A third Paris religious house turned into a prison during this fevered priest-hunt of August 1792 was the Abbey of Saint Germain des Prés, a 6th century foundation on the south bank of the Seine famous for the work of such patristic scholars as Jean Mabillon (1632-1707) and Bernard de Montfaucon (1655-1741). The community were too well-known to escape the attentions of the search-parties, but they had vacated the building before these arrived. The abbot, Ambroise Augustin Chevreux, had, however, been traced and he was one of the three Benedictines consigned to the Carmes. The Abbaye (as it was simply referred to by the local people) had already received as prisoners a contingent of officers of the royal bodyguard (the "Suisses") deemed to have opposed the revolutionary cause by their defence of the royal family on August 10. The clergy who were destined for the Abbaye were first taken to the municipal headquarters (the Mairie) and herded there in a loft until arrangements could be made for their transfer. One of the last to be arrested and taken there was no less a dignitary than the Paris papal internuncio, Mgr. de Salamon. As events turned out he escaped the slaughter that took place in due course at the Abbaye and he wrote a memoir of his experiences soon after his release. Here is how he describes his arrival at the Mairie under armed escort early in the morning of August 27:

I was taken through the stable yard and up to the second storey of the building into a fairly spacious loft, the ceiling of which, however, was so low that anyone five feet six inches in height could not comfortably have remained standing. It was full of prisoners, about eighty I should say. They were packed together lying on straw. They hardly noticed me at first but were complaining to one another about the straw not having been changed for four days. The only light came from a very few narrow and barred windows and the overall effect was of an eerie gloom. The place was a real death-cell.

I recognised the parish priest of Saint Jean-en-Grève, a man worthy of veneration both for his virtuous life and his advanced age. I saw also Mgr. Godard, vicar general of Archbishop Fontanges of Toulouse. Both had to remain stooping when they stood for they were both six feet tall. Also there were Mgr. de Bouzet, vicar general of Reims, brother of a rear-admiral, the Abbé Sicard of Strasbourg, the Abbé Gervais of the Paris curia, and many other well-known persons.

The above-mentioned parish priest of Saint Jean was a very jovial man as well as a very saintly one — he was a proof, incidentally, that God is pleased with a kind of piety that does not exclude joy and amiability and indeed prefers it to the kind of severe attitude which seems to be permanently censorious of others. He told us amusing stories which made us burst out laughing, so much so that, speaking for myself, I almost did myself harm, and this despite all the reasons I had to feel miserable. Anyone would have thought we were lying on feather-beds in a palace! This went on until one in the morning and I felt constrained to call out, "Come, Father, that's enough! We must get some sleep." And immediately he stopped the flow of his stories and fell silent. Nor did the good Lord lose out in all this: at four o'clock our story-teller was up, or rather, on his knees (unable to stand because of his

height) saying his prayers and then, when there was enough
light, reciting his breviary.

Salamon's account continues with the story of the transfer
of a majority of the priests to the Abbaye. The Louis
Pierre Manuel he mentions was the procurator general
of the Parish city council. He was a writer whose *Essais
historiques, critiques, littéraires et philosophiques*, published
in 1783 when he was thirty-two years old, had propounded
subversive ideas which had gained him a three-month spell
in the Bastille. He was an enthusiast for the Revolution
but, a few months after the incident Salamon is describing,
Manuel refused his vote for the execution of Louis XVI and
so became suspect to the Jacobins. On August 21, 1793 –
almost exactly a year after we meet him here – he was
arrested and imprisoned in the same Abbaye to which he
was now despatching the priests, and was guillotined the
following November 14:

At last came Saturday, September 1, 1792, a day of horrible
memories. Manuel, an official of the Commune, came up to
the loft to make an announcement, remaining however at the
entrance as if we were all plague-stricken, or perhaps he was
unable to bear the suffocating, fetid atmosphere. He told us
that the city council had decided that we were to be transferred
this evening. He said that this was the reason for his visit to us
and he even left a copy of the act concerned, a printed paper
the size of those posted on walls around the city.

The news made almost all of my companions happy,
thinking only of the fact that at last we were going to
get out of our present wretched situation. Some said, "So
we're to leave here this evening, and perhaps we are going
to be deported so we shall need to obtain some money for
the voyage." Others thought, "No, we are going to join the
clergy already in the Carmes prison, but we shall be better
there." Shortly after, yet another priest was brought in, Canon
Simon of Saint Quentin, a man over eighty years of age. He
had wanted to see his seventy-five year old brother already
incarcerated with us. He was allowed to enter, but when he
made to leave he was told, "You're a priest so you may as
well stay since you have come; you'll be transferred with the
others very soon."

At eleven o'clock, an official of the commune, wearing the tricolour sash, came and called out loudly: "We shall take the sixty-three who have been here longest; let these come forward and give their names." Now, although I had been among the last to arrive, I quickly stepped forward and had my name taken. I don't quite know why I did this but I was asked no questions. It was surely an inspiration from heaven for, if I am still alive, it is because of what I did then, as will be seen later ...

We were made to go down, one after the other, into the courtyard and then were packed in sixes into the coaches waiting for us. So the dismal cortege started out. It was as if an execution by torch light was going to be carried out. We were guarded on all sides as if we were criminals on the way to the gallows, and the gloomy silence, combined with the darkness of the cloudy night, deepened the horror of this funeral march.

We went along the Quai des Orfèvres, crossed the Pont-Neuf, and passed along the Rue Dauphine as far as the Buci crossroad, whereupon someone in my carriage remarked, "So we're not going to the Carmes after all; we're heading in the direction of the Abbaye ..." And, in fact, we arrived in front of the tower which was serving as the prison for the military ... We moved on and I said, "Where are we going then?" but I had hardly said this when we turned into the Sainte Marguerite side street which led directly into the courtyard of the Benedictine monastery. Throughout the journey we had been escorted not only by the armed guards but also by a crowd of the local populace who, however, remained silent and seemed to follow us only out of curiosity. We were taken to a large hall which served as a kind of barrack room for the national guards, and there we were received with the most boorish insults from some of these men wearing the national uniform ...

It was already the small hours of September 2 when the group had arrived and their twenty-four companions left behind at the Mairie were to follow them later that day, but in circumstances which initiated the so-called September Massacres. The government had foreseen September 2 as a day for rallying the revolutionary spirit among the citizens of Paris. News of the advance of Brunswick's invading troops was being received with less than the frenetic excitement which the reality warranted. Precisely on the morning of Sunday the 2nd, the town-criers announced that Verdun, less than 200 miles east of the capital, had capitulated, and the self-appointed Paris council – the Commune – gave orders for the sounding of the cannon, for drum-rolls at the main crossroads of the city, and speeches everywhere summoning the citizens to their patriotic duty. Metropolitan sang-froid was transformed; it became dangerous to seem less than feverishly indignant. The committees of the various Sections were in session all day and outlandish propositions were voted with enthusiasm. One such (recorded for the Section Grange-Batelière) demanded that " all former counts, marquesses, dukes, barons and all nobles and financiers" be sent against the enemy but "positioned alongside patriots who would keep a close eye on their behaviour".

But the frantic proposition voted by the Poissonnière Section manifested the prevailing notion that the non-juring clergy were no less anti-revolutionary than the aristocrats. The proposition was worded to the effect that "all conspirators against the State" then held in the prisons of Paris should be put to death before the departure of the citizens volunteering to march against the enemy, and that refractory priests not already in prison, together with the wives and children of aristocrats who had emigrated, should be placed unarmed at the front of the volunteers "so that their bodies could serve as a rampart for the true citizens who were going to exterminate the tyrants and slaves".

A delegation of representatives was despatched to the committee rooms of all the other Sections to obtain their support for this proposition. The party arrived at the Luxembourg Section at about 2.30 in the afternoon only to find that events there had rendered their visit purposeless. The Luxembourg had adopted for this special session of September 2 the interior of the vast Saint Sulpice church so as to ensure room for the expected attendance of large numbers of the local citizenry. Speeches from the pulpit followed one another in rapid succession, anyone having the right to declaim at a signal from the chairman. The minutes record a particularly dramatic intervention by a certain wine-merchant called Louis Priere. He proclaimed that he was in perfect agreement with the need for patriotic citizens to march to the defence of the country, but that he personally would not stir a foot until Paris was disencumbered of the individuals held in the prisons, "especially those held in the Carmes". The implications were sufficiently awe-inspiring to prompt a murmur of hesitation among some of the listeners, one of whom, a watchmaker by the name of Carcel, ventured to say that there were no doubt guilty persons in the prisons, but that there could be some also who were not guilty and that assuredly honourable citizens would not wish to stain their hands with the blood of innocent people. Carcel's words were listened to with enough respect to encourage him to make a formal proposition that a commission of six persons be elected from those present to examine the records of the prisoners and to bring to the courts only those who had charges to answer. The chairman, Joachim Ceyrat, was not in favour of this conciliatory approach. "All," he pronounced, "who are in the Carmes are guilty and it is time the people did justice to them." And with blatant abuse of the authority of the chair he forthwith put the wine merchant's sentiments into the form of a proposition, that "before the departure of the volunteers from Paris the prisons be purged by the shedding of the blood of all who were held in them". And Ceyrat's menacing and roving gaze ensured a huge majority in favour.

But it was one thing to vote the proposition and another to implement it. Discussion on this terminated with a temporising measure: three members of the Section committee would report the decision to the headquarters of the commune, thus ensuring, say the minutes of the meeting, "that all be done in a uniform manner". One of the three appointed delegates, a lawyer called Lohier, ventured to ask how, precisely, it was intended to dispose of the prisoners "in a uniform manner", to which Ceyrat impatiently replied, "Par la mort!" – a phrase which has ensured for this minor official himself, in the history books of the Revolution, a kind of immortality he could have done without.

But here again events were moving with a rapidity that made a mockery of any attempt at a uniform, let alone judicial, procedure. Even while discussion was in progress at Saint Sulpice, the killing had begun at the Abbaye and we must now go there to observe the tragic spectacle. To enable us to do so we have, besides Mgr. Salamon's account, some minutes of the recording clerk of the Paris commune, one Méhée, and a memoir of a priest who, like Salamon, narrowly escaped the slaughter, the Abbé Roch Ambroise Sicard, Director of the Home for Deaf-Mutes (it was his dedication to that work which won him his reprieve). The three accounts do not always coincide and Gérard Walter, who uses all three in his critical study of the September Massacres, is duly cautious. But, as Walter says, Méhée's position gave him a privileged status for knowing what happened, and Sicard's record for integrity encourages confidence in his narrative, due account being taken of the evident emotional stress under which he wrote. As for Salamon's version, the portion we have already quoted suggests an inherent credibility.

2

AT THE ABBAYE

As Mgr. de Salamon has told us, only two thirds of the priests held at the Mairie were transferred to the Abbaye during the night of September 1. In what seems to have been an exercise in whetting the people's appetite for bloodshed, orders had been given for twenty-four of the most recently apprehended to be held back for transfer the next day in broad daylight. The idea was to parade the twenty-four through the streets on the way to the Abbaye in the expectation that the sight of them would provide the needed stimulus to the people's patriotic emotions. The departure was timed for about 2.00 p.m. One of the prisoners concerned was the Abbé Sicard and his account will serve as our guide. Sicard was directed with five others into the first of the waiting carriages, and when the rest were duly loaded the procession moved off, escorted by soldiers. Sicard recorded what happened then:

> They told us amidst a thousand insults that we would not reach the Abbaye, that we would be handed over to the people who would do justice to us, their enemies, and would cut our throats en route.

A crowd of onlookers gathered and began to walk alongside the carriages, the guards calling out to them: "Yes, these are your enemies, the accomplices of those who have delivered up Verdun to the enemy and who only await your departure to murder your wives and children!"

Méhée says in his account that during the journey one of the priests, exasperated beyond endurance, lashed out at one of the guards with his walking-stick and that he

43

was promptly despatched "with three thrusts of a sabre", an incident carried out so promptly that the slow progress was not even halted.

When the carriages arrived at the Abbaye a group of armed men were already waiting in the courtyard, "with orders," says Sicard, "to begin the killing with us". One priest made a futile attempt to escape, jumping from the first carriage and running into the middle of the crowd, but he was lynched there and then. Two others made a similar attempt with the same result, but a fourth seemed to succeed. Sicard's story appears to call for a willing suspension of disbelief at this point. He says that he and the remaining companion in the first coach crouched down at the far side of the vehicle, hoping that the killers would assume that their carriage was now empty and would turn their attention to the next. And this is what happened, so that Sicard was able, in the melee, to leave the scene unnoticed and to present himself before the Section committee to claim their protection. The abbé's story of what happened then again leaves us wondering whether he has not improved on the reality. He says that a would-be assassin rushed into the committee room and raised his pike to thrust it into the priest when a member of the committee placed himself between the weapon and the abbé and bared his chest saying: "Your blade must pass through me before it reaches the Abbé Sicard. You are not going to kill one of the country's most deserving men, one who has been a father to so many poor children who can neither hear nor speak!" The words were effective enough even though, as Sicard goes on to say, it took three more days of formalities for him to be set free. The historical fact, anyway, is that Ambroise Sicard survived the Revolution and died in 1822 at the age of eighty, a member of the French Academy, a Chevalier of the Légion d'Honneur, a member of the Order of Saint Michel and the author of works which had made a notable contribution to the methods of teaching deaf-mutes.

How, meanwhile, had Mgr. de Salamon and his sixty-two companions fared since we left them in the improvised guard room inside the Abbaye? The internuncio resumes his narrative at daybreak after their arrival in the small hours of the night:

It was September 2, that date which must remain for ever a day of horror and mourning in the annals of France. It fell on a Sunday. I have to admit that I had not adverted to this, but a saintlier priest than myself, the good Curé of Saint Jean-en-Grève, remembered it for us. He said to us (after we had tidied the room) "Gentlemen, today is Sunday. It is certain that we shall not be allowed to celebrate or hear Mass. I suggest, therefore, that we kneel down for the time a Mass would last and raise our hearts to God." Everyone applauded this and we immediately knelt to pray. There were also a few laymen with us, the President of the Superior Council of Corsica, a magistrate of the Paris Parlement, a hairdresser, a manservant of the Duke of Penthièvre and five or six deserters from the army . . .

When we had rendered our homage to God with much fervour, we started to walk up and down the room in twos or in small groups. We discussed our situation, the fate that awaited us, and especially the privations we were being made to suffer already. There was not so much as a chair on which to take a rest. At one point the prison superintendent came in and said: "The nation is now responsible for your keep, but your arrival was unexpected and there is nothing prepared for you today. You will have to make your own arrangements as far as meals are concerned. I've brought along this caterer for you."

The Abbé Godard, Vicar General of Toulouse, and I (since we both seemed to be more alert to the situation than the rest) spoke to the caterer and told him, "Prepare meals for forty sous per person, and bring them in two hours time. We'll answer for any who can't pay." Apart from the army deserters there were, in fact, two or three priests among us who seemed quite penniless and, although we were still unsure about what was going to happen to us, this was certainly a time to practise charity. (I would mention, in passing, that in the various prisons I have had occasion to visit, I have always noticed great union among the inmates, and much generosity; whatever one had was shared with those who had nothing.)

During the time we were waiting for the meal we walked about rather in a crowd. Everyone was talking at the same time and no one could really catch what was being said. Myself, I found a quiet corner where there was a small bench and I sat there pondering vaguely what was happening to us and, as I well recall, feeling very anxious and sad.

Well, the caterer arrived and set up a very long table with benches on either side and, at 2.00 in the afternoon, the meal was brought in. It was a meal that was soon to be rudely interrupted ...

The interruption was caused by the arrival of the delayed contingent at the Abbaye and the terrifying sounds of the slaughter that took place in the courtyard. Salamon says that once again it was the saintly and jovial Curé of Saint Jean-en-Grève, (he names him here) Marc-Louis Royer, who took the initiative, proposing that the moment was come for the priests to make their immediate preparation for death and to hear one another's confessions. The account continues:

I myself knelt before the Abbé Royer himself, but my sad confession was interrupted by a fearsome supervisor, a man who delighted in frightening us with false stories. "The people are getting more and more furious," he shouted, "there are two thousand men trying to get in here!" And later, "It's just been announced that all the priests held at the Carmes have been massacred!"

This heart-rending news caused us all to kneel before the Curé of Saint Jean-en-Grève and beg him to grant us general absolution *in articulo mortis*. The saintly man, a tall commanding figure, stood before us, prayed silently for a few moments, and then told us to recite the Confiteor and make an act of faith, an act of contrition and an act of the love of God, all of which we did with great fervour. He then pronounced the words of general absolution. As we knelt there in profound recollection, the Abbé Royer addressed a few words to us: "We may consider ourselves," he said, "as persons ill unto death, even though we are in full possession of our faculties. We must omit nothing that could win God's mercy for us. I am therefore going to recite the prayers for the dying and I invite you to join me in asking that God may have mercy on us." He began with the customary litany, we answering the invocations with intense feeling. The manner in which this worthy priest then intoned the first prayers, "Go forth, Christian soul, from this world, in the name of the Father almighty who created thee ..." moved almost all of us to tears.

At about midnight the priests were taken to another part of the building to submit to a formality of judgment. Salamon describes the walk in the dark across the courtyard and through the garden, and then continues:

> At last we reached the monks' quarters and were led to a low-ceilinged room with glass-panelled double doors and a view into the garden. In the middle of the room was a large table covered with a green cloth, some sheets of note-paper with writing on them, and an inkstand with pens. Several men were seated around this table and were in such earnest discussion that they paid no attention to us. The one at the head, evidently the chairman, was wearing black and his hair was powdered.

Our author does not name this personage, but he is known to have been Stanislas Maillard, a character who had figured prominently in the episode of the taking of the Bastille and whom popular talk had built up into a hero of the patriots with the nick-name of "Tape-dur", the "Hard-hitter". The image, according to Gérard Walter, hardly corresponded to the reality. He was a "pauvre diable", condemned by his doctor to an early death from tuberculosis of the lungs, and desperate to have his niche in history. His courage and intelligence were both undisputed, as well as his ability to sway a crowd by his eloquence. But this self-acquired role as chairman of the Abbaye tribunal was the nearest he got to an official rank in the revolutionary movement. He died two years later at the age of thirty-one.

Salamon (having, as we have noted, pointed out that the attention of the men at the candle-lit table was absorbed by their discussion) continues:

> I made my way unnoticed to the side of the room furthest from the door. There was a window there, closed and having a recess forming a window seat. After a little while, the chairman turned to the right and addressed the person nearest the door, the first in line. It was the Curé of Saint Jean- en-Grève. His interrogation was short, like that of all who followed him: "Have you sworn the oath?" The curé replied, with the calm of a conscience at peace, "No, I have not sworn it." Immediately a blow of a guard's sabre was aimed at his head, but it was a glancing blow which served only to remove his wig and reveal a balding head,

a head which the years had respected but which the weaponry of the assassins was now to shatter. Blow followed blow to head and to body, and soon the victim lay on the floor, a corpse. The assailants dragged him by the feet out of the room and returned shouting, "Vive la Nation!"

It seems appropriate that Marc-Louis Royer, the priest who, as Salamon's account has shown, was the natural leader of the group, thus led the way in accepting a violent death for conscience's sake. The historian, Joseph Grente, points out that at a memorial service held in 1803 for the priests of the diocese of Paris who had died in the September massacres, the panegyrist singled out the Abbé Royer for particular mention, saying that for more than thirty years he had guided the parish of Saint Jean-en-Grève with wisdom and, by his charity, his zeal and his kindliness, had re-enacted the lovable life of Saint François de Sales and, by his courage, that of "the holy pontiff of Canterbury".

Salamon, observing the proceedings undetected from the obscurity of his window seat, continues:

> It was the turn next of Canon de Bouzet, Vicar General of Reims, the brother of a rear-admiral whom I have since come to know well. The chairman asked him, "Have you sworn the oath?" "No," was the reply, in a voice so faint I could hardly hear it, "No, I have not." "Take him away!" was the order given, and immediately several of the assassins surrounded him and, opening the glass doors leading into the garden, pushed him through on to the killing-ground which was on a level with the room floor. I saw his two arms raised to ward off the blows of the sabres and pikes that rained down on him. I turned away, thinking to myself that I also could not escape death, since I had not sworn the oath. An instant, and Canon Bouzet was no more, and the shout "Life to the Nation!" rang out again.

The internuncio's narrative continues with further names of victims (Jean André Capeau, a canon of the diocese of Avignon, attached to the parish of Saint Paul in Paris "where everyone venerated him", Pierre Louis Gervais, secretary to the former Archbishop of Paris, and others ...) until he reaches the case of Louis Benoît Simon, and here for the first time the question is raised about the difference between the two oaths, that of fidelity to the Civil Constitution and the so-called Liberty-Equality oath. When Canon Simon stood in front of Maillard's tribunal, the routine question was put: "Have you sworn the oath?" His prompt reply took everyone by surprise. "Yes, I have," he said, and he presented a signed testimonial in proof. The paper showed that Simon had sworn the Liberty-Equality oath, and one of the self-styled judges pronounced: "This oath is no good; we want to know if you have sworn the clergy oath!" But one of his colleagues challenged this and a heated discussion followed which ended with the discharge of Canon Simon.

The incident is interesting in that it illustrates the uncertain understanding, both of the clergy and of the improvised magistrates, of the nature of the Liberty-Equality oath. The question turned on whether this, like the Civil Constitution formula, was incompatible with fidelity to the Church and the Holy See. The wording (quoted on an earlier page) seemed to exclude any religious commitment, and a number of theologians whose orthodoxy was above suspicion had readily expressed the view that the new formula was extraneous to religion and could be pronounced with a clear conscience because the pastoral needs of the faithful required the continued ministrations of the priests. A letter of a leading ecclesiastic of the time, Jacques André Emery, superior general of the Society of Saint Sulpice - "the conscience of the Paris clergy" his biographer calls him - is quoted to this effect.

But there was an alternative opinion which saw the new formula, whatever the neutrality of its wording, as a contribution to the de-Christianising intentions of its devisers, and when news of the controversy had belatedly percolated through to the more than 150 clergy incarcerated at the Carmes their concern had been to obtain an official ruling. Their first thought had been to turn to the three prelates imprisoned with them: their view, in the circumstances, could be taken as a safe guide for action. According to Gérard Walter, the prelates were embarrassed by the question. "They understood very well that a formal condemnation of the new oath would be equivalent to a sure death-sentence for themselves and for their fellow-prisoners", and this was a responsibility they were unwilling to assume. They had decided to submit the case to the Pope's representative in Paris, the same Mgr. de Salamon that we know. But at the time concerned, the latter was already himself in custody at the Mairie prior to his transfer to the Abbaye. He too had proved to be disconcerted when the messenger found him, on August 28, and presented the question as formally submitted to him by Archbishop Dulau. The internonce, says Walter, had sent a recent report to the Holy See concerning the developing situation and expressing his personal opinion that the revolutionaries' aim was "the annihilation of all religion". He had received no reply as yet, but he expected that any mention in it of the new oath would be negative. Salamon's answer to the archbishop was (again in Walter's terms) "hesitant and evasive, and he concluded by declaring that the pope would surely not be favourable towards the oath in question and that as far as he, Salomon himself, was concerned, he would not permit himself to blame anyone who pronounced the oath, but that he personally was quite determined to refuse it." It was a reply which, concludes the historian we are quoting, effectively sentenced to death "three hundred Catholic priests representative of the flower of the French clergy" - a generalisation, however, which Marcel Guilhem questions, suggesting rather that things had gone so far by the time the massacres began that it was doubtful whether even the pronouncing of the disputed oath would have made any significant difference to the final tally of deaths.

The interrogations and killings went on at the Abbaye into the small hours of September 3 (but the great majority of prisoners there were, as has been mentioned, royalists and Swiss guards). There was an interruption at about 2.00 a.m. for "refreshments" for the judges and the assassins - two barrels of wine brought in from a local vintner on the Rue Saint Benoît - after which the business was resumed "with redoubled energy". But in the meantime some members of the tribunal had decided to call it a day and failed to reappear after the interval. Some of those that remained were for sending men to their homes to bring them back by force, but others preferred to get on without them: "It's their loss if they don't want to take their share in the nation's vengeance,"

they are quoted as saying. The chairman, Maillard, himself
withdrew at about 5.00 a.m. but "with the assurance that
he would be back in an hour". His place was taken by a
nobody called Dougazon, but his colleagues decided to take
a rest themselves, and Salamon notes that during Maillard's
absence no one was judged or killed.

The chairman duly returned as daylight was beginning
to enter the room. "Let's get it finished!" he said as
he took his place at the head of the table, and the few
remaining prisoners were brought in. All this time the
papal internuncio had remained, as he hoped, concealed
in his hiding place, trusting to find a moment to escape
unnoticed. But the increasing light betrayed his presence
and he was duly arraigned before Maillard. Historians have
been severe with Salamon for having at this moment, by a
subterfuge, allowed his instinct for self-preservation to get
the better of his opportunity to die a martyr's death. He
claimed to be a simple lawyer whose enemies' calumnies
had landed him in the Abbaye. (He had, in fact, obtained a
doctorate in civil law before his ordination to the priesthood.)
Surprisingly Maillard, who recognised the prisoner for who
he was, nevertheless accepted the defence and discharged
Salamon. Mercifully, comments the latter himself, he was
not asked whether he had sworn the oath! It remains true that
historians are indebted to the internuncio. His "Mémoires",
published by Plon of Paris, with Introduction and Notes
by the Abbé Bridier, in 1892, and his correspondence with
the papal Secretary of State, Cardinal Zelada, discovered in
the Vatican Archives and published in 1898 with impressive
editorial flair by the Vicomte de Richement, provide indispensable information about the events in Paris during the
fateful years 1791-1792.

A profoundly sad postscript to the Abbaye story is the
information, based on official documents and quoted by
Gérard Walter, that the men who had carried out the
massacre, "robust and solid individuals, aged from 30 to
40 and belonging to various trades, wheelwrights, locksmiths,
carpenters, shoe repairers, even hatters and watchmakers"
claimed, "as a reward for their services as the nation's
avengers", a shareout of the victims' belongings, and when

this was refused them they demanded payment in cash. The sum fixed by the commune headquarters was 34 livres per man, but on condition that there was no pilfering of money, watches or clothing from the corpses of the men they had massacred.

3

AT THE CARMES

Unlike the Abbaye, where the great majority of the prisoners were laymen, the Carmelite monastery was used almost
exclusively for the incarceration of clergy, between 150 and
180 according to varying accounts. There were three exceptions, of whom two were Brothers of the Christian Schools,
Nicolas Leclercq, whose religious name was Brother Solomon,
and Jean Baptiste Istève, who likewise had a religious name
derived from the Old Testament, Brother Abraham. The
ground of their arrest may be inferred from a document
concerning Istève, discovered by Alexandre Sorel in the
archives of the Paris Police headquarters and published by
him in *Le Couvent des Carmes:*

> On Tuesday, August 14, 1792, the fourth year of liberty, Jean
> Baptiste Istève was brought to the general and permanent
> headquarters of the Luxembourg Section. He was a so-called
> Brother of the Christian Schools, aged 37, residing at the home
> of M. Cornet in the Rue Princesse. He had been denounced
> by the voice of the people for publicly teaching young persons
> principles at variance with the Constitution and urging them to
> keep away from the parish religious services; also for having been
> refractory with regard to the law of *patentes* and for not having
> sworn the oath. The Committee appointed M. Yosse to conduct
> a search at the residence of M. Istève where, however, nothing
> was found. But in view of the facts mentioned above, the person
> concerned being more than suspect, the Committee ordered that
> he be consigned forthwith to the Carmelite monastery.

The document bears the signature of Joachim Ceyrat whom
we have met. Brother Istève, in the event, was to escape the
massacre, but his confrere, Nicolas Leclercq, Secretary

53

General of his Congregation, was among the victims of the Carmes slaughter. Leclercq, Brother Solomon, was an assiduous letter-writer and his correspondence, much of it preserved in his Congregation's central archives, is a valuable source of information about the day-to-day life in Paris during the period directly leading up to the September massacres. No fewer than four notable biographers have deemed Leclercq's life worthy of full-length treatment, three writing in French, the fourth in English. The pioneer work is by the Abbé Hyacinthe Chassagnon who later became the bishop of Autun (the see dishonoured by Talleyrand); his biography was accorded the mention "Couronné par l'Académie Française". The second biographer was Georges Rigault, whose later nine-volume history of Brother Solomon's Institute won the prestigious Grand Prix Gobert of the Academy. And as recently as 1990 Marcel Guilhem has told the Lasallian martyr's story afresh. The one English biographer was the late Dr. W.J. Battersby whose book was published by Burns Oates in 1960.[1]

Chassagnon quotes a long letter written by Nicolas to his sister Marie Barbe on the Feast of the Assumption, August 15, 1792. It was the last of many to his family at Boulogne (who filed them all carefully and later donated them to Nicolas's congregation) since on the evening of the 15th a search party arrested him at the community residence in the Rue Notre Dame des Champs, a few minutes walk away from the parish church of Saint Sulpice. The letter begins:

> Greetings to you and a happy feast day! I pray God that you may spend it in good health with all your dear family, and in the peace and calm which are not easily come by these days. Well, at least let our submission to God's will make up for

---

[1] A reprint of Battersby's work has been issued this year, 1992 (in view of the bicentenary) by St. Mary's Press, Winona, USA. An interesting echo of the Revolution's repercussion on the United States occurred in 1988 with the publication, by Gateway Press, Baltimore, of DESCENDANTS OF AUGUSTIN LECLERCQ, a meticulously researched and beautifully produced history of the flourishing families descended from the children whom Nicolas's widowed brother, Augustin, took to the safety of Gallipolis, Ohio, in 1790 — two years before his Lasallian brother's martyrdom.

other consolations. Let us accept whatever it may please Him to send us and remain faithful to Him. The trials we have to suffer here are transient, but the reward we hope for will be eternal. We should make up for the religious duties our present circumstances prevent us from fulfilling, by means of spiritual reading, prayer and meditation ...

The third non-cleric imprisoned at the Carmes was an aristocrat, Charles Régis Mathieu de La Calmette, Count de Valfons, commanding officer of the Royal Champagne cavalry regiment, retired the previous year. He had lodged with the Abbé Jean Antoine Guillemenet, a curate of the parish church of Saint Roch. A document held at the Paris police archives records his arrest and suffices in itself to explain and justify his presence among the distinguished band of confessors of the faith assembled at the Carmes. Cited by Grente, the minute reads as follows:

October 9, 1791, arrest and interrogation of Ch.-Régis Valfons Mathieu. Holding a rosary in his hands, he declared himself a member of the Catholic, Apostolic and Roman Church, ready to suffer for his religion. He had led the riot that took place in front of the Irish seminary and also, a fortnight previously, the one in the Rue des Carmes. He was referred to the Police Department which in turn sent him to the Public Prosecutor of the 5th criminal tribunal. He was granted bail on condition of presenting himself on every occasion required.

Grente mentions two of the replies that Valfons gave to the tribunal during his interrogation. One was that he had retired from the army "partly because of infirmity, but principally because he had not been able to swear the required oath"; and, asked what his present occupation was, he replied: "The service of God with all my strength."

Like the two Lasallians, therefore, Count Valfons was a worthy companion of the three prelates and a hundred and fifty or so priests who made up the Carmes total. The reference to his having led a riot outside the Irish seminary points to an interesting feature of the life in Paris of the hunted clergy and their followers. There were two Irish seminaries in the French capital at the time, one in the Rue des Carmes, the other in the Rue du Cheval Vert.

Both readily welcomed the non-juror priests and their flocks to their religious services. Letters of Nicolas Leclercq are quoted by Chassagnon to ilustrate this aspect of Paris life at the period we are concerned with:

> Today, feast of St. Vincent de Paul, I went to the Irish College for Mass. Almost everyone present received holy communion ...For my thanksgiving I stayed for a second Mass, celebrated by a young priest, a very angel to look at. (July 19, 1791)
>
> Last week at the Irish community there was the Forty hours devotion, with a sermon each day. On the Sunday two sermons were given simultaneously, one in the library, the other in the refectory, and both places were crowded. (September 15, 1791)
>
> The chapel of the Irish seminary is quite small but it has two altars and Mass is celebrated at both continuously from 6.30 a.m. to 11.00 or noon, and there are always communicants at every Mass. Today, an ordinary Sunday, there were so many communions at the High Mass that I had time, during the distribution, to read the Formula of Honourable Amends of which I sent you a copy. (January 22, 1792)

The Irish seminaries, in common with other non-French foundations, were exempted from the laws affecting religious practice. A decree of October 29, 1790, quoted by Duvergier, reads:

> Establishments for study or teaching; or simply of a religious nature, of foreign foundation in France, will continue to exist as before.

But this official protection did not prevent the harassing of the French "refractories" and "fanatics" who availed of the foreign communities' hospitality. These had often to run the gauntlet of insults and blows from hostile crowds. O.J.M. Delarc, in his monumental work *L'Eglise de Paris pendant la Révolution Française*, quotes a letter of Father Walsh, superior of the Rue des Carmes Irish seminary, addressed to the municipal authorities, complaining about the scenes of violence taking place outside his establishment. No doubt it was one such occasion that was referred to in the charge against Count Valfons, a spurious charge based on some intervention by the ex-army officer aimed at protecting the harassed faithful making their way to the Irish college for their devotions.

The story of the massacre at the Carmelite monastery has a particular interest in that the building which was the scene of the episode, No. 70 Rue de Vaugirard, remains largely the same today and is an indispensable stopping place for tourists or pilgrims interested in the religious life of the French capital. The classical domed church is as it was when the refractory clergy were herded there in August 1792. The door leading to the sacristy brings one on to a corridor which opens on to a small landing with five steps on either side descending into the garden. Two Latin words have been inscribed below this landing: HIC CECIDERUNT – "This is where they fell" – for the prisoners, after a pretence of a trial at a table in the corridor, passed through this door and down the steps where their slaughterers awaited them.

Eye-witness accounts are available to tell us what happened. One of them was written by the Abbé Pierre François Vidal de Lapize de La Pannonie, who (as his name suggests) was born into an aristocratic family in the *département* of Lot on December 21, 1761. He did his clerical studies at Saint Sulpice and graduated in theology at the Sorbonne. He escaped the Carmes holocaust but with wounds sufficient to keep him in hiding with friends in Paris until well enough to move. On September 30 he obtained a passport for England and was able to sail for Hastings on October 13. A work by Canon François Xavier Plass, entitled *Le Clergé Français réfugié en Angleterre*, describes the warm welcome accorded to him and the many other emigrants who made their way to safety across the Channel. Each new group of arrivals had stories to tell of their own or others' experiences, and an early emigrant, a Jesuit historian called Augustine Barruel, took upon himself the task of assembling and checking the various accounts and eventually publishing them from London in 1794 under the title *Histoire du Clergé pendant la Révolution Française*. (He dedicated the work to "the British nation which, in a singular manner, has distinguished itself by its generosity to the French clergy".) It was Barruel who persuaded La Pannonie to write a memoir of his experiences, as La Pannonie indicates, without naming Barruel, in his opening words:

> The memory of the massacre carried out at the Carmes prison in the Rue de Vaugirard, and my own experience of what happened, evoke such horror in me that I would be unable to relate the details if I did not think it my duty to defer to the advice of a clergyman who is as enlightened as he is devout, and who assured me that my account could contribute to the edification of the faithful and to the glory of the Church. With this alone in view I am going to set down quite simply the facts as I experienced them, without allowing myself to add any reflections — which, in any case, the facts will suggest of themselves.

A facsimile reproduction of La Pannonie's very legible manuscript was published, with an introduction by Mgr. De Teil, in 1913, by Desclée, Paris, and it is from this that I translate in the extracts to be quoted here. The memoir is used in all the monographs of the September massacres and there is evident consensus as to its reliability. Henri Welschinger, a member of the Institute of France and a specialist of the Revolution, says of it that "the truth cries out from every page".

There is a second eye-witness account of the Carmes episode, also much quoted by the historians. The author of this was Canon Berthelet de Barbot, Vicar General of the diocese of Mende. His memoir was published in full by the French Academician, G. Lenôtre, in his work *Les Massacres de Septembre*. The general correspondence between Berthelet's account and La Pannonie's encourages confidence in the veracity of both, but they are independent memoirs of the personal experiences of two different men and the information they contain is complementary as well as corroborative.

Both priests were arrested during the first round-up on August 11, and each offers details of the period of detention leading up to the climax of September 2. La Pannonie speaks of the foul language and mockery the prisoners of the Carmes had to endure from the men guarding them, men whose particular sense of humour prompted them to sing snatches of the plainchant Mass for the Dead "no doubt," says La Pannonie, "to let us know what to expect in a short while". Berthelet says that the request to celebrate, or assist at, a Mass was denied throughout the period of the detention, but La Pannonie says that the favour was granted once, on the first Sunday after their arrival, "but, seemingly to diminish the joy we felt at being able to assist at the sacred mysteries, we were told soon afterwards that the only Mass on the following Sundays would be celebrated by a juror priest for the guards". La Pannonie mentions the detail that Mgr. Dulau was a special target of the insults of the guards, one of whom "had the audacity to follow the archbishop everywhere in the church, puffing clouds of tobacco smoke into his face. The venerable prelate offered no response to this unspeakable insolence other than an inexhaustible patience and words full of meekness and charity". La Pannonie continues:

> With the number of prisoners increasing day by day, the Section authorities thought that they should grant us a morning and an evening stroll of an hour each in the garden of the Carmelite fathers; this under the close supervision of the numerous guards. I am bound to say, however, that these same guards, who ordinarily wore a fearsome and threatening expression, quite soon softened their attitude to us, so struck were they by the sight of so many innocent victims awaiting with patience the fulfilment of God's designs on them. I even saw one myself who could not restrain himself from lamenting our lot and protesting out loud at the injustice of our detention. More than once I felt obliged to urge them to be more prudent, assuring them that we had no complaints to make and that our only sorrow was to be slandered to the ordinary people whose best friends we had always been.

Our author also describes the arrival at the prison of the clergy arrested at Issy by Lazowsky's squad:

> At about 10 p.m. on August 15, the feastday of Our Lady, we suddenly heard some frightful shouting and musket shots coming from the courtyard. We thought then that it was all up with us and we withdrew into the sanctuary to offer God the sacrifice of our lives and to place ourselves once again under the protection

of the august Queen of Martyrs whom the Church was honouring that day. But it was not yet the moment of Providence. A new contingent of clergymen was arriving, dragged by Finisterre men from their retirement home of St. François de Sales or from the Sulpicians' seminary at Issy. No words can express my feelings at the sight of those reverend old men who were hardly able to walk upright. The cruel treatment they had received during the transfer would make the most insensitive person shudder with horror ... When we had recovered a little from our shock we set about giving our new guests all the help they needed after their ordeal. We were well repaid subsequently for our pains by the beautiful example these saintly retired men gave. The serenity, patience and resignation reflected in their faces sufficiently revealed the peace within their souls.

Berthelet's account of the initiation of the massacre is the more circumstantial of the two:

Sunday, September 2. Some of us were visited that day by relatives or friends who shook our hands and shed some tears but did not dare to voice their fears. The activity of the guards watching over us, the shouting which reached our ears from the neighbouring streets, and the cannons sounding the alarm, all gave good reason for anxious concern. But our confidence in God was complete. At 2.00 p.m. a Section official hurried in to where we were, took a roll-call and sent us into the garden. We descended by a single flight of stairs almost next to the chapel of the Blessed Virgin which forms part of the church where we were imprisoned. We reached the garden passing through lines of other guards who were not wearing uniforms but were armed with pikes and had red caps on their heads; only their officer in charge was wearing the uniform of the national guard. Hardly had we reached this walking area, which was bordered by the cloister, when some people, looking through the windows of the cloister, started insulting us with vile and bloodthirsty threats. We withdrew to the furthest part of the garden between a line of hornbeams and the wall which separates the property from that of the Sisters on the Rue du Cherche-Midi. Some of us found a refuge in a small oratory placed in a corner of the garden, and we had just begun to say some prayers there when suddenly the garden gate was thrust open with a bang, and seven or eight wild youths rushed in, all wearing belts with pistols in addition to those they were carrying in their left hands; each was brandishing a sabre with his right hand.

The first priest they met and struck down was the Abbé de Salins who was absorbed in reading a book and had seemed oblivious of what was happening. They felled him with sabre strokes and then proceeded to kill or mortally wound all whom they found in their way, without pausing to make sure they were dead, so eager were they to reach the group of clergy gathered at the end of the garden. They advanced on them shouting "The Archbishop of Arles! The Archbishop of Arles!" That saintly prelate thereupon spoke these few words to us, inspired by his lively faith, "Gentlemen, let us thank God for calling us to seal with our blood the faith which we profess; let us ask of Him a grace that we could not hope to obtain by our own merits, the grace of final perseverance." At this point, Père Hébert, Superior General of the Eudist congregation, demanded, for himself and for all of us, the right to be tried. The answer he received was a pistol shot which broke his shoulder; we were all scoundrels they shouted, as they continued to howl, "The Archbishop of Arles! The Archbishop of Arles!"

But for the actual murder of the Archbishop all the historians of September 2 use the narrative of La Pannonie who was fortuitously involved in the incident. (He is mistakenly described by one writer as the Archbishop's secretary and by another as his Vicar General.) His own account of how he came to be at the prelate's side at the fateful moment is worded simply thus:

I had long had the honour of taking my walk in the company of the virtuous Archbishop of Arles, an advantage I availed of as often as I could, because I was so impressed by the good example he never ceased to give us.

And so the two men were together in the garden when the assassins approached, shouting the prelate's name:

I did not leave the Archbishop's side. The strength and calmness he showed in the presence of the danger that threatened us sustained me in the midst of my alarm. Our guards abruptly disappeared. The assassins traversed the garden armed with muskets, bayonets, pikes and pistols. They cut down anyone in their way. One of them came ahead of the others and stood in front of the Archbishop and myself. "Are you the Archbishop of Arles?" he said to me, quivering with fury. I made no other reply than to shrug my shoulders. "It's you,then!" said the raging fellow, this time addressing the Archbishop. "Yes, it is I," he replied immediately, his countenance at once steadfast and modest. "So!" said the monster, "You're the one that caused all that blood to be shed at Arles?" "I?" replied the Archbishop, "I am not aware of ever having harmed anyone." "You haven't harmed anyone, have you, you blackguard? Well, I'm going to harm you here and now!" And forthwith he pounced on him like a raging tiger and dealt him a mighty blow to the head with his sabre. At this first stroke, the Archbishop joined his hands and covered his face. Without a single word of protest he accepted from this brute the death for which he had so well prepared himself during his captivity. A second assailant, eager to share the glory of his comrade, plunged his pike into the body of the illustrious martyr.

As this bloody scene was enacted I moved away to the small chapel of the Blessed Virgin which is in the garden, and there I joined a certain number of my companions. The attackers gathered around us with their muskets and pistols. I saw the Bishop of Beauvais fall nearby and I offered him no help, believing him to be dead; but it was only that his leg was broken.

The astonishing thing, certainly, is that I did not hear a single murmur from those whom I saw being massacred. Several of those who had taken refuge in the chapel accepted death in the act of offering to God the sacrifice of their lives. When the assassins had satisfied their fury a little, they ordered everyone else to assemble in the church, firing their guns all the time. During this move, I saw the Benedictine, Dom Massey, fall at my side and I was grieved not to be able to do anything for him. Back in the church, pursued by the howls of our assailants, we fell to our knees at the foot of the crucifix which was the one and only sign of religion left there.

The situation had become so confused that some of the younger priests (forty or so, according to Barruel) were able to escape by climbing over the garden wall. Word of these escapes reached Ceyrat (he who had declared that all the clergy detained at the Carmes were guilty) and he sent a deputy, Jean Paul Violette, to give a semblance of order to the melee by setting up a tribunal of judgment — not, however (comments Gérard Walter) to waste time examining the case of each prisoner, but simply to pose the question, "Have you sworn the oath?" and, in the case of a negative response, to pronounce the sentence of death. The Abbé Berthelet takes up the story at this point:

An official of the Section called Violette (he was one of the Luxembourg committee members) arrived, with the mission, it seemed, to halt the massacre. He set up a table, with the register of prisoners, near the door which led into the garden. He seated himself there and summoned the priests before him, two by two, first to identify them and then to see if they persisted in refusing the oath. He then made them move along the corridor which ended at the steps going down into the garden. Assassins were waiting there for them and slew them as soon as they appeared, shouting out each time, "Life to the Nation!"

From the very beginning of this species of execution, staged in such a frightful manner, the priests inside the church had no further doubts about what fate awaited them. And yet, continuing in prayer before the altar, they seemed untroubled. As each name was called in turn by the commissioner, they stood up promptly, some with the calm serenity of a pure conscience and total trust in God, others with a certain haste as of men eager to give their lives for Christ. Some went forward with eyes lowered, continuing their prayers and interrupting them only to answer the official, then continuing them calmly as they approached the steps, still praying as the blows fell; others had a breviary or a bible in their hands, conscious of the divine promises which filled the books they held and showing by the expression on their faces their expectation that such promises would be fulfilled when they received the fatal blow. As they reached their assassins they looked at them with an angelic expression full of gentle charity mingled with compassion for such frenzy and blindness. A heavenly nobility marked these priestly heroes as they received the mortal strokes which took them from the persecution of men and from the evils of this world. Several of them, as they left the sanctuary to appear before the commissioner, men on the threshold of paradise, turned their gaze on the crucifix on the altar and spoke the words of Jesus Christ, "My God, forgive them, they do not know what they are doing."

Thus, in this place, died as true martyrs three illustrious prelates, a very great number of clerics, and a devout layman.

The commissioner himself was moved by their heroism. Two days later he admitted, as if in spite of himself, to some priests he had reprieved and who were being held at the Section headquarters: "I couldn't understand it; nor would anyone else have been able to if they had witnessed the same thing. Your priests went to their death as joyfully as men going to their wedding."

Both eye-witnesses conclude their accounts with a fairly detailed explanation of how they came to escape the massacre. Berthelet, having reached the steps where the assassins were waiting, was recognised by one of these who lived in his neighbourhood and he intervened to save him. La Pannonie was rescued "miraculously" (his term) by one of the national guards whom he did not know but who "stood by me with the utmost solicitude, showing me every sign of compassion and concern. He even declined my offer of 500 livres which I had on me, saying that he would be sufficiently compensated if he succeeded in saving my life and that if he did not succeed he had no wish to profit by anything belonging to me".

G. Walter, in his critical study, puts the time taken for the total operation at the Carmes at less than two hours, and he explains this "vertiginous rapidity which at first sight seems beyond belief" by "the orderliness and promptness with which the priests faced the final combat."

Early the next morning two wagons arrived to collect the corpses for burial in the Vaugirard cemetery at the end of the long street in which the monastery was situated. A single common grave had been dug in advance (the grave-diggers had been hired — according to a minute found in the police archives of the Seine *département* — three days prior to the massacre and had received 300 livres for their work). A certain Daubanel, who was given the responsibility for the burial, reported that all the corpses were duly thrown into the common grave, that quicklime had been scattered over them and that the grave had been duly filled in. A rumour went around, however, that many of the bodies had been disposed of in a deep well in the grounds of the monastery itself, and this tradition persisted without, however, being taken very seriously by historians because of the extant document bearing Daubanel's signature. But three-quarters of a century later — in 1867 — the construction of a new thoroughfare, the present Rue de Rennes, necessitated excavations in the monastery grounds and, truly enough, a considerable quantity of human bones were disovered where the oral tradition had claimed them to be. They were reverently gathered and, in due course, placed for the veneration of pilgrims, in a glass-fronted casket in the crypt of the church, with nearby an inscription of Tertullian's famous challenge to the persecutors of the early Christians: "Sanguis martyrum semen Ecclesiae — The blood of the martyrs is the seed of the Church".

4

AT SAINT-FIRMIN AND LA FORCE

The seminary of Saint-Firmin was the only prison other than the Carmes which was intended exclusively for the custody of non- juring clergy although, by chance, as at the Carmes, a layman found himself among the eighty or so clergy held there. This was Jean Antoine Joseph de Villette, a retired officer (like Count Valmont) who had found permanent lodging at the seminary and whose devout Catholic practice there had caused the seminary staff to refer to him as "the blessing of the house". When the search party told him that, as a layman, he could leave the premises before the exits were sealed, his attested reply was, "No fear! I'm too happy here to want to leave!"

In fact, from the first arrests on August 12 until near the end of the month there was a fairly relaxed atmosphere among the detainees who, it seemed, were under the impression that they were simply hostages. A colourful personality among those consigned there was Claude Ignace Laurent, a parish priest of the diocese of Chartres who, like so many others, had come to Paris when ousted from his parish at Brétigny and who had found residence in the Navarre seminary where he had studied. After the meek, if admirable, responses given to Maillard at the Abbaye and to Violette at the Carmes, it is difficult not to warm to the account of Laurent's spirited exchanges with his interrogator, a certain Charles Mathieu Hue. This latter personage, according to a contemporary character sketch quoted by La Gorce, was a polite man, sharp-eyed but of friendly aspect and approachable, but his smile was sardonic and his mildness deceptive: he was capable, in cold blood, of sending fellow-citizens to their deaths without any feeling of personal animosity.

But the Abbé Laurent was not overawed by him and, even if our source for the encounter is a report by Laurent himself, there is nothing in it to raise doubts as to its essential truthfulness. He began by declaring that, yes, he was a priest, a parish priest, in fact, and that he had refused the Civil Constitution oath. He added, however, that the law, as it then was, allowed him to refuse it. He had left his presbytery and locality the day he was dispossessed and had been living for eighteen months quietly in Paris, unknown and minding his own business. He then continued, unperturbed by the sceptical smile of the man facing him:

"I refused the Civil Constitution oath and I would refuse it again, should the occasion arise, because I cannot compromise where conscience and honour are concerned. But I have no quarrel with the republican government. I have even less quarrel with it than you, citizen-judge. At any rate, I was in favour of democratic government long before many other people who now, since August 10, like to boast of their republicanism. I have never been able to resist a certain predilection for this form of government which is suited to idealistic souls and strong characters, and I declare to you, in all frankness, that if I were as convinced that the majority of the French people were as worthy of a republic as I believe myself to be, my desire for a democratic France would be stronger still.

"I have felt that desire ever since the arrest of the King at Varennes. At that time I said quite openly that he should have been let go, since he was leaving the country; or that, if it was deemed preferable at that time, he should have been simply dethroned and offered a quiet existence as a private individual in retirement − a role for which he was well suited. That was the moment to proclaim a republic and it would certainly have been of more value than to bring Louis XVI back to Paris to insult him and heap all sorts of bitterness on him, but to retain for him the title of king and replace him on the throne − a fallen monarch as ruler of our people!

"Fellow-citizens, I am far from repudiating the Republic

and hence I sincerely applauded the decree which recently imposed the liberty-equality oath. Far removed as I was from pronouncing the civil constitution oath, I would be quite ready to pronounce the new one. As I see it, it entails only a political commitment and has nothing to do with dogma; it is a commitment which, at last, draws a line between the social area and that of religion; it enables us, not only to be, but to be seen to be, good citizens, yet without compromising the principles proper to our state. I therefore declare to you that I would pronounce the liberty-equality oath here and now − if I were not under arrest. But were I to do so now, being under arrest, you would deem me, and rightly so, a coward."

It was a bold speech and it won a round of applause from the soldiers standing by. But Charles Mathieu Hue, sitting at the table across from Laurent, showed no sign of emotion but remarked that, with such eloquent protestations, Monsieur l'Abbé had it in him to be a dangerous fellow. In the present circumstances, he went on, it was necessary to take all precautions and a few days at Saint Firmin would do a supporter of the Republic no harm. Laurent takes up the story:

He even said that I had nothing to worry about: no harm would come to me provided I was not one of "the Château conspirators". "A conspirator!" I replied, quietly but firmly, "You know in your heart and conscience that I am no conspirator! And neither am I a fool to be taken in by your assurances. I know what fate to expect. I am under no illusions. Persons like me are not important enough to be held as hostages; we are under arrest to be victims of a holocaust!"

Hue continued to play what his prisoner calls "his hypocritical role", even inviting Laurent to share his lunch, an invitation which the abbé, not to be upstaged, accepted. And at the end of the meal the arrest was confirmed, but in unusual terms: "Take Monsieur l'Abbé to Saint Firmin," Hue told the guards, "but in a fraternal manner and without your weapons."

Laurent's memoir speaks of the moment of his arrival

at the seminary-prison and the passage is also worth quoting:

> I found there a whole crowd of clergymen whom I knew and who welcomed me with real affection. They included former superiors and teachers of mine, colleagues and personal friends. They were, or appeared to be, very cheerful, with just a few exceptions. The Abbé Gros, parish priest of Saint Nicolas du Chardonnet, who had been like a father to me for fifteen years, was the first to remark on my own downcast appearance. "Come now," he said, "here we must leave our worries at the door and be determined not to take a gloomy view." "Oh," I replied, "I'm not gloomy, only serious-minded as befits someone who is being led to his death."

In the event Laurent, unlike his interlocutor, was not to be one of the victims of the Saint Firmin massacre. He managed to make his escape in the mayhem which characterised this particular onslaught. He survived for another twenty-seven years in the course of which he had a period as parish priest of Saint Leu in Paris and, according to Grente, was, under the Empire, appointed to the bishopric of Metz (but René Schneider in *Le Diocèse de Metz* says merely that he "administered the diocese" during a three-years absence of the incumbent, Mgr. Jauffrey).

So Laurent's memoir is not quoted by the historians beyond the point of his conversation with the Abbé Gros. The rest of the story is based on documents found in the Paris police archives but also on another personal account (already briefly referred to) by one of the priests imprisoned at Saint Firmin who also escaped, or rather, was rescued. This was the Vincentian bursar of the seminary, Père Boullangier. The Section authorities had found it convenient (and economical) to leave him relatively free, within the building, to provide for the material needs, not only of the regular residents of the seminary, but also of the increasing number of priests brought in from elsewhere. Boullangier fulfilled this duty with warmth and efficiency, helped by gifts of food and money which he was allowed to receive from sympathisers outside.

His memoir has been cited with reference to the arrests

of some of the detainees at Saint Firmin. His account of what happened inside the improvised prison when the massacre became imminent is mostly taken up with his own experience which led up to his being able to escape (though he speaks throughout of "the Bursar" in the third person), but it sufficiently evokes the general count-down period to be worth quoting:

On Sunday morning, September 2, all Paris was talking about a massacre which was to take place that day. The only people who knew nothing about it were those who were going to be massacred. Placards giving notice that the non-juring priests were going to be deported had reassured these; they had no suspicion that death was so near. And yet Monsieur Henriot, the officer in charge of a troop of sans-culottes, had told them that as criminals they were all due to die. But the very openness with which he made these bloodthirsty threats had made them think he was only trying to frighten them.

At 8.00 p.m. on that Sunday, the Bursar of the seminary, who had authorisation to go in and out of the kitchen, was stopped on his way into it by a butcher's boy whom he did not know except by sight, though his employer was not a supplier to the Seminary. This good youth took the Bursar's arm and said, with tears in his eyes, "Father, save yourself. They are going to kill you all tonight. My master is grief stricken at the thought of your fate, but he dare not come in person to warn you."

The Bursar could not believe that such an atrocity was possible and he suspected a trap. He went straight off to the Superior to tell him what the lad had said. The Superior replied that such a thing was impossible, but he added that he must send one of the domestics to enquire at the Section office, situated in the Rue Saint Victor, whether there really was reason to fear for the Seminary.

The Bursar returned to the kitchen, did the business he had gone for, and then went to the larder where he found the butcher's boy who again took hold of him and pleaded with him to leave the house. He said that all the prisoners at the Carmes had been massacred, that assassins were now on their way to the Seminary, and that in another quarter of an hour it would be impossible to escape. Just then two other young men arrived on the scene, one of them carrying a rifle with bayonet, and these also urged the Bursar to leave. But he said to them, "What about the guards at the entrance? Don't they count for anything?" One of the three youths replied, "We're talking about a mob of four thousand on their way here, and how do you suppose the guards will keep them out? Anyway you can't count on the guards — there are lots of them who have no love for you."

The narrator says that at this point he finally became alarmed and went off again to speak to the Superior. In the meantime the messenger who had been sent to enquire at the Section office had failed to return. Boullangier decided to take his chance of escape. He went back to the three young men and with their help managed to get out into the street. He says that he there offered a louis d'or to the butcher's boy who refused it, saying that he was satisfied now that he had done what he had hoped to do.

Although Boullangier's eye-witness account of the events inside the Saint Firmin building necessarily terminates there, he continues his narrative with details of the actual massacre. As he says himself, a few other prisoners later escaped also and it was from these that he learned the supplementary information. He says that a gang of cut-throats arrived at about 5.30 on the morning of the 3rd. They began by rampaging through the premises, gathering up the prisoners as they went, all except five priests whom Boullangier names (Lhomond, De Letang, Lafontant, Bouchard and Desmoulins — all associated with the parish of Saint Nicolas du Chardonnet in which the Saint Firmin seminary was situated) and who, he says, "were granted the protection of the law". Our author offers no explanation of this unexpected semblance of law and order, but he comments that the detail proves that the operation had been planned by the authorities.

Planned it may have been, but the execution of the plan reads like the work of a mob gone berserk and out of control. "At no moment," says Gérard Walter, "did any members of the Section committee present at the scene of the massacre intervene to stop the grisly proceedings: the 'nation's avengers' were able to operate with complete freedom."

The Superior of the Saint Firmin seminary was, as has been mentioned, the Vincentian Louis Joseph François, a saintly man but also a staunch defender of the rights of religion. He had once written in one of his pamphlets that had made him a marked man for the Jacobins: "Death by starvation is a misfortune, but not so great a misfortune as to die an apostate ... Swear the oath? Death, rather, by far!" The invaders of the seminary now found him in his room on the top storey. The death of the Superior would make an appropriate start to the operation. The window of his room was thrown wide open and the unresisting François was carried to it and thrown out on to the street below, to be finished off by the crowd waiting there. For the first time in the various accounts of the September massacres mention is made here of the violent interventions of women in the work of the assassins. Armed with kitchen implements they helped to deal successively with the victims thrown down from the windows of the seminary. One of them, it is reliably reported — Pierre de La Gorce quotes it — earned on this occasion the nickname "La Tueuse" — The Killer — and she was referred to by that name for the rest of her life. It is to be hoped that a detail of female malevolence mentioned in one account, and quoted by Joseph Grente, is no more than a melodramatic embellishment prompted by a sense of outrage: some of the women, it was claimed, gouged out with scissors the eyes of the corpses.

The Abbé Gros, whom we left urging Laurent to cheer up, was not thrown out of a window; he was beheaded inside. A story about him says that during the massacre a sympathiser offered him a chance to escape, but Gros replied: "These people are aware that I am here and I know that they are after my blood. If they don't find me they'll turn the place upside down, and any others of the prisoners who are hiding will be found and slaughtered. Better I remain here."

The cry "Life to the Nation!" resounded throughout the building as the bloodbath proceeded. One of the victims was Pierre Claude Pottier, Assistant General of the Eudist Congregation and later Rector of the Seminary of Rouen, about whose career Grente has some interesting details. Eighteen months earlier, on January 16, 1791, Pottier had sworn the liberty-equality oath, believing it to be permissible and being anxious to continue his pastoral ministry if at all possible. But less than a week later he pronounced a retraction, of which the text, held in the municipal archives of Rouen, is quoted by Grente:

> I, the undersigned, a priest and Superior of the Seminary of Rouen, certify and declare that, for grave and pressing reasons of peace and security, of my own free will, I resign my charge as a public functionary, a charge which, for similar reasons, I have hitherto fulfilled with openness and good faith. Persuaded now by new considerations that have been put to me, I hereby disavow and retract any civic oath pronounced by me, and notably that which I pronounced on the 16th of the present month in the metropolitan church of this city. I desire that this act be made public by the newspapers. Rouen, January 22, 1791.

Grente records that a solid combined tradition of the Rouen archdiocese and of Pottier's own religious congregation retains details of what led the sincerely-intentioned priest to make such a volte-face within less than a week. The morning following the Rector's swearing of the liberty-equality oath he found himself alone in the seminary chapel when he went there to preside at the morning prayers. He forthwith made the rounds of the corridors knocking at the doors of the seminarians' rooms. He opened one door and, finding the student still in bed, told him to get up and go to the chapel quickly. The reply he received was, so to speak, his moment of truth: "Sir, we students no longer acknowledge you as our Superior. You have left the fold of the Church and we cannot now pray with you." It was a stunning blow and, to recover his balance, Pottier set off for a visit home. When he arrived, so the tradition goes, the door was opened by his mother but she held it ajar only long enough to say, "Go away, apostates are not welcome here!"

The story is representative of the many personal traumas that afflicted the lives of individuals at this period when the de-Christianising forces of the Revolution were at work. The irony of the confused situation bids us call Father Pottier's "horrible massacre" (the words used in the record), with him urging his murderers to repent until they finally silenced him, a happy ending to what was judged to be a momentary wavering in his journey of faith.

As in the case of the previous massacres, the number of victims at Saint Firmin is variously estimated. La Gorce puts the total at seventy-five priests together with the one layman, Jean Antoine de Villette. The same authority says that fifteen (he seems to be giving round-figure estimates) managed to escape, either by scaling the surrounding wall or by concealing themselves in the building, familiar to them, until the assassins departed. All was over by 4.00 p.m. The bodies of the victims were despoiled of their belongings and then thrown on to wagons "as logs of wood are thrown", an eye-witness told Boullangier) and were carted off for mass burial.

Mortimer-Ternaux, author of a multi-volume *Histoire de la Terreur*, using documents relating to the subsequent trials of the "Septembriseurs" (a word that the massacres added to the French language) describes the macabre ritual of the doling out of wages for "the work" done at Saint Firmin. One official ventured to make difficulties about this, but quickly changed his attitude when the spokesman of the group awaiting their pay gave a meaningful glance at the window out of which the last priests had been thrown. When the money was handed over "the killers went off to a nearby wineshop to share out the profits of the day, absolutely as if it were the most ordinary business possible". One witness testified that there was a problem about breaking down the louis d'or for the share-out and that he personally was asked if he could provide change – a request, he said, which he lost no time in fulfilling.

September 3 witnessed also a wholesale massacre at the official Paris prison known as La Force which was situated between the Rue Pavée and the Rue du Roi de Sicile (it was demolished in 1850). The buildings were in two sections, the Petite Force, to which women were assigned, and the Grande Force, reserved for male political prisoners. This probably explains why the five priests who were held there were the only clerical "offenders" not to be assigned to one of the three improvised prisons we have visited. All five were suspected of anti-revolutionary activity over and above any refusal of the oaths.

The five concerned were: Jean Baptiste Bottex, a former parish priest of the diocese of Belley; Jacques Flaust, also a parish priest but of the diocese of Paris; Michel François de La Gardette, a curate of the parish of Saint Gervais in the capital; Bertrand de Molleville, another diocesan priest, under suspicion as being the brother of a minister in Louis XVI's government; and Hyacinthe Le Livec, a Jesuit and chaplain to the Convent of the Daughters of Calvary, Paris. The Abbé Flaust escaped death by pronouncing the liberty-equality oath (he argued that it was only the opinion of some people that this oath was not compatible with the faith, an opinion not shared by all competent persons, and he declared that he saw no reason why he should "sacrifice his life for an opinion"). De Molleville also escaped death, though how he did so is not clear. The remaining three were killed.

The Abbé Bottex, who had been a member of the Constituent Assembly, was arrested in the first place on suspicion of conspiracy. A letter was found in his possession written to him by the Abbé (and future Cardinal) Maury, a former fellow-member of the Constituent and an implacable defender of the Church's rights there. But when Bottex came before the tribunal at La Force, he was cleared of the charge, since the letter was found to contain no incriminating evidence. However, before pronouncing the acquittal, his judges asked him to demonstrate his "patriotism" by pronouncing the liberty-equality oath. This Bottex refused to do and promptly received the death sentence.

A document exists concerning the interrogation of Michel-François de La Gardette which led to his incarceration at La Force. It is a letter he was able to write to his family after his arrest, and extracts from it are quoted by Grente. If the letter accurately records what happened, we are in the presence of an exceptionally courageous man, one whom an observer unfamiliar with the supernatural gift of fortitude might describe as "too outspoken for his own good". When the police interrogator told him that among the people of his neighbourhood he was under suspicion of anti-revolutionary procedures, he replied, "It is true that I am under suspicion, but only by the intruder clergy and their false Catholic followers". Among his papers, which had been confiscated by the police, was a written statement protesting against the Civil Constitution oath. "I was happy," he comments in his letter home, "that they had found it as well as some other papers which state my principles, for they are principles I would readily proclaim from the housetops!" In reply to the warning by his interrogator that he was not helping himself to obtain an acquittal, he said, "So be it. I am prepared to defend my faith with my life. I love my God, my King and my Country. Send me to my death, but I shall still be above you to defend all three!"

The Jesuit Hyacinthe Le Livec, in addition to being a non-juring priest, was incriminated as having been the spiritual director of the Princess de Lamballe, who was a close friend of the queen, Marie Antoinette, and who was herself to be the victim of a particularly horrendous murder at La Force on this same occasion. De Guilhermy's Jesuit Martyrology says of Father Le Livec: "He had accepted with heroic courage the suffering of exile and penury in order to remain faithful to his Society ... His virtue, learning and meritorious qualities had caused him to be held in the highest esteem in Germany. As chaplain to the Daughters of Calvary and as spiritual director to the Lamballe family he was regarded as a saint."

INTERLUDE:
A CONTEXT OF TERROR

Just a fortnight after the burial of the last victims of the September massacres, the Legislative Assembly gave way to the new governing body of France known as the National Convention. Its first act, dated September 21, 1792, was the formal abolition of the monarchy and the proclamation of a Republic. Two political ideologies confronted each other within the Convention. One of the parties, of radical tendency, was known as the Montagnards, simply because these occupied the higher level of seating in the assembly chamber (in the Tuileries palace left available by the imprisonment of the royal family in the Temple). The other, more moderate, party had been given the sobriquet Girondins because its most prominent members happened to be the elected members of the *département* of the Gironde. The Montagnards were dominated by a triumvirate of Georges Jacques Danton, Jean Paul Marat and Maximilien de Robespierre, all of whom had played a part in the de-Christianising process under way and in the explosion of violence of September 2.

Having abolished the monarchy, the Convention was obliged by its destructive logic to dispose of the still living monarch. On December 11 the long-suffering Louis XVI ("Citoyen Capet") was brought to trial before the assembled members of the Convention, transformed for the purpose into a Supreme Court. Historians combine to praise the dignity he demonstrated in this situation. The charge was conspiracy against the nation and, despite an eloquent defense by his lawyers, he was found guilty by a majority of 683 votes. The question next put to the vote was whether he be sentenced to death or to imprisonment and exile. On January 20, 1793, a majority of 70 came down in favour of immediate execution and the sentence was carried out by guillotine two days later.

The regicide triggered events of far-reaching significance. A European coalition, led by Britain, posed an increasingly dangerous threat from outside and, within the country, an uprising in the Vendée region signalled warnings to the Convention that the people were far from wholly behind them in their efforts to make the republican dream a reality. The government's reaction was to establish, on March 10, a Revolutionary Tribunal with two subsidiary committees, one of General Security, the other of Public Safety, both of which would deliberate in secret. Stemming from these, a proliferation of committees of surveillance were set up in municipalities throughout France, with the duty to delate suspects. The General Security's purported role was to safeguard the lives and properties of the people, that of the Public Safety was to guide foreign policy and the defence of the country against enemies from without. The two Committees, in collaboration with the Revolutionary Tribunal, were the agents of the period of terror which, in the years 1793-1794, further disfigured the story of a great nation.

Precise dates are given for this lurid period: March 10, 1793 (the establishment of the Revolutionary Tribunal) to July 27, 1794, the arrest of Robespierre who, by then, was the only surviving member of the triumvirate: Marat had died on July 13, 1793 at the hands of Charlotte Corday, and Danton, arraigned by Robespierre himself on a charge of financial misdealings, had been guillotined on April 6, 1794.

The Reign of Terror, as history has named it, was marked by two phenomena: the wholesale use, against all enemies, proved or suspected, of the regime, of the expeditious instrument of execution, the guillotine, an invention of the Revolution, of which it remains in popular imagination the sinister symbol; and a reckless intensification of the attempt to de-Christianise a nation whose Christian faith was rooted in the days of St. Irenaeus, the Church's first great theologian.

The overall number of executions carried out during the

fifteen months of the Terror remains a matter of conjecture. A statistical study by an American writer, Donald Greer, and published in 1935 under the title: *The Incidence of the Terror: A Statistical Interpretation*, is still quoted by historians who confront the question. But Greer's estimate of 17,000 victims was based on only one third of the executions, according to Marc Bouloiseau who suggests a total of 50,000 as likely.

The Convention early turned its attention to the religious cult which was thus far tolerated provided its ministers had sworn the oath. The day after its installation at the Tuileries, it proclaimed "The Era of the Republic", thereby, says Pierre Pierrard, "manifesting in an official manner its wish to break with France's Christian past". The first anniversary of the events of August 10, 1792, was celebrated as the Feast of the Unity and Indivisibility of the Republic, but without the Solemn High Mass and Te Deum at Notre Dame, traditionally at the centre of public festivals. The painter, Louis David, a member of the Convention, was entrusted with the devising of a liturgy for the ceremonies and he made the glorification of Nature the theme. "Of Christ and His gospel there was no mention" (J. Leflon).

Another major step in the same direction was the abolition of the Gregorian calendar "a repertoire of lies, duplicity and quackery" which "assigned a so-called saint to every day of the year" — according to the playwright Fabre d'Eglantine who was entrusted with the task of producing a new calendar more in keeping with the principles of the Revolution. The new system divided the year into twelve months, each of thirty days, with five supplementary days set apart for the celebration of feasts of the Republic. The year began with the autumn equinox, September 22-23. The months were given new names associated with nature: the first, September 22 October 21, was *vendémiaire* (the "grape-harvest" month); the second, October 23 November 21 was *brumaire* (the "foggy" month) and so on. Each month was divided into three "decades" of ten days each, and the days were named according to their numerical sequence, *primidi, duodi* etc. Sunday was effectively abolished, the new day of rest being *decadi*, the tenth day. The system lasted thirteen years, the Gregorian calendar being reinstated on January 1, 1806.

On November 7, 1793 (17 brumaire, Year II) the "intruder" bishop of Paris, Gobel, whom we have met, presented himself with eleven of his "episcopal vicars" before the Convention assembly and announced that he and his colleagues, "yielding to the imperious voice of public opinion", renounced, there and then, the exercise of their functions as ministers of the Catholic religion. The statement was acclaimed and all the clerical delegates present, as if by pre-arrangement, thereupon formally abjured their religious prejudices − all except the redoubtable Henri Grégoire (whom we have also met), the intruder bishop of what had been the diocese of Blois, who resisted all pressures, whether blandishments or threats, to resign.

Three days after the Gobel debacle, the Cathedral of Notre Dame was desecrated by a celebration there in glorification of Liberty and Reason. A lofty structure was built up in front of the sanctuary and on a throne sat the goddess of Reason − an unnamed actress, dressed in white robes and blue mantle and wearing the red bonnet which had become a trademark of the Revolution − while the assembly vied in singing her praises and pledging fealty. An element of buffoonery entered into the proceedings and the guiding spirits of the Convention were not amused. Robespierre dismissed the business as "a masquerade".

It was Robespierre who saw that a belief in the existence of God was not something that could be obliterated by absurd manifestations. He also saw that such a belief, combined with an acceptance of the immortality of the soul, was the mainstay of moral and social order. This conviction, however, did not diminish his detestation of the Church and its clergy. He was all in favour of the pressure put on the constitutional priests (whose taking of the oath had left them free to conduct the liturgy for the people who chose to worship in their churches) to renounce their priesthood. He supported a motion, voted through on November 20, exempting priests who married from all penalties and awarding them an increment to their salary of 800 livres.

It was again the Incorruptible (a term applied to Robespierre with complimentary or pejorative overtones according to the applier) who introduced a new cult to displace that of the goddess Reason. On June 8, 1794 (20 prairial, Year II), a grandiose ceremony, devised again by the painter David, was carried out in Paris, to the glory of the Supreme Being. The presiding dignitary was Robespierre, conveniently elected president of the Convention four days before, and it was he who pronounced the discourse and generally performed the functions of high priest.

His colleagues soon realised that, by electing him president of the Convention, they had created a dictatorship and that the protagonist concerned was a man of blood. They quickly came to feel that they themselves (and not only the hated clergy and religious) were − as potential rivals − targets of the Incorruptible's attentions. It was said at the time that members of the Convention avoided their own homes as much as possible, for fear of being arrested there; and that when they found themselves in Maximilien's company they assumed a distracted air for, said one of them, "I would not want him to think that I was thinking something". But fear easily turns to aggression and the growing hostility to Robespierre within the Assembly reached boiling point on July 27, 1794 (9 thermidor − the "hot" month − Year II) when a fusillade of accusations was aimed at him and his attempts to reply were shouted down. He and his few friends, Saint-Just, Couthon, Le Bas, were placed under arrest at three o'clock that same afternoon. In the evening of the next day they were decapitated in the Place de la Révolution, except Le Bas who cheated the guillotine by shooting himself.

It was in this context of terror that the Christian martyrs whose story remains to be told stood firm to their consciences and their calling. And first, the religious Sisters against whom the charge was "fanaticism", which was the de-Christianisers' word for "fidelity".

PART II
THE VIRGIN MARTYRS

5

THE RUE DE GRENELLE
CONTEMPLATIVES

As it happens, the first group of Sisters to claim our attention, chronologically, were spared the final sacrifice at the eleventh hour by the events of "9 thermidor" (the historians' shorthand for the downfall of the Robespierrists). But "martyr" is the Greek word for "witness" and the group of Carmelites and one Visitation nun with whom we are concerned here were certainly witnesses to the power of the Spirit and to the fortitude they were given to confront the harassment they suffered throughout the period of the Terror. Their story is particularly well documented and the sources include not only an important dossier held in the National Archives at Paris, but also a personal account of the events by one of the Sisters which makes compulsive reading. The major historian of the operations of the Revolutionary Tribunal in the capital, Henri Wallon, says of the arraignment of these contemplatives that "their trial manifests Christian faith with a simplicity and strength worthy of the earliest confessors and martyrs of the Church."

The initial inroad into their life of prayer occurred precisely on the day the massacres were taking place in the Carmelite monastery which had housed their confreres. Late in the evening of September 2 a squad of armed men appeared at the gate of the convent in the Rue de Grenelle and demanded entrance. The gatekeeper remonstrated, "The Sisters have retired to sleep. You will terrify them!" "We are not concerned with the Sisters," was the reply, "We are looking for a calotin who has escaped and is hiding somewhere here." The concierge opened the gate and the men made for the entrance to the building and began to bang on the door leading into the cloister. It was opened from within by the prioress who was brushed aside with the three Sisters who were with her. The search for the escaped priest proved fruitless and was called off at midnight.

Less than a week later, September 8, a second house search was made with the purpose of surprising any *réfractaire* who might be hiding there. Again the yield was nil, but the chagrined pursuers took the opportunity to remind the Sisters that the law no longer allowed the wearing of the religious habit and that the sooner they conformed the better it would be for them. Only three days after that, all the entrances to the convent were forced open and a mob of vandals, collected for the purpose, made their way through the building, leaving damage everywhere. The Sisters were told to quit within three days or be evicted by force.

The nuns used the interval to make what preparations they could and, in accordance with the threat that had been made, two commissioners arrived on the 14th to escort the community out of the house. The thirty-five religious had already decided to break up into groups of five or six, with a member of each group in charge, so as to continue their religious life to whatever extent circumstances would allow. Thanks to the discreet negotiations of some non-juring priests in the neighbourhood (their names are given in the sources — De Launay, ecclesiastical superior of the Sisters, Legris-Duval, Bechet, Vicar General of Paris, and others) refuges had been found for the groups in houses whose proprietors were in sympathy. Almost inevitably the refuges soon became known to the Section authorities and periodic raids were made, always with the official object of seeking refractory priests. One such refuge was in the Rue Mouffetard, and the Section chose Good Friday, March 29, 1793, to carry out a search there — led by none other than Claude Lazowsky whom we last met rounding up the aged clergy and the students at Issy. No priest was found, but the altar of repose of the previous day was discovered and duly noted.

The Sister in charge at the Rue Mouffetard was Camille de Soyecourt, a lady of noble birth, whose father was to be guillotined a year later for the crime of being an aristocrat and therefore an enemy of the Revolution. The danger attached to Camille's name, however, did not prevent her from presenting herself at the Section headquarters on the Saturday to lodge a complaint about the confiscation by Lazowsky's men of some papers which included letters of her own. She was promptly led off to the police headquarters for interrogation, specifically concerning the priests who had been welcomed at the Rue Mouffetard. Camille's refusal to give names provided grounds for her arrest and incarceration at the women's prison called the Sainte Pélagie. The document minuting her arrest is in the Paris police archives and has been published by Henri Leclercq among others:

> We, the administrators of justice, in consideration of the refusal of the said Soyecourt to declare the names and residences of the priests who have celebrated Mass at the said house, Rue Mouffetard, which indicates a connivance with refractory priests, the moreso since the citizen Soyecourt was in charge of the community there and so most certainly knew the names and residences of those priests; and since therefore her responses to our questions cannot be sincere, we order that the citizen Soyecourt be placed in custody at the Sainte Pélagie prison until such time as the names and addresses of the priests concerned are known.

At the prison Camille found three of the Sisters of her group already there, and also another Carmelite of the Pontoise community who had joined them in Paris. An anecdote of this sojourn at the Sainte Pélagie well illustrates the light-hearted way in which the Sisters accepted their lot. One of them, Joséphine de Carvoisin, declared that she was going to fast on bread and water, to make herself more ready to appear before God's judgment seat. "Oh no, Sister Joséphine," the others teased her, "a victim for sacrifice has to be nice and plump. And besides, this is Easter time and to fast is contrary to the spirit of the Church." "Well," replied the 60-year old Joséphine, "I prefer to wait and sing my alleluias in heaven. What a joy it will be to mount the scaffold! Whatever have we done to deserve such a favour?"

But the threat of the guillotine was not yet immediate. The small group of Carmelites were transferred to the tribunal of the Sainte Geneviève Section, where it was hoped that new interrogations would bring to light the whereabouts of the elusive priests. It was a vain hope. The minutes show that Camille de Soyecourt was more than a match for the men who tried to break down her refusal to name names.

The sessions sometimes lasted several hours, on one occasion from 5.00 p.m. to midnight, during which Camille finally lapsed into silence and broke it only when her interrogator asked why she was now refusing to answer questions and she replied, "Because I am waiting for you to tire of repeating the same old things". During another session papers were produced that had been confiscated at the Rue Mouffetard. An extract from a letter signed "Abbé de Floriac" was read: "Our nation must be overcome, and when it revolts it must be vanquished at any cost to self . . ." "Well, Citizen Soyecourt," said the interrogator, "so our nation must be overcome, must it? What have you to say to that?" "Can you not read?" was Camille's reply, "The word is 'nature' not 'nation'. It's spiritual direction." In yet another session the questions turned on a collection of Sacred Heart badges found also at the Rue Mouffetard. The interrogator told Camille that these were emblems of anti-revolutionary activity. Her reply is the most extended and enthusiastic one in the dossier: "The Sacred Heart of Jesus? Oh, now I can answer with complete freedom, without implicating anyone! I am proud to tell you that I made those badges myself, and if you call that a crime and are going to condemn me for it, why then I shall be sure of dying for my faith! The Sacred Heart of Jesus is dearer to me than life itself and if by my death I could make Him better known and better loved, ah then my happiness would be boundless indeed!" Her questioner, trying hard to maintain the initiative in the uneven contest, interrupted her to say, "How many of these emblems have you made? We need to know the number!" "Oh," replied the imperturbable contemplative, "I've made so many, and given away so many, that it would be quite impossible for me to state a figure."

The Mouffetard group had been in custody since April 1,

but on May 11 the authorities, apparently admitting defeat, discharged them. But the surprise house searches continued and our story of the Rue de Grenelle Carmelites now moves to another of the havens found after the expulsion from their convent. This was in the Rue Cassette, a street at right angles to the Rue de Vaugirard and minutes away from the scene of the Carmes massacres. A search there, conducted on November 29, 1793, led to the arrest, two days later, of the entire group of seven Carmelites and a Visitation Sister who had taken refuge with them. The National Archives dossier of their case, W. 321, d.491, lists their names: Victoire Crevel, in charge of the group, Louise Thérèse de La Biochaye, Joséphine de Carvoisin, Chrétienne Donon, Rosalie de Joubert, Philippine de Lesners and Angélique Vitasse (whose name will reappear prominently in our story) and the Visitandine, Madame Chenet. The charge against them was that they "refused to swear the oath of liberty and equality, and were counter-revolutionary fanatics who intrigued with refractory priests – those men who destroy the people in the name of heaven – against the Revolution and against the eternal principles of liberty and equality on which the Revolution is founded".

The house-search had revealed a paper which, in the terms of this charge, was particularly incriminating. It was a leaflet headed: *Advice to Religious Virgins Consecrated to Jesus Christ* and beginning: "It is in the name of Jesus Christ and His holy Mother, and of the entire Catholic Church, that a minister of Jesus Christ humbly requests you to heed the advice which the love of our divine Master prompts him to offer you . . ." The essence of the leaflet was a vehement warning against swearing the liberty-equality oath which the unnamed author of the piece condemned uncompromisingly (too much so, in the view of the Benedictine scholar, Henri Leclercq, considering the body of respectable opinion which allowed it a personal interpretation: unlike the Civil Constitution oath – Leclercq notes – it had not been formally condemned by the Pope).

The Rue Cassette Sisters apparently knew who the author of the document was, but they were unanimous in their refusal to reveal his name under pressure of repeated interrogations.

Delarc, who prints the piece in full, suggests that the author was the ever busy Père de Clorivière who, according to his biographer, Jacques Terrien, had found shelter precisely in the Rue Cassette house where the Sisters had found a home shortly before. (The hiding-hole he had contrived in the foundations of the house places him, it would seem, in not unworthy succession to his Jesuit confrere, Nicholas Owen, of an earlier English persecution.)

The Rue Cassette nuns were taken first to the bureau of the Section, then to the Bourbe prison, and from there to the central office of the Revolutionary Tribunal. Here they underwent an intensive interrogation of which one of them, Sister Angélique Vitasse, has left a written record. She compiled this at the request of a lady of the vicinity, Madame Bergeron, a devout Catholic who had rendered whatever charitable services she could to the inmates of the Bourbe prison and was later arrested herself for having given shelter to a non-juring priest. The Vitasse document was found in a search of Madame Bergeron's house and it now forms part of the dossier at the National Archives. Angélique's account is a remarkable document, representing such a power of memory and narrative skill that Delarc, who quotes it in full, feels it useful to cite beforehand the official summary of the interrogations (also in the dossier) as evidence of the accuracy of the nun's version. The account is lengthy but the detail of its information seems to justify a translation of much of it here:

The friendship you have honoured me with, Madame, and the kindnesses you never stop rendering to my Sisters and myself, are strong reasons indeed for me to satisfy your wish. In doing so, I count on your indulgence, knowing my incapacity for the task. But I do it with the confidence of a child who knows that it need fear no criticism from its mother.

I think you already know how our arrest came about. It was for not having taken the oath. We spent five hours at the Section bureau where we were threatened with being sent separately to the workhouse or to the Bicêtre prison, or to the guillotine, but were finally despatched to the Bourbe prison. We reached there an hour after midnight on December 1, bereft of even the most necessary things. Some ladies there very charitably let us share their quarters for the rest of the night. The next day, and the following three days, the corridors and a vast common room (with a hundred or so men there) were our dwelling places. But when our charitable ladies vacated their own room they let us use it for saying our office together.

Every evening we were led around looking for a room to sleep. Some of the rooms had been parlours and had no locks to their doors. We were lent four mattresses and just a blanket each. The cold, and all the other discomforts, caused our Visitation nun to become ill, and thereupon we were given another smaller room with a fireplace. We obtained permission for things to be sent into us, but when we had eight mattresses spread out it was difficult to pick one's steps between.

Our sick Sister developed bronchitis and a high temperature and it was really sad to see her suffering so much. We were kept indoors all day and we had to wait three or four hours if we needed anything. We had asked for a doctor to come and bleed our patient, but he was made to wait two hours before being brought in and he said he wasn't going to be trapped like that again. In fact, he never came back and we were powerless to give Sister the treatment she needed. We really feared we were going to see her die there in front of us. God must have permitted this to show how virtuous the dear sufferer was: her patience and resignation were so perfect that she was an inspiration to us all. She herself spoke words of encouragement and joined us in reciting the prayers for the dying with a quite admirable peace and tranquillity. Then the Lord, having given us such a great example of virtue, brought it about that a doctor, who was a prisoner in the same establishment, was allowed to visit Sister every day and he brought her back to health quite soon.

We had been ten days in this one room when the administrators came to see us. They were so appalled at our state that they immediately had us transferred to another apartment where we were as well off as anyone can be in a prison. We remained there, in relative peace, for about six weeks, experiencing the goodness of Providence every day in the form of help given to us by the generosity and kindness of people who brought us things before we had thought of asking for them.

Well, we had been at the Bourbe prison about two months, resigned to all God's designs on us, thinking only of blessing Him for the kindness with which he watched over us, when, one day at two o'clock in the morning messengers came to take our Sister Victoire to the office for questioning. We heard no more of her for two hours, which worried us very much. Then they came for Sister Louise Thérèse Biochaye. We were told that we would all be going, one after the other, but the messengers did not know why. In fact the Sisters duly left in turn and none of them came back, which meant that we had no idea what was happening. We became more anxious than I can express.

At five o'clock in the evening they came to bring myself down together with Sister Chrétienne and our Visitandine. The other five, who had already been questioned, were coming back up and I made to hand one of them the key to our room, but one of the guards accompanying us watched me with a threatening glare, and so I was unable to find out anything. We were kept waiting until six o'clock because our interrogators were having dinner. The time we passed in the waiting room was no small ordeal for us since the place was crowded with different people who had nothing in common with us.

At seven o'clock a guard came for me and led me into a large room. At two sides of a table in the middle were seated two men [Henri Leclercq supplies their names: Antoine Marie Maire, a judge of the Revolutionary Tribunal, and Raymond Josse, the minuting secretary.] I was told to sit. I was then asked my name, my age, the places I had lived in, and how long it was since I had left my convent. Then one of the two said to me, "I am a judge of the Revolutionary Tribunal. You must know that the tribunal has been established to judge and condemn to death all who are found hostile to the Republic, and that when the Republic is firmly established the tribunal will exist no longer and all its judges will return to the same rank as their fellow-citizens."

He had put on his spectacles in order to see me better, and both men looked at me very intently as if to see whether I showed any signs of fear. But since God was powerfully upholding me I did not feel the least emotion of any kind. I simply nodded my head as if to say, "All right," but I said nothing — at which they seemed surprised.

"Have you taken the oath?"

"No."

"Why?"

"Because it is against my conscience and my vows to do so."

Then he passed me a handwritten paper which had been found with a young lady during a search of her house, and she had said she had got it from our Sister Sainte Victoire. He asked me if I knew it:

"I heard it read at the Section bureau on the day we were arrested."

"Do you agree with what it says?"

"Yes."

"Where did this paper come from?"

"The Sister to whom it was given told me that she could not recall who had given her it."

"Do you know who wrote it?"

"She who was given it did not know. How should I know?"

"Are you allowed to tell lies in your religion?"

"No."

"Very well. Did priests ever come to see you at the Rue Cassette?

"We did have friends who sometimes came to see us there."

"I am not asking you if you had friends who came to see you. I am asking you specifically if priests came there. Answer me! Did priests come to see you?"

"Sometimes."

"Were they bishops? Did they have any rank?"

"No."

"Did you make your confession to them? Did they say Mass?"

"Sometimes."

"Often?"

"No."

"How many came?" (The secretary added: "Did two come?")

"Yes."

"Tell me where they live."

"I don't know."

"Their names?"

"I won't tell you."

"Why?"

"I don't wish to."

Here the secretary gave me to understand that if I did not give the names the consequences would be regrettable for me.

"Nothing will happen to me except what God permits."

The judge: "It isn't God who is judging you! It's myself and the other judges of this tribunal!"

"It is God who will permit the judgment you will pass on me."

"Such stubbornness! You are willing to sacrifice your life for them, something you would not do for your own father!"

"Pardon me. I would certainly give my life to save that of my father, and I would do so also for you."

"That's not true. You would not do so for me."

"Pardon me. I would not wish to save my life at the expense of yours."

"So! You will not give me their names?"

"No."

"They are guilty, then, since you do not want to name them?"

"No, they are not guilty of anything. You only want to know who they are so as to do them harm, and that is why I won't name them."

"Did they come to hear confessions in your convent?"

"No."

"Who are the persons who told them about you?"

"I cannot tell you."

"Why?"

"I am the youngest Sister and I mind my own business. So I cannot tell you who they are."

"I am not asking you if you mind your own business, or if you wish or are able to tell me. I am asking you formally the names of the persons who told the priests about you."

"I won't tell you."

"You have to tell me!"

(I made no reply to this.)

"What you say has to be written down. Now, answer me!"

"Very well. Write down that I did not wish to answer you."

"Is it not true that citizens Suzanne and Rousselle lived with you at the Rue Cassette?"

"No."

"Are you cold?" (He said this with an air of great kindness.)

"No."

"Well then. So you won't take the oath?"

"No."

"You think you are better than the others?"

"No, citizen."

"Do you think you are below the others?

"Yes, I think that is where I belong."

"It's those priests who have turned your head. They want to put you against us, and if they could they would lunge a sword into each one of us. They are seditious men who gather meetings everywhere to work up a revolt."

"I have never known anyone who thought like that."

"You're like them. You'd be glad to see all sorts of calamities fall on us!"

"I wish no harm to anyone. I desire what is good for everyone."

"All right, then, take the oath! We are not asking anything else of you, only that you regard all men as your brothers and that you will contribute as far as you can to gain for them the liberty that alone can make them happy, and that you will defend their rights."

"I am a woman. How could I defend anyone's rights?"

"You would do so as far as it depended on you."

"I'd live at peace in my cell, not interfering with anyone else's business. The oath would be useless for me. It would be swearing in vain."

"Would you not want to prevent someone from robbing your neighbour?"

"Oh, surely I would if I were able."

"Do you not believe that all men are equal, and do you not acknowledge them to be your brothers?"

"I have long believed in such equality. But I recognise also that there are superiors to whom I must show submission."

"Where are they, these superiors?"

"You have dealt with them so efficiently that I do not know where they are."

"How can you wish to obey men who are dead? And if they are dead, what way can you obey them?"

"The explanation is that I obey God in their person and when they die others take their place, and God, who is always living, is the One I obey in each of them."

"So much for your obedience! They've abandoned you here and are at their ease somewhere while you are in danger of all kinds of misfortune. Come, swear the oath!"

"No, I will not."

"You have a sincere look on your face, but those old women have turned your head."

"My Sisters have not turned my head. God and my conscience have always guided me."

"You have held meetings to foster a revolt against us!"

"We have never concerned ourselves with politics. We were living in peace and tranquillity. We kept together because we loved one another and because it was less costly. When we went to obtain certificates of residence the Section authorities never made any difficulty about our living together."

"You are living at the nation's expense."

"If you hadn't taken what belongs to us we wouldn't be living at the nation's expense."

"What's that you say? You owned something, did you?"

"What belonged to us was in common and I had my share like everyone else."

"Is it true that you gave up your state allowance?"

"In so far as we had to take the oath to qualify for it."

"Well, what did you live on?"

"We trusted in Providence."

"Oh yes, Providence! The fact is there were people who helped and supported you."

"No, but I know that God never abandons those who trust in Him. Anyway, I have employment."

"Well, if you have employment it is because of the liberty which you are unwilling to swear for. It is we who leave people free to be employed. If we did not want it, you could do nothing about it."

"I could not work if I had no hands. But God has given me hands and it is to Him that I am indebted for the employment they provide."

At this point he handed me again the paper found with Sister Sainte Victoire. He asked me to read it and then said:

"Have you noted carefully the first four lines?"

I had not noticed anything more special about those lines than about the rest of the document. I looked at him as if to ask him what he meant. He turned to the secretary and said:

"Just read the first two lines for her and stop there."

"'It is in the name of Jesus Christ and His holy Mother, and of the entire Catholic Church, that a minister of Jesus Christ humbly requests you ...'"

He looked at me and I looked at him, for I did not understand what he meant any more than the first time. So he said to the secretary, "Read it again for her."

Then he said to me, "'minister of Jesus Christ'. It's a priest then that wrote it?"

He was looking at me very hard, still wearing his spectacles.

"Apparently," I replied, "since he says so."

Then, with a terrible expression on his face, "And you agree with the principles of someone you do not know? You are not even sure who wrote it? And supposing it was a criminal who wrote it?"

"What would that matter, provided what it says is good?"

"Tell me the names of your priests!"

"No, I will not."

"We know them."

Here the secretary said, "You will be very surprised when we bring them before the tribunal." And the judge, "Your Sisters have been more open than you. They have given us the names."

"Well, that should suffice for you."

The secretary: "It's your interests we are concerned about. Our knowing the names makes no difference to the fact that if you persist in refusing to give them, the result will be serious for you."

I adopted an attitude of not being unduly concerned.

The judge: "Since your Sisters have given us the names nothing is going to happen to them; that's settled. Now you give us them too."

"I won't have had anything to do with it."

Here he touched my hands: "Are you cold?"

"No."

"Your feet?"

"A little."

He had an armchair brought and also some wood to get the fire burning well.

"So, you will not take the oath?"

"No."

"Why?"

"I have already told you. It is because it is contrary to my conscience and to my vows."

"For goodness' sake! Look, obey the laws of the Republic, submit to them and you will be practising your vow of obedience. You have made a vow of poverty, but God does not forbid you to have what is necessary. You will have your state stipend but you can still live simply: just buy very ordinary and cheap things, avoid unnecessary expenses – and there's your vow of poverty practised! You have taken a vow of chastity. Well, who's stopping you from remaining a virgin? You will be free to marry if you wish, but you will be equally free not to marry if you don't wish to. If you belonged to my household I would be the last to prevent you from living just as you wish. I practise chastity also, but that does not stop me from rendering service to the Republic, nor have I renounced marriage. You need to know that however many convents there were in France before, there is now only one and it is called The Republic; for there all men are equal, all are brothers, and each is free to live as he wishes."

The secretary turned to me: "You see how kindly he is speaking to you? He has the tender affection of a father for you and he only wants to see you happy."

"I am very grateful."

"Well, come then, name your priests."

"I won't name them."

The secretary: "I can't bear to write down your answers, it pains me so much. It is so clear to me that you will suffer for them and go to the guillotine."

"So much the better! I shall get to heaven all the quicker."

"Oh yes, heaven! And a fine welcome you will have! God will not want to receive you. You disobey the law and pay no heed to what His Son said about rendering to Caesar the things that are Caesar's."

"He also said that we must render to God the things that are God's. Well, God forbids me to swear the oath, and since He is above all others, my obedience is to Him first."

"Oh, come on! Name your priests!"

"I shall not name them."

The judge, with a laugh: "Oh yes, you will name them."

I, speaking very firmly, "No, no, I shall not name them."

The secretary: "What an abyss you are falling into! You will be taken before the Revolutionary Tribunal, and you don't know what it's like to appear there. You will be seated on a chair on a raised platform before all the judges and a great crowd of people, all with their eyes fixed on you. You'll be asked the same questions as we are asking you, and we shall see then if you have the courage not to reply! But if you persist in the same frame of mind, you will be deported to Guyana among savages . . ." and he acted as if there were worse things that he preferred not to add. But whilst he was saying all that, I was thinking that God would be my strength and would not abandon me. I even think I said that to him, but I am not quite sure.

The judge: "Are you keen on being deported?"

I was not aware that Sister Victoire had answered that same question by saying that we would be welcomed in a convent in Flanders. I made no answer myself, but just showed by my demeanour that they could send me wherever they wanted as far as I was concerned.

"You still will not take the oath?"

"No."

The secretary: "You will have only yourself to blame. Why don't you want to take the oath?"

"I have already told you."

"Tell us again!"

"It is because it is against my conscience and my vows to do so."

"So then your vows are against the law?"

At this moment God abandoned me to my weakness and I could not find a single word to reply. I even felt afraid that if I did answer it would go against me and so I said nothing. He put the same question again and insisted on a reply. I said that I was not a theologian and that I could tell him nothing else than that I would not take the oath because my conscience would not let me and because I considered it to be contrary to my vows.

"Very well, now I want you to tell me if that means that your vows are contrary to the law."

"It seems so," I said, and my answer made him laugh.

"Ah," he said to the secretary, "write that down, 'It seems so'. And write also that according to the admission of the citizen, the priests are the reason why she will not take the oath."

"But I've kept saying the very opposite to you!"

The judge, to the secretary, "Write it all the same, for I'm sure of it."

"It is not true."

"I know you haven't said it, but I believe that it's the case."

I said to him in a very determined tone of voice: "What you believe and what is the fact are two different things. I object to what you have said being written down!"

He said to the secretary, "Oh well, add that she objected to that."

He asked me if we had a defence lawyer. "None to my knowledge," I said. He named one for us and told me that he would come the next day to confer with us. He said that we would be allowed a few days to think things over and that then we would be taken before the tribunal. At last, after two hours of questioning, they let me go.

Our Visitandine came after me but, being hard of hearing, she was not kept long. She was very firm, however, about refusing the oath, and since she had kept very much to her room it was easy for her to despatch the questions they asked. But they did ask her who her confessor was, and she said he was dead. "Of what illness?" they said. "You massacred him at the Carmes," she replied. They objected to this and said he was certainly not dead. She said it would give her much joy to see him again, and she asked them to tell her where he was living. They quickly realised that she was making fun of them. They asked her what the name of her confessor was, and since she was quite sure he was dead, she gave them his name. Whereupon they wrote down that according to her admission this was the clergyman who had written the document found with Sister Victoire. She had, of course, said nothing like that at all. When she was dismissed from the room she told the guard who was leading her to walk more slowly since she was still getting over her illness. His answer: "Oh well, when they do for you, it won't be such a misfortune, will it?" At which she laughed and said, with the utmost sweetness, "You are quite right!"

At the end of my interrogation I had heard them saying between them that they would have to bring Sister Victoire back, once all had been questioned. Now I had not felt able, without lying, to deny that priests had visited our house, and I wanted very much to let her know this and also that I had given no names. Well, Providence gave me the opportunity. When Sister Chenet came out of her interrogation she was very tired and, in addition, was suffering from a cyst on her neck. She was in much pain and needed to take some medicine. I explained all this to the concierge and begged him to let me go back with her, and by insisting I got the permission. Sister Chrétienne was still being questioned while we were going back and I just barely had time to say what I wanted to Sister Victoire, because the judge, suspecting what had happened, had sent for her straight away ...

Sister Vitasse's account continues for some pages more,

but sufficient has been quoted to exemplify the procedures of the tribunals which the Convention had set up, not only in the capital but elsewhere up and down the country. Needless to say, Sister Victoire's group of Carmelites, with their admirable co-opted Visitandine, were found guilty. But a further document enables us to sample the terminology with which the prosecution case was put against these innocent women. The state prosecutor at the Paris Revolutionary Tribunal was one Antoine Quentin Fouquier-Tinville of whom the *Grande Larousse* tells us that "he carried out his duties with a merciless zeal that earned him the nickname of 'Purveyor to the Guillotine'. He brought the same zeal to bear in upholding accusations against his own relative, Camille Desmoulins, and also against the Queen . . . Arraigned himself, after 9 thermidor, he claimed that he was only the instrument of the Committee of Public Safety, but he was condemned and guillotined."

Here, translated from the procès-verbal contained in the dossier and published by Henri Leclercq, is his speech which, if composed by a novelist, might well be deemed overdone:

> Antoine Quentin Fouquier-Tinville, public prosecutor of the Extraordinary Tribunal, declares that, by decree of the revolutionary committee of the Observatoire Section, on 10 frimaire last:
>
> 1. Victoire Crevel, aged forty-six, born in Paris,
> 2. Jeanne Louise Colin Biochaye, aged forty-one,
> 3. Marie Elizabeth Eléonore Carvoisin ex-noble, aged sixty-two, born in Crépy-en-Valois,
> 4. Adélaide Marie Joubert, aged forty-five, born in Paris,
> 5. Angélique Françoise Vitasse, aged thirty-two, born in Paris,
> 6. Marie Louise Philippe Lesnier, aged thirty-six,
> 7. Anne Donon, aged forty-two, born in Capeny, all ex-religious of the former convent of Carmelites, living in Paris, Rue Neuve Sainte-Geneviève (*sic*) and Thérèse Julienne Hélène Chenet, aged fifty-eight, ex-religious of the former convent of the Visitation, Rue du Bac, have all been summoned before the Revolutionary Tribunal as charged with consorting together and scheming to trouble the State by provoking civil war with their fanaticism. From

the investigations carried out both by interrogations and by the information in papers addressed to the public prosecutor by the revolutionary committee of the Observatoire Section, it is established that the said Crevel, Biochet (*sic*), Carvoisin, Joubert, Vitasse, Lesnier, Chenet and Donon, all ex-religious, instead of living at peace within the bosom of the Republic, which had provided for their subsistence, and instead of obeying the laws, adopted the idea of residing together in the same house, Rue Neuve-Sainte-Geneviève, and of making this house a refuge for refractory priests and counter-revolutionary fanatics, with whom they plotted against the Revolution and against the eternal principles of liberty and equality which are its basis.

It is further established that the criminal assassins of the people, in the name of heaven, whose names and residences the said Crevel, Biochet and the rest have stubbornly persisted in refusing to reveal, thereby hindering the Republic from being able to seize those cowardly conspirators, and so fostering the progress and success of their liberticidal machinations against the Fatherland, have, thanks to such fanaticism, imbued the said Crevel, Biochet and the rest, with their own anti-revolutionary spirit, their principles of mendacity and imposture, and the most utter aversion for liberty and equality, and so have brought them to the point of avowing themselves boldly in rebellion against the laws of the country which had undertaken to provide for their subsistence and needs.

Meanwhile it appears from a statement of the above-named Chenet that one of these conspirators was a certain Rousseau de Roseicquet, an ex-Jesuit whom, together with his colleague d'Herville, the law has struck with its sword, and that he was their adviser who, more than anyone else, inspired them with the audacity, despite their sex, to declare themselves enemies of the Republic. It seems even that this corrupter of all morality, public and private, was the author of the fanatical and incendiary document which was found with the ex-religious, a document in which the poisoner of minds dares to declare that liberty and equality − those offspring of heaven − are contrary to all religion and that the Church has condemned them, an execrable imposture to which he adds the advice, or rather, the order, to any ex-religious who might have taken the oath, to retract it, and forbidding those who had not taken it, to submit to the law, enjoining on them rather to forego their stipend. This abominable piece of writing has become, for the accused, their one and only code of behaviour and they have made their own its blasphemous statements against liberty and equality; they have made profession of its seditious and counter-revolutionary maxims and have become thereby the accomplices of the infamous schemer, the abettor of despotism and of royal and sacerdotal tyranny. Under interrogation they have admitted that this writing, hostile as it is to national sovereignty and destructive of all submission to the laws and constituted authorities, had become their rule of conduct, and they manifested no fear in thus denouncing their country and declaring themselves the enemies of the government which protected them and which had ensured, by its beneficence, their means of existence.

In accordance with the above exposition, the public prosecutor accuses the above-named ex-religious of having conspired against the unity and indivisibility of the Republic and against the security and internal order of the State, by gathering refractory priests together in their dwelling place, Rue Sainte-Geneviève, for schemes designed for the upheaval of the State and the provocation of civil war by fanaticism, arming citizens against one another and against the exercise of legitimate authority, all of which is contrary to article 2 of the second section of Title 1 of the Penal Code.

Pronouncing the verdict against the nuns, the judge began by saying that there was no form of death cruel enough for such fanatics as they were, but that, since they had previously lived retired and tranquil lives, they would not be kept in prison. Since, however, they had refused to state the names and addresses of the refractory priests who had visited them, it was as if they had harboured them, and the law decreed the punishment of deportation not only for all refractory priests but also for those who had given them refuge and thereby incurred their guilt. The sentence therefore was deportation in accordance with the terms of the law, as well as the confiscation of whatever goods they possessed, for the profit of the State.

The group were transferred on February 11, 1794, to the Salpêtrière prison to await deportation. They were still there when the Robespierrist regime collapsed and they were then removed to the Bicêtre where they remained for another few weeks before being finally discharged in November. They found refuge then in the Convent of the English Nuns (the "Dames anglaises") in the Rue des Fosses-Saint-Victor. But that is another story which has, in fact been related in a monograph by F.M.T. Cedoz, entitled *Un Couvent des Religieuses Anglaises Paris, de 1634 a 1884*, published Paris 1891. Two other communities of British origin had already found refuge there, the Benedictine Sisters of the Rue du Champ de l'Alouette and the Ladies of the Immaculate Conception (known, from the colour of their habits, as the Blue Nuns — a sobriquet later to be applied to Mother Potter's Sisters). Cedoz describes the happy relationship that bound the four groups at this period, each of them maintaining their own community life in a section of the large building set apart for them, but coming together for meals and recreation. The arrangement lasted into the following year, 1795, but our Carmelites finally obtained authorisation to move to Flanders and to join the Carmelite convent there at Termonde.

As for the other members of the original Rue de Grenelle convent, their story has been told in no fewer than three biographies of Camille de Soyecourt, the valiant woman whom we left expressing doubts about the literacy of her interrogator, the "Carmélite au grand coeur", as she was called by the Academician, Cardinal Baudrillart, and whom her contemporaries, as well as subsequent tradition, credit with the restoration of Carmelite life in France after the vicissitudes of the Revolution.

6

MONSIEUR VINCENT'S
DAUGHTERS OF CHARITY

It is not fortuitous that, of the four best attested cases of the harassment and murder of women religious during the Revolution — the four that make up this second part of our account — three are to do with contemplative nuns and only one with those of an "active" or, in current usage, "apostolic" congregation. The earliest hostile moves, those of the Constituent Assembly, were aimed at the former, as is clear from the wording of Jean Baptiste Treilhard's speech (referred to on an earlier page) introducing the bill for the suppression of religious vows. (The speech was printed by order of the Assembly, and is reproduced *in extenso* by A. Aulard in *La Révolution Française et les Congrégations*.)

The "apostolic" congregations of women were a relatively recent phenomenon in the history of the Church. St. Vincent de Paul was the great innovator in this respect and when, in 1633, he assembled a small group of young women to be trained by the widow, Madame Le Gras, the future illustrious St. Louise de Marillac, it was with works of charity in view. The name he gave the new congregation was Daughters of Charity, Servants of the Poor. They were to live in the "world" and not in a cloister, to emulate the pursuit of perfection associated with the religious life without being "religious" themselves. "If one day," Monsieur Vincent told the pioneer group in his picturesque way, "someone among you were to put about the idea that you should become Religious Sisters, oh then your Company would be ready for Extreme Unction. Beware of that idea, and as long as you have life in you, reject it. Whoever says 'religious Sisters' says 'cloistered nuns' and the Daughters of Charity must be free to move about anywhere ...But for this very reason they must aim for an even higher degree of perfection than their cloistered sisters — two degrees of perfection for every one of theirs."

He did not want the Daughters to use the word "Congregation" for themselves, but rather "Company" or "Confraternity". The house of formation was not to be called a "novitiate" but a "seminary". There was to be no grille in the parlour ("*Your* grille is the fear of God.") no veil ("*Your* veil is holy modesty."), no special habit, just the kind of everyday dress they wore before entering though, for the sake of uniformity, these were to be of similar pattern. It was only seven years after the foundation that the idea of vows was introduced, and implemented two years later when Louise de Marillac, with three companions, pronounced for one year vows of poverty, chastity and obedience, and of fidelity to the corporal and spiritual works of mercy.

It was after the Legislative Assembly took over the powers of government from the Constituents on October 1, 1791, that the apostolic congregations, of women as well as men, received the unwelcome attentions of the lawmakers. They are referred to in the Assembly's documents as "les Congrégations séculières", a term which, in fact, reflects what Monsieur Vincent had in mind, although it does not convey precisely what the term "Secular Institutes" does now.

The first assault was aimed at the teachers. Jacques Gaudin, elected by the département of the Vendée to the Legislative, and spokesman for the committee for public education, introduced, on February 10, 1792, a draft of "a decree for the suppression of secular congregations". The proposed first article began:

> The corporations known in France by the name of "ecclesiastical secular congregations", such as (here are named seventeen male and six female congregations, all of which included education, at one level or another, in their apostolic work) and in general all secular congregations of men and women, ecclesiastical or lay, other than those solely dedicated to the service of the hospitals and the care of the sick ... are extinguished and suppressed as from the date of this present decree.

The second article further particularised the exception clause:

> Provisionally excepted from this suppression are houses of charity of both sexes, and all persons attached to the service of the poor and the care of the sick, due regard being given to the arrangements deemed necessary by the administrative bodies.

These and the remaining six proposed articles (specifying the practical measures to be taken to implement the act of suppression) were the subject of debate at sessions of the Legislative Assembly during a period of six months, a debate notable for a prolonged and devastatingly skilful speech by Pierre Anastase Torné, the constitutional bishop of the *département* of Cher, urging the outlawing of religious dress for all congregations, and for a brief intervention by J.B. Lagrévol objecting to the exemption clause for the nursing congregations.

When the amended draft became a decree, by vote of the Legislative on August 18, 1792, the exception clause had disappeared: the wording of the first article was very similar to that of the draft (with some additions to the names of the congregations mentioned as examples) but with the crucial change of the phrase "other than those" to "even those".

But another delegate, Claude Le Coz, had warned the Assembly of the effect on the people whose interests they were supposed to be protecting, of the wholesale suppression, first of the teaching congregations "You will immediately deprive 600,000 children," he said, "of the means of learning to read and write") and now of the nursing congregations. The delegates must have been at least generally aware that, for example, Monsieur Vincent's Daughters of Charity numbered more than 4,000, with over a hundred novices in training. They were at work in 429 establishments in France (with 20 others in Poland and 1 in Spain). To outlaw them and other nursing congregations would create an even more serious immediate problem for the people than the suppression of the educational institutes.

Hence the wording of the second article of the voted decree was as follows:

Nevertheless, in hospitals and houses of charity the same persons will continue, as before, the service of the poor and the care of the sick, but as individuals and under the supervision of the municipal administrative bodies, until such time as the public assistance committee will, without delay, provide a definitive arrangement.

The Superior General of the Vincentian Sisters, Antoinette Duleau, had foreseen the developments and had already, a few months earlier, prepared the Sisters for the action to be adopted. Her circular letter of April 9 had concluded:

In order to be able to continue to serve the poor, co-operate with whatever may be decently required of you in the present circumstances, always provided that there be nothing contrary to religion, the Church or conscience.

It was an admirably reasonable directive which the Sisters showed much discretion in implementing. They avoided drawing attention to themselves, and because their dedicated service of the poor could not be more consonant with the Revolution's ideology they were generally left unmolested.

But one of their communities was situated in an area in which the local agent for the Committee of Public Safety had acquired a reputation for bloodthirsty zeal in the fulfilment of his charge. If ever the ancient adage *corruptio optimi pessima* had an example to justify it, it was the career of Guislain François Joseph Lebon. Born at Arras September 25, 1765, he became a pupil of the French Oratory and, in due course, joined the Congregation. An early appointment was as professor of rhetoric at Beaune where, says Alfred Maury in the *Biographie Universelle*, his devotion to the teaching of the young, his ardent charity and the purity of his morals won him the warm sympathy of everyone who came to know him. From the outset of the Revolution he was its committed supporter, but his uncritical enthusiasm caused a rift with his Oratorian superiors and in May 1790 he withdrew definitively from the Congregation. In July 1791 word reached him that his mother had had a mental breakdown, caused by the news that her priest son had sworn the Civil Constitution oath. Lebon returned home to remain and care for her and his father. He was elected constitutional parish priest of nearby Neuville-Vitasse, but by August 1792 the parishioners had almost completely deserted his church and he resigned and married. He was thereupon elected Mayor of Arras (he was still only 27 years old) and substitute deputy to the national Convention.

Lebon's biographer assures us that despite the ex-Oratorian's enthusiasm for the Revolution his general attitude thus far was moderate rather than aggressive. In illustration of this it is said that on the question of the penalty to be meted out to Louis XVI, Lebon argued that the deposition of the monarch was itself an adequate retribution for whatever guilt attached to him. In fact, when he was made agent of the Committee of Public Safety for the two *départements* of Pas-de-Calais and Nord, his reputation for moderation caused concern at Paris, and in due course he received a message from his masters there urging him "to guard against the seduction of a false and badly understood humaneness".

He took the warning so much to heart that he soon earned himself a nationwide notoriety for implacable cruelty. Dom Poulet, in volume IV of his *Histoire du Christianisme* says of him that he became convinced that the safety of the nation lay in the work of the Committee he represented. His own secretary reported that Lebon was "seized with a kind of fever" for sending victims to the guillotine. Lebon himself sent word to Louis de Saint-Just, a henchman of Robespierre in Paris, that "the machine is working splendidly — the relatives and friends of the émigrés have quite monopolised the guillotine!" In the town of Cambrai 150 citizens were "shortened" (Lebon's term for beheading) in six weeks. After the thermidor debacle of the Robespierrists Lebon was one of the terrorists brought to justice. When the recital of his deeds was read out to him, he is reported to have said, "You should have blown my brains out there and then". And when the executioners were preparing him for the guillotine, to which he was condemned on October 9, he remarked to them, "It isn't me you should be preparing but the men in Paris. I only carried out their orders". And extant letters from those men to Lebon and to other *agents en mission* (as they were officially called) support, if they do not validate, his remark.

Among the 150 victims despatched by Lebon at Cambrai were four Daughters of Charity. Their convent was at Arras, Lebon's birthplace, established there by St.Vincent himself in 1656. There were seven in the community, and their ministry to the people included visiting the sick, dispensing medicines free, and even maintaining a gratuitous school for the children of the poor. In the spirit of their Superior General's instruction they went about their business unobtrusively, as individual charitable ladies, dressed in quiet secular clothes.

But their persistent absence from the intruder priest's services at the parish church could not escape notice and on November 14, 1793 (24 brumaire Year II, in the new terminology) their house was visited by two town officials, Jacques Philippe Duponchel and Charles Joseph Effroy, with instructions (according to the report they drew up for their committee) "to notify the citizens formerly known by the name of Daughters of Charity that they must pronounce the oath prescribed by the law within a period of fifteen days". The report continues:

> On our declaring this to them, they all replied that there was no need for a prescribed period: they had no intention of taking the oath ever. In consequence of which we deemed it necessary to establish an inventory of the furnishings and effects of the house for submission to the general committee of the municipality, and this we forthwith proceeded to do, accompanied by Citizen Madeleine Fontaine, Directress of the establishment.

The inventory, signed by Sister Fontaine as well as by Duponchel and Effroy, runs to 2000 words and reads like an auctioneer's catalogue (it is reproduced in full by Dom Henri Leclercq O.S.B. in the eleventh volume of his 15-volume history of the martyrs of the Christian Church). Almost all the articles listed were self-evidently stores for the works of charity maintained by the Sisters.

The search was a first threat to the safety of the convent. Just a week later, on November 23, the town council of

Arras issued an ordonnance which included the following clauses:

The administrators of the district of Arras considering that, at a moment when the people of France are demolishing and proscribing the prejudices of superstition, overturning the altars raised to falsehood and fanaticism, and having no longer any gospel save reason and nature, it would be a crime against humanity to entrust our fellow-citizens and sick brothers and sisters to the care of crazy and fanatical women, who cherish endless hopes for the return of their pious and hypocritical impostors, and who importune heaven by their prayers for the ruin of the Republic and the triumph of its enemies;

And considering that these nuns can, by a thousand means, when caring for the dangerously ill, speak of God and His angels and saints, of hell, purgatory and paradise, and so can influence the minds of the sick and thereby hinder the progress of public spirit, turning those who should be the defenders of the Republic into its enemies, or driving terror into the souls of weak people and shaking even the strong;

Considering further that it is only sane philosophy not to leave in our hospitals persons so dangerous, fanatical and counter-revolutionary, and that such women can inflict a death on the sick more serious than their illness by their superstitious and fanatical make-beliefs;

Hereby decree that the nuns attached to the hospital known by the name of Hotel-Dieu and to the so-called House of Providence, will withdraw from these houses within three days of the publication of this decree.

Sister Fontaine forthwith gave her six companions the option of returning to their families but only one, Sister Contacheaux, accepted to do so. But the superior made it a matter of obedience for the two youngest members, Rose Micheau and Jeanne Fabre to leave, believing it her duty to spare their youth the ordeal which she saw confronting the community. This left four to face the test of their fidelity, Madeleine Fontaine herself, aged 71, Marie Lanel, 48, Thérèse Madeleine Fantou, 46 and Jeanne Gérard, 41.

The expected warrant of arrest was not long in coming. On February 14, 1794, the administration "in consideration of the fact that the women attached to the so-called house of charity ... remain obstinate in refusing to take the oath prescribed by the law, decrees that the Sisters be placed under arrest as suspects". The four were taken first to the abbey Saint-Vaast for registration and then, ironically, to the Providence hospital which had been taken over as a temporary prison. On April 4, they were summoned before the surveillance committee to answer a charge that anti – revolutionary newspapers and pamphlets had been found in their residence. The charge was based on a delation by one André Mury, who claimed that his daughter Eugénie had found such publications hidden in the convent, several titles being specified, including the *Gazette Marchand*, the *Courrier Boiteux* and a copy of *Délibération et Adresse des Catholiques d'Alais*.

The minutes of the four, quite brief, interrogations are available and the overall impression they give is that the two interrogators (named as Citizens Pater and Boizard) were, if not sympathetic, at least objective in their attitude. The questions concentrated on the presence of the proscribed literature in the convent, and the answers were evidently accepted as given. Sister Jeanne Gérard was questioned first and, when asked if she knew why she had been placed under arrest, answered that she had no idea. To the question whether she was a reader of the *Courrier Boiteux* etc., she replied simply, "No". As if to give her an opportunity to clear herself and her three companions, it was suggested to her that perhaps someone had introduced the papers into the convent as a hiding-place, but Jeanne replied that she knew nothing to that effect. Only one question was marginal to the point at issue: "Have you sworn the oath?" and to this she offered more than a simple negative, "No, because I did not think I was obliged to."

Marie Lanel was less reticent in responding to the few questions put to her. Did she know why she was in custody? No, but she suspected that it was because she had refused to swear the oath prescribed for religious, but her reason for that refusal was that she was not a religious in the strict sense of the term, not having pronounced solemn vows and believing herself free to decide about the oath. One of Sister Lanel's answers has diamond-brightness: asked what persons she had consorted with during her time as a member of the community, she replied, "None, except the poor". Only once did the interrogators seem to wish, but respectfully, to catch her out in her replies. Were newspapers taken in at the convent, and had she read any of them? No, said Marie, no newspapers were taken in, and the only publications she had read were the government and municipal decrees. Had she not read the *Gazette Marchand* and the *Courrier Boiteux*? No. Had she seen the bundles of newspapers discovered in the convent, and could she say if they belonged to the Sisters? No, they did not belong to the house, and the only newspaper she had ever read among those named was the *Courrier Boiteux*. "But, Citizen Lanel, you are contradicting yourself; a moment ago you denied having read the *Courrier Boiteux*." "No, I meant that I had not read it at the convent."

Similar questions were put to Thérèse Madeleine Fantou and similar answers were received, but when she was asked if she read newspapers she spiritedly replied that she was kept too busy looking after the poor to be able to read newspapers; and when asked if she knew who might have planted the journals in the convent she answered that so many people came into their courtyard, seeking help, that anyone with a grudge against the Sisters could have done it easily.

The remaining interrogation, that of the Superior of the group, Madeleine Fontaine herself, was no more protracted than those of the other three, and the one question addressed specifically to her as the one in charge – had she subscribed to any of the journals named? – received a negative reply with the addition that the Sisters had neither the money to buy, nor the time to read, newspapers.

Despite the consistent denials of all four of the nuns, the municipal surveillance committee, having received the minutes of the interrogations, concluded (no doubt with consciousness of the report they would have to make to Joseph Lebon) that the said minutes justified a "violent presumption" that the named Fontaine, Lanel, Fantou and Gérard had hidden in the house formerly inhabited by them, counter-revolutionary gazettes, tending to excite revolt and instigate civil war in the region.

The four unlikely-looking fire-raisers were assigned to the Beaudets prison where they remained in close confinement for eighty-two days, up to June 25. In the meantime evidence was found to prove that the newspapers had been hidden in the convent without any knowledge of the Sisters, but Mury, who had made the original accusation, reiterated the charge, suggesting that a new chimney had recently been installed in the convent and that no doubt the opportunity had been taken by the Sisters then to secrete some forbidden literature. Unbelievably (if the minutes did not oblige belief) the committee duly ordered a search of the new chimney and later solemnly signed a report "that the most scrupulous (their word) search having been made, nothing was found".

Now enters on the scene Citizen Lebon, busily supplying the insatiable guillotine at Cambrai with victims. On June 25 his agent at Arras received a peremptory note from Lebon's right hand man, J.Caubrière, the public prosecutor at Cambrai:

> Brother, on receipt of this present communication,despatch hither the four former Daughters of Charity whose papers have been forwarded to the representative. Do not delay an instant ["Ne perds pas un moment"]; send them at speed. I count on your zeal for the due punishment of conspirators. I shall expect them early tomorrow morning.

The same day an instruction was sent to the officer in command of the gendarmerie at Arras to have the four Sisters escorted "under sound and secure guard, to Cambrai, there to be handed over early tomorrow to Citizen Caubrière, public prosecutor of the criminal and revolutionary court".

An order prompted by Joseph Lebon was not one to be trifled with and the four ladies were soon on their way. But before leaving the prison, Sister Fontaine remarked to those left behind (and expecting a similar summons every hour), "Have no fear. You will not be sent for execution. We four shall be the last victims of Cambrai". Then she handed the contents of her purse, seven livres, to one of them with the request to ensure that it was given to the two young Sisters Micheau and Fabre when they returned to Arras to continue the community's service to the poor. The transport wagon left Arras at 1.00 a.m. At one point in the journey during a halt made for changing the horses, another wagon arrived with a convoy of women, condemned to Lebon's guillotine for the crime of "fanaticism". "Be of good heart, ladies," said Madeleine Fontaine to them, "God has taken pity on you and your lives will be spared. We four Sisters will be the last victims of the Cambrai guillotine."

The Arras wagon passed through the Cantimpré gate of Cambrai at 8.30 a.m. Soon after, the formality took place of a brief appearance before the local tribunal. According to an eye-witness report by a certain Flandrin, the four innocent women were lined up together and offered their liberty if they agreed to swear the oath. As one, they shook their heads. "But if it were necessary to do so for the safety of the Republic?" they were asked. "Our consciences," replied Madeleine Fontaine, "forbid us to swear the oath." And sentence of death was duly pronounced. A piquant detail is the wording of the motives for the death sentence:

> Citizen Fontaine is condemned as a pious anti-revolutionary, who kept hidden under a heap of straw a pile of brochures and newspapers imbued with the most unbridled royalist spirit, who has further refused the oath, and who has even insulted the district commissioners by saying that there are no more devils left in hell since they are all busy on earth. Citizens Gérard, Lanel and Fantou are sentenced as her accomplices.

It remained to prepare the victims for the sacrifice. Their hands were to be tied behind their backs, but the executioners found them all clutching their rosary beads. The man in charge, one Darthé, ordered the men to remove "those lucky charms" by force, but one of the men suggested placing the beads on the heads of the Sisters as crowns. The eye-witness says that this was intended as mockery, but the Sisters readily co-operated with the suggestion: the idea that their heads would fall into the basket adorned with the beads they had lovingly fingered so often, strongly appealed to them. On arrival at the scaffold they first knelt on the ground for a few moments. Then, one after the other, each climbed the steps. Sister Fontaine was the last, and when she stood on the platform she turned to the crowd and said, "You who are Christians, listen. We four Daughters of Charity are the last victims of this guillotine. Very soon the persecution will cease, this scaffolding will be pulled down and the altars of Jesus Christ will once again rise in glory."

It was June 26, 1794. There were still four weeks to go to 9 thermidor, but whether or not Joseph Lebon had wind of the anti-Robespierre moves in Paris, the historical record is that Monsieur Vincent's four disciples of Arras were indeed the last persons to suffer the monstrous injustice of the Cambrai guillotine.

A few other Daughters of Charity are remembered in their Congregation (their Company, as they would call it themselves) as victims of the Terror. Marie Anne Vaillot and Odile Baumgarten, who worked in the town hospital at Angers, were found to have refused the oath. When asked at her trial why she refused it, Marie Anne gave the now-expected reply − that her conscience would not allow it − but added a few words which did not go down well with her interrogator, one Vacheron: "I have made the sacrifice of leaving my parents when very young to serve the poor; I have made the sacrifice of leaving aside my religious habit to wear the clothes you see me in. I have even made the sacrifice of accepting to wear this tricolour cockade ..."

Vacheron's paroxysm of rage and threat at these last words quite frightened Sister Vaillot and she hardly found breath to say, "You can deal with me as you wish." "Write that down, secretary," shouted the interrogator, "'we can deal with her as we wish'!" And then, to the gendarme standing by the Sister, "Take that emblem of patriotism from her!" Finally, to Marie Anne, "Don't you know that death is the penalty for people who are refractory to the law?" To which, now more composed, Sister Vaillot replied, "I have told you, you can deal with me as you wish". Vacheron hardly bothered to question Odile: "I suppose you have nothing different to say from your sister?" "Nothing," replied Odile, and she too was relieved of the cockade.

Their execution was fixed for four days later, February 1, 1794, but the manner of it was not by guillotine but by firing squad. The two Sisters were tied by the wrists to each other. Odile was trembling. "Be brave, Sister," said Marie Anne, "I wouldn't change places now with anyone in the whole world!" The captain of the firing squad (perhaps his family had known the charitable ministry of the two victims) spoke to the Sisters: "Citizens," he said, "there is still time to escape death. You have served your fellow human beings well. Are you now, for the sake of a formula, going to throw your lives away and be unable to continue serving the poor you love? Look, you don't need actually to pronounce the formula. I'm prepared to testify that you have pronounced it, and I can assure you that all will be well with you." "Oh but, citizen," answered Marie Anne, "not only do we not want to pronounce the oath, we do not want it to be said that we have pronounced it. We are not all that attached to this sorrowful life. If the only way to save our lives is to take the oath well, then, we prefer to die." And the order to fire was given.

At Dax, approximately as far south of Angers as Angers is from Arras, another of St. Vincent's disciples, Marguerite Rutan, had been in charge of the Saint Eutrope hospital some fifteen years when the local surveillance committee turned its attention to her. Among the poor whom she served she had the reputation of a saint, but to the committee her religious status was compounded by the fact that she was of aristocratic birth. The charge on which she was arrested was that "by her *incivisme* (another word coined at this time and meaning a lack of the spirit and sentiments of a supporter of the Revolution) she had sought to undermine the revolutionary and republican fervour of the soldiers treated at her hospital; and that, being a notorious aristocrat, she had none of the qualities required for fulfilling humane and beneficent services to a free people".

She was led to the guillotine in the Place Poyanne in company with a refractory priest whose name is not given in the record. As he was placed in position under the blade, a guard told Marguerite to turn her eyes away. "Oh no," she replied, "the death of an innocent man is worthy of a witness." When the executioner made to uncover her neck, "No,no, please!" she cried, "don't touch me. I can do it myself!"

Yet other names are remembered of the well-loved Company of the "butterfly nuns", as they came to be called — Anne Catherine Tisserand, executed at Mayenne, Jacquette Paujade and Thérèse Hanot who died in prison, the former at Cahors, the latter at Brouage — but out of over 4000 the total number was a tiny minority, and one of their historians, Dom Maur Cocheril, attributes this to the probability that the security guards, originating mostly from the "petit peuple" to whom St. Vincent's Daughters of Charity devoted their lives, had ways of enabling them to escape detection.

7

THE MARTYRS OF ORANGE

One of the most famous Roman remains to be seen in France - Louis XIV called it the finest monument in his kingdom - is the theatre of Orange, a small town nestling at the foot of a hill six or seven miles east of the Rhone and 15 or so north of Avignon. The theatre dates from the time of the Emperor Augustus, of whom a 12-foot contemporary statue dominates the interior,and it is considered the best preserved Roman building outside of Italy. The backdrop is a decorated wall 125 feet high and 340 feet long, the auditorium a vast semicircle of 180 feet radius, and the remarkable acoustics of the building make it a tourist attraction not only for its archaeological interest but also for the "Son et Lumière" and theatrical performances given there during the summer season. But from 1673 until about 1800 it was used as a prison, and it is under that guise that we meet it in the story of the thirty-two contemplative nuns whose choice of the guillotine rather than what they saw would be a defilement of conscience and a betrayal of their calling, is now to be told.

So the surveillance committee of the area had a ready-made place to hand for the pre-execution detention of persons judged to be anti-revolutionary in sentiment or action. Known locally as the *Cirque*, it was to be the ante-chamber to scenes more sanguinary than anything the Greek or Roman tragedies had offered there centuries before. In a period of forty-five days, June 19 to August 3, 1794, a total of 332 persons were sent from there to the guillotine standing a hundred yards away in the square inappropriately named Place de la Justice.

Of that particular holocaust thirty-two victims were consecrated women representing not one, but four congregations.
Of differing foundations and traditions, they were of one
heart and one mind in their conviction that death was
preferable to a violation of conscience. We shall meet them
individually during the course of our narrative - for they *were*
individuals, each self-evidently possessed of deep spiritual
strength and each a witness to a personal relationship with
God and with their chosen Spouse, Jesus Christ. A good
deal has been written about them by French historians:
references in this chapter will be particularly to Canon
Julius Méritan and Dr. Joseph Goubert, the former the
principal authority on the subject, the latter a populariser
of Méritan's researches but whose small volume had the
honour of a preface by the Academician Louis Madelin,
himself a much-quoted historian of the Revolution. Among
the organizers of the anti-Christian activity in the Provence
region, and specifically in the *département* of Vaucluse, the
name of Etienne Christophe Maignet has first place. His track
record of ruthlessness had sufficiently commended him to
the Convention for him to be named their "representative
in mission" in that area. He had been elected delegate to
the Legislative Assembly in 1792 and there had voted for the
execution of the King without delay and without reference to
the people. He was a friend (from the same *département* of
Puy-de-Dôme) of Georges Couthon, the crippled henchman
of Robespierre, who deemed him the ideal man to make the
Terror felt in the south of France. He was one of the few
Robespierrists to survive the Dämmerung of 9 thermidor
and, after unabashed political adventures, including a spell
as mayor of his native town of Ambert where he was received
as a hero (though it is on record that amidst the vociferous
welcome one woman climbed on to his carriage and shouted
at him, "Have you brought your guillotine with you?") he
died in 1834 at the age of 76.

It was Maignet who, in a letter dated May 10, 1794,
was instructed by the Committee of Public Safety in Paris
to establish a People's Commission at Orange "composed
of five members, namely the Citizens Fauvety, Melleret,
Fonrosa, Fernex and Ragot, to try whatever enemies of

the Revolution are found in the surrounding region, and particularly in the *départements* of Vaucluse and Bouches-du-Rhône".

Méritan offers a profile of each of the five appointed members of the Commission. Jean Fauvety, named as chairman at the age of 31, had shown such early zeal for the revolutionary movement as to be appointed personally by Robespierre to the Paris tribunal. Less than a month (on June 6) after being named chairman of the Orange committee he was writing to Claude Payan, organiser of the people's commissions in the Comtat Venaissin:

> The Committee is in place. In a few days you will be hearing that it is no less terrifying than just. Its mandate is to make the whole of the South tremble with fear and to exterminate all who fall into its hands, making the rest expire with fright.

Just a month after that, on July 7, he wrote again to Payan:

> I could do with another ten men on the committee to make things go as I should like. Even so we are making progress. We have done more in these early days than the Nîmes committee has done in six months - 197 trials in eighteen days!

This letter concludes with an expression of misgiving about the commitment of two of his colleagues, one of whom, he says, is "obsessed with formalities", the other "inclined to be soft to the priest-prisoners, and insisting on proofs". "God grant," he concludes, "that Fernex and I never ail thus. If that should happen, our committee would do no good at all."

The two "lukewarm" members of the Commission who worried Fauvety were Fonrosa and Melleret. Roman Fonrosa, born at Die, March 8, 1733, was, in fact, a trained lawyer, having qualified at the University of Orange itself. His *curriculum vitae* included a period, in 1790, as mayor of Die. At 60, he was the oldest member of the Orange commission and, as Fauvety had implied, his age and training had made him over-concerned, from his chairman's point of view, with the niceties of legal procedure.

Payan reacted to Fauvety's complaint by sending a

peremptory note to Fonrosa pointing out, among other things, that:

> The People's Commissions are revolutionary tribunals whose business is to deal with facts without worrying too much about legal formalities. Their task is to hit the conspirators without mercy, and any member who dares to acquit someone who is guilty should tremble with fear!

But Fonrosa was not to be bullied. He wrote back to Payan that the law had at all times been his guide as to his duties and opinions, that he had no intention now of departing from that principle, and that he believed that there are different degrees of guilt. It is on record that Fonrosa, by arranging for his own arrested fellow-citizens to be transferred for imprisonment to Valence, in the neighbouring *département* of Drôme, he saved a number of them from the guillotine, including Mgr. de Chambon, who later became Bishop of Amiens.

The other member of the judiciary committee who, in a phrase of Fauvety's report "fell somewhat short of the Revolutionary ideal" was Jean Pierre Melleret. He fell so far short that Fauvety addressed a complaint to his bosses in Paris:

> Melleret is absolutely useless. Sometimes he actually thinks that one or other of the counter-revolutionary priests should be acquitted. He talks of "proofs" as if he were a judge of some law-court of the *ancien régime!* He passes his viewpoints to Fonrosa and worries him, and then the two of them try to worry the rest of us! We often have quite lively set-to's. Doubtless Melleret is a patriot, but he is in the wrong job here.

But both Melleret and Fonrosa remained members of the Commission (perhaps because the Paris men thought that their feet-dragging presence gave a semblance of respectability to the excessively expeditious proceedings of the Orange trials).

Anyway, Fauvety's other two colleagues more than restored the balance. Fernex, a silk-worker of Lyons, had sat on the revolutionary tribunal of that city, a tribunal which, according to the official statistics, condemned 1684 persons to death in less than five months. Méritan cites (but without naming him) a historian of the Lyons tribunal for the statement that "Fernex was the one official of the tribunal from whom it was never possible to draw the slightest sign of feeling". A reported saying of his, frequently repeated, was, "My life is on offer for the triumph of the Revolution." "But," remarks Méritan drily, "before offering his own life he offered the lives of countless others." There is an extant letter of Fernex to Robespierre of which the following is an extract:

> Whenever we get a chance to take vengeance on those who thought they were safely hidden - the upper-class, the businessmen, the priests, the aristocrats - we hardly ever make a mistake, as you will see for yourself; we ensure due punishment for their treachery and we let them see, from the beginning of their trial, what the outcome will be.

He escaped the thermidorean reprisals of 1794, but nemesis caught up with him the following year when, on February 15, he was recognised in the Place des Terreaux at Lyons and was manhandled by the crowd and thrown, not quite dead, into the Rhône.

As for the fifth member of the Orange tribunal, Ragot, the description of him in the records savours of caricature. "He was drunk every day," we are told, "and appeared to be asleep during the trials. As each discussion closed, his neighbour had to nudge him to ascertain his vote. Ragot, hardly opening his eyes, murmured gruffly, 'Death!' and drew his finger across his throat. Then, apparently, he fell asleep again."

But a letter he wrote to his immediate chief, Maignet, is lively enough, as a sample sentence shows:

> Rejoice! Heads are falling by the thousand, and walls are going up fast for the firing squads!

A "monster", no doubt, as the same record calls him, if the information is historically exact. But his dramatic repentance when his own death-sentence was pronounced was claimed by the crowd who witnessed it as an early and stupendous miracle owed to the thirty-two virgin martyrs he had sent to the guillotine. The priest who ministered to the victims on the day of Ragot's execution has left a memoir of the event, and Méritan quotes the relevant lines:

> In 1795, on a day in June, Ragot, a carpenter of Lyons, one of the revolutionary judges of the tribunal of Orange, having heard the sentence of death pronounced against him and his colleagues, called out to the people around him, asking if there were a Catholic priest among them, one who had remained faithful, willing to hear his confession. At 5.00 a.m. on the day he was to be guillotined, a priest came to his cell and received his confession. Later, the undersigned Catholic priest called at the prison to offer spiritual succour to the condemned. He was directed particularly to Ragot, as one of the most contrite, but learned from him that he had already made his confession. The priest spoke to him of the persecution he himself had suffered, and this prompted the prisoner to question whether the priest who had come to him earlier might be one who had sworn the oath. He was told that the priest concerned was reported to have done so, whereupon Ragot begged to be allowed to make his confession again, which he did, to the great edification of the undersigned ...

Such then were the five men before whom the thirty-two religious Sisters espoused, in the classic terminology of the consecrated life, to Christ, appeared for judgment. We must now tell how this most incongruous of confrontations came to take place. And, first, how in the ways of Providence, as they themselves would have seen it, the group came together from diverse localities and backgrounds to stand as one in witnessing to the values that transcend the forces of evil.

The town of Bollène had the honour of being the birthplace of seventeen of the thirty-two martyrs. Of the others, four had been born in Sérignan and one in each of the following townships, Courthezon, Tulette, Laudun, Saint-Laurent de Carnols, Livron, Val Ste-Marie, Bouvante, Baume-de-Transit, Richerenches, Montdragon and Pierrelatte. But from the families they had left in those thirteen towns to follow their vocation they had found their new homes in just four religious families: the Ursulines, founded in Italy by St. Angela Merici in 1535 and established in France since 1574; the Sacramentines, founded at Marseilles in 1639 by Fr. Antoine Le Quien, O.P.; the Bernardines (the term often applied to the Cistercian Sisters from the founder of the Cistercians, St. Bernard); and the Benedictines. The four Congregations are listed here in that order according to their numerical representation among our thirty-two martyrs: sixteen were Ursulines, of whom ten belonged to the convent of Bollène, three to that of Pont-Saint-Esprit and one each to those of Carpentras, Pernes and Sisteron; thirteen were Sacramentines, all of the one convent of Bollène (not surprisingly popular tradition often refers to all thirty-two Sisters as the Martyrs of Bollène, though the more correct appellation is the Martyrs of Orange, the place where the deaths took place); two were Bernardines of the Abbey of Sainte-Catherine at Avignon, and one a Benedictine of the Abbey of Caderousse.

Numerically, then, the most fully represented individual convent was that of the Sacramentines at Bollène. At the outbreak of the Revolution it had twenty-three choir Sisters, five serving Sisters and two novices. Up to 1792 the convent was left undisturbed but in April of that year the municipality of Bollène was instructed to implement the law against religious women. The officials, themselves sympathetic to the Sisters, obtained a stay of execution for two months, but in June the administration was obliged to make the prescribed visitation. The officials were received by the Superior, Madame de La Fare, and, says the procès-verbal, all the Sisters declared that "a thousand deaths would be preferable to the liberty offered them of renouncing their vows". But the customary searches of the house were made, and from that time the community were in daily expectation of being evicted.

The other Bollène convent with which we are concerned, that of the Ursulines, had, like that of the Sacramentines, been left untroubled for a relatively long period and during it their Sisters who had been evicted from two of the other Ursuline convents mentioned above found a precarious refuge there. But the order to quit duly came in October 1792 and the Mother Superior, Marie Anastasie Rocquard, who had rented a house in anticipation of this moment, gathered her group there to continue the community life as normally as possible.

One of the refugee members of the group was from the Ursuline convent at Pernes. This was Sister Madeleine of the Blessed Sacrament, Dorothée Madeleine de Justamond, one of four de Justamonds who are named among the thirty-two martyrs, two of them Madeleine's sisters and one her aunt. The aunt, Marie Madeleine de Justamond, was an Ursuline like her niece, but of the convent of Pont-Saint-Esprit from which thirty-five choir nuns and five serving nuns were evicted in October 1792. Some of these returned to their families, but Marie-Madeleine, with five companions, two of whom, Marguerite d'Albarde and Anne Cartier, were to be among the thirty-two martyrs, having heard that their sister-Ursulines were managing to continue a community life at Bollène, made their way thither and joined them.

The two other Ursuline martyrs were to meet their Sisters, not at Bollène, but in the prison at Orange. Marie Anne Depeyre was a member of the Carpentras community, all of whom were evicted in 1792, and all of whom, including Marie Anne, returned to their families. Marie Anne's devout life and active charity in her native town of Tulette, led to her being delated as a "fanatic" and she was arrested on March 27, 1794, and transported directly to imprisonment at Orange. Thérèse Gonsolin, superior of the Sisteron Ursulines, likewise returned to her home when her convent was pillaged, and she too was arrested in March 1794 and arrived at the Orange prison on the same day as Marie Anne Depeyre.

The two Cistercians were Marguerite Eléonore de Justamond and Madeleine Françoise de Justamond, sisters of Dorothée Madeleine and nieces of Marie-Madeleine. Their abbey of St. Catherine at Avignon dated back to 1060 and had been visited by St. Bernard himself. It had become one of the richest of the many monastic foundations in the City of the Popes, and it was the first to be vandalised by the revolutionaries. The two de Justamonds returned to their native city of Bollène, not, however, to their family but to Madame de Roquard's refuge. The one Benedictine of the thirty-two martyrs belonged to the Abbey at Caderousse which had a community of about fifteen when their eviction took place. Sister Suzanne Agathe Deloye returned to her family at Sérignan and was arrested there on May 10, 1794 and transferred to the prison at Orange: she was to be the first to mount the guillotine scaffold, on July 5.

The first place of incarceration to which the nuns were consigned as they arrived at Orange successively, from March 23 to June 13, was the former parish presbytery. It is referred to in the documents by the French equivalent of that, *La Cure*. There were five other places of detention and, at the time of the arrival of the Sisters, there were approximately 330 detainees awaiting trial. Predictably, the contemplatives promptly organised themselves into a community, happy to have a fixed residence now, even if by courtesy of the Orange watch committee, and even if its permanence seemed likely to be of short duration. It was from there that they would be summoned in turn, to answer charges before the unlovely quinquevirate whose acquaintance we have made, and thence to be consigned to the *Cirque* to await execution.

No rationale is discernible in the order with which the Sisters were summoned to judgment. It might have been expected that they would be called all together and judged and despatched as a group, but this did not happen. Pierre de La Gorce suggests that, by separating them out, the judges hoped to break the resistance of at least some of them. Whatever the motive, only one Sister was summoned on each of the first two days of the "trials", July 5th and 7th, only two on each of the next two sittings, 9th and 10th, and only then, as if it was evident to the judges that there would be no weak link in the chain, were greater numbers called, four on July 11th, four on 12th, six on 13th, seven on 16th and five on the last day, July 26th.

They seem to have been selected each day almost at the random decision of the guards sent to escort them. It had certainly nothing to do with the alphabetical order of names, nor the dates of arrest (Thérèse Gonsolin, who had been the first to be incarcerated, as early as March 23, was the last to be judged and executed). Nor was it a matter of what Congregation they belonged to, although a certain degree of grouping is apparent here: the first to be called, as has been mentioned, was Suzanne Deloye, the only Benedictine of the group; the second was a Sacramentine; two days later two Ursulines were called and the day after that two more

Ursulines of the same Bollène community, and so on . . . The surprising thing is that , despite such seeming haphazardness in the proceedings, the minutes were kept and have survived in archives, and it is thanks to them that Méritan was able to establish a calendar of the protracted travesty of justice and also to record sayings of the Sisters which come to our 20th century ears with the naive but inescapably moving tones (as Latreille suggests) of the Golden Legend.

The tribunal sittings took place in a large disused chapel situated between the *Cure* and the *Cirque*; a door on the east side of the building admitted the victims for judgment, one on the right side admitted members of the public wishing to assist at the trials. On the altar, still in place, a bust representing Liberty and wearing the emblem of liberty, the red phrygian bonnet, occupied the place of the crucifix. The judges' seats were arranged in front of the altar. The proceedings for each trial began with the indictment by the public prosecutor, delivered from the pulpit built into the west wall. The public occupied two galleries running one along each wall. The nave was occupied by guards, present to ensure good order and also to serve as escorts as required.

The state prosecutor at Orange was a formidable individual by the name of Viot. His indictments of the nuns assumed a stereotyped character, so much resembling each other that Méritan cites only the following one, with the comment that the substitution of the successive names would suffice to differentiate them:

> Citizen Judges, I bring before you for accusation the indi-
> vidual Marie Madeleine Guilhermier, an ex-religious. She has
> constantly shown herself to be an enemy of the Revolution.
> She has refused to take the oath to which the law obliged her
> and by means of her fanaticism has concurred in impeding the
> progress of the revolutionary government, and so has declared
> herself a partisan of despotism and of the tyrants in coalition
> against the Republic.

The prosecutor's statement was followed in each case with the interrogations by the chairman of the tribunal, Fauvety, and these likewise present, in the minutes, a stereotyped character, relieved only by the occasional unexpected (unexpected especially by the judges) responses or comments of the contemplatives standing calmly before them. We shall listen in to some of those responses in a few moments. Then came the verdict - each worded in more or less the same terms in the case of the Sisters. Méritan quotes the one pronounced against two of the Ursulines of the Bollène convent, tried on the same day, 22 messidor (July 10), Marie Gertrude de Ripert d'Alauzier and Sylvie Agnès Romillon:

In the name of the people of France, the Commission pronounces judgment as follows:

The public prosecutor, plaintiff in the trial, has, in public audience, accused of conspiracy: Marie Gertrude Alauzier, ex-noble, aged about 38 years, ex-religious of the so-called Order of Saint Ursula of the convent of Bollène, native of the place and resident there, not having sworn the oath; and Sylvie Agnès Romillon, ex-religious likewise of the said Order of Saint Ursula of the said convent of Bollène, not having sworn the oath; both of them warned, arrested and charged. The accusation is presented in these terms: [here the prosecutor's indictment is set out.]

Having heard in public audience the replies of the accused to the questions put to them, the Commission declares that Marie Gertrude Ripert Alauzier and Sylvie Agnès Romillon are convicted of being instigators and accomplices of the aforementioned conspiracy and in consequence the Commission sentences them to death. It orders that, within twenty-four hours, they be delivered to the executioner and be put to death in the Place de Justice of this town. It further orders that their possessions be seized and confiscated for the profit of the Republic.

It ordains that the present act of judgment be printed and displayed throughout the territory of the Republic, all at the request, and by diligence of, the State prosecutor.

Once sentence had been pronounced, the condemned were led, not back to the *Cure* prison, but along a short street to the *Cirque* which served, as has been said, as the ante-chamber to the Place de Justice where the guillotine and its operator, Antoine Paquet, awaited the victims. The contraption had been transferred there at the beginning of June from Avignon where it had exhaustively dealt with the convicted "conspirators" of that city. Méritan reproduces the act of June 3rd by which the people's commission of Orange had arranged the transfer, and other works appertaining:

> In consideration of the wish of the people's representative [Maignet], and in consideration of the installation this morning of the people's commission, all authorities are requested to furnish expeditiously all that may be needed for the commission to begin its important operations.
>
> The instruction of the nation's agent [Maignet] is that the municipal administration of Orange be responsible for:
>
> 1. the carrying out of the work required for installing the guillotine;
> 2. the choice of a place suitable for the burial of the corpses of the executed and the excavating of the pits needed, all precautions being taken that the air be not infected;
> 3. the provision of the required number of men and wagons for the transport of the said corpses;
> 4. the provision of a sufficient quantity of quicklime for throwing into the pits.

The oral and written tradition of the locality provides the unexpected detail that the official charged with the supervision of the *Cirque* was a humane, even compassionate, man named — appropriately, as it seems — Charles Noble. It is from his evidence, no doubt, that we know of the mission of mercy exercised by the Sisters among the successive groups of prisoners who were condemned on the same days as themselves and moved with them into the ancient theatre. The hearings ended each day at noon, but the executions did not begin until 6.00 in the evening, and during the hours of waiting, the cheerful serenity of the Sisters for whom the daunting stone structure was less an antechamber to the scaffold than one to the paradise for which they longed, worked marvels of comfort and resignation on their fellow-victims. They moved among these companions, some of whom were hysterical with fear, others hunched in attitudes of stoical despair, speaking words of Christian love which rarely went unheeded. A story is related of one Sister (but her name is not given) who knelt an hour in prayer before a man who sat blaspheming and cursing the injustice he had suffered but who, as the Sister prayed, grew calm and, after the long struggle, began to pray with her. Another story is about one of the Sisters — and this time her name was known and has been handed down, Rosalie Bes, a Sacramentine – condemned on July 11. Rosalie had managed to keep with her, ever since her arrest on May 2, a packet of sugared almonds (the "confetti" often still distributed to guests at marriages in Italy and France and elsewhere) and she went among her fellow-victims offering them with a smile and the words, "Today is my wedding-day". The reported saying of one of the guards on duty at the *Cirque* has a ring of authenticity about it: "Can't understand it at all. Those idiot women went to the guillotine laughing!"

But before the guard concerned had the occasion to be baffled by a demonstration of the folly of the Cross the women he spoke of had made their separate appearances before Fauvety's tribunal and a rapid montage of some of those appearances (based on the combined researches of Méritan and Goubert) will enable us to make a closer acquaintance with this remarkable group of wise virgins at the culminating point of their lives of contemplation and Christian love.

Marie Suzanne de Gaillard, aged 33, a Sacramentine from the age of 18, arraigned alone on July 7, was asked if she was willing to swear the oath. "I cannot," she replied, "I have sworn my oath to God and men cannot release me from that. And anyway I know of no more glorious liberty than to be able to live my vows. To swear the oath you ask of me would be truly a crime for me."

Marie-Marguerite de Rocher, Ursuline, aged 39, thanked the judges after they had pronounced the death sentence, saying that she "had more reason to be obliged to them than to her parents because her parents had given her only the life to be lived here below whereas her judges had just ensured her a life of eternal happiness".

Marie-Gertrude d'Aulazier, whose death-sentence, delivered jointly with that of her sister-Ursuline Sylvie Agnès Romillon, we have read, had been seen weeping the evening before she was called before the judges, and when her companions sought to comfort her she reassured them: "They are tears of joy! I have this assurance deep within me that I am going to be called tomorrow and that therefore tomorrow I shall see my God."

The Sacramentine, Rosalie Clotilde Bes, she with the packet of sugared almonds in her pocket, heard the sentence of death and immediately turned to the three companions arraigned with her on July 11 and said, "Think, Sisters, this very day we are going to meet our heavenly Spouse, we who have done so little to deserve such happiness." And, showing the ring of her profession day: "The promise made to us with this pledge is now about to be fulfilled. Let us trust that our blood, in union with that of the divine Victim, will wash away our infidelities and make us less unworthy to enter our heavenly home."

She was followed by another Sacramentine, Elizabeth Pélissier and her case is, in a way, the most surprising of all. Like some other contemplatives we read about in the lives of the saints, she had a talent for versifying and also, less commonly perhaps, for composing simple melodies. In the more tranquil times of the Bollène community Elizabeth could always be counted upon to provide a song to celebrate a feast day or a jubilee celebration. And now in the forbidding surroundings of the *Cure* prison, so far from finding her muse silenced, she was inspired to compose an "Ode to the Guillotine", a song she was to sing walking from the *Cirque* along the narrow street to the Place de Justice (switching to the Magnificat only at the foot of the guillotine steps). Joseph Goubert reproduces the ode in full, five stanzas, each of eight trochaic tetrameters, rhyming *abab cdcd*. Here, as a sample, is the concluding stanza:

> Qui te craint, O guillotine,
> A mon avis, a grand tort;
> Si tu nous fais grise mine
> Tu nous conduis à bon port.
> Si tu nous parais cruelle
> C'est pour notre vrai bonheur:
> Une couronne éternelle
> Est le prix de ta rigueur.[1]

---

[1] It is a mistake, I think, to be afraid of you, O guillotine; Your aspect is forbidding, but you guide us to haven-home. If you seem cruel to us you intend our true happiness. For the prize your rigour wins us is an unfading crown.

Marie-Thérèse Talieu had been for twenty-three years a serving Sister of the Sacramentine community. Having firmly refused the offer to pronounce the oath, she was asked by Fauvety, "Did you love the King?" Her reply, delivered, says the record, in a strong voice: "I love my neighbour! I love my neighbour! I love my neighbour! Ask me no more, for I have nothing more to say. I am a simple ignorant person." No doubt, the "simple, ignorant person's" reminder to Fauvety and his fellow-judges of the catechism of their schooldays went home.

Tried and condemned on the same day was another serving Sister of the Sacramentine community, Marie Cluse, aged 32. Marie was endowed with remarkable beauty, so much so that one of the guards on duty in the *Cirque* told her that if she would agree to marry him he would contrive her escape. The particular "golden legend" reply *he* received was: "Do your job, Sir! I have an appointment to dine with angels tonight!"

The last to be tried was Thérèse Gonsolin, superior of the Ursuline convent at Sisteron. She had been held at the *Cure* since March 23, 125 days of suspense and hardship, and had watched each of her thirty-one companions leave her to go to their deaths. She had heard the roll of the drums at 6.00 in the evening, signalling the fall of the blade on her sisters and their fellow-victims, and had joined her diminishing band of companions in reciting a Te Deum. When her own turn came, she was more than ready. To Fauvety's opening question, "Who are you?" she disdained to identify herself, as expected to, by giving her name. "I am a daughter of the Catholic Church" was her reply. And to his next question, "Will you pronounce the oath?" she answered "Never! I was asked to do so at Sisteron but I refused because my conscience would not allow it." And when Fauvety persisted, "But the law requires you to do so," he received a further free lesson in ethics: "Human law," said the valiant woman standing before him, "cannot command things that are contrary to divine law."

And to close the admirable chronicle of these thirty-two virgin martyrs, whose love of God was stronger than death, just two vignettes from the scene of the guillotine itself, one amusing, the other moving, and both concerning Sister Henriette Faurie, one of the three Sérignan Sacramentines. Five companions were condemned with her on the same day, July 13. As the six stood at the foot of the scaffold waiting their turn to climb the steps, one of them, who regrettably is not named, had, according to the record, a sudden scruple (but perhaps she was wanting to make the others smile?), "Mon Dieu!" she cried out, "We haven't sung Vespers!" "Don't worry about that, my dear," said Henriette, "we're going to sing them in heaven today." And at the moment when Henriette was standing on the platform awaiting the executioner's instructions, the crowd below parted to allow a young girl to rush to the front, sobbing and shouting, "Henriette! Henriette!" It was the martyr's sister, arriving from her home in Sérignan, just in time for a last glimpse of her nun-sister. Henriette simply smiled down at her and said, "Au revoir, Félicité, kiss Mummy for me and tell her I'll be waiting for you all in Paradise."

And for the epilogue let us quote some words of Professor André Latreille of the University of Lyons, commenting specifically on the story of the thirty-two martyrs of Orange:

> Such episodes are not without interest for history. If one did not linger over them for a moment one would risk misjudging the religious physiognomy of France at the end of the 18th century and the quality of people that the country still possessed in the remotest corners of its provinces and among its ordinary populace. It would be to undervalue the strength of resistance that the attempt at dechristianisation met in the depths of the country's soul ... Such examples inspired a devotion which won a great number of the people over to the side of the "refractories" who then acquired an ascendancy against which the constitutionals, still less the founders of sects, had nothing to set in opposition. And this prestige was to be maintained long after the crisis, and from it emerged the religious renaissance of the beginning of the 19th century.

8

CARMELITE DIALOGUES

The story of sixteen members of a Carmelite convent of Compiègne, a town 60 miles north of Paris, who went to the guillotine in the capital on July 17, 1794, is more widely known — or less widely unknown — than that of any other of our French Revolution martyrs. Two authors and one composer of international repute found inspiration in it for their genius. The German writer, Gertrud von Le Fort, published a novel based on it in 1931, giving it the title *Die Letzte am Schafott* and this was early translated into French under the same title *La Dernière à l'Echafaud* (and into English with a modified title *Song at the Scaffold*) and a dramatisation of this by Georges Bernanos was published in 1949, the year after his death, but with a new name *Dialogues des Carmélites*. and under that title Francis Poulenc completed in 1956 an opera which, according to the Encyclopedia Britannica, "is considered one of the finest of the 20th century": it had early acclaimed productions at London's Covent Garden and the San Francisco Opera.

Le Fort's treatment of the story represents a subtle and powerful blend of fact and fiction evoking superbly the mingled tragedy and triumph of the episode. For the historical facts we have two principal sources, a contemporary memoir of a member of the Community, Françoise Geneviève Philippe, Sister Marie de l'Incarnation, who, being absent on an errand of obedience, escaped the arrest; and a critical study by Victor Pierre, an authority on the Revolution.

The Carmel at Compiègne had been established in 1641 under royal auspices. Louis XIII's wife, Anne of Austria, had given the founding community hospitality in a wing of the royal château there and had often visited them with gifts, accompanied by her infant son, the future Louis XIV. The Sun King himself continued to visit the community when he had succeeded to the throne and it was a usual haven for other members of the royal family, the princesses even, on occasion, taking over one or other Sister's routine chores to enable her to share in some celebration.

Eventually a monastery was built apart and given the name of the Carmel of the Annunciation; it was officially inaugurated on the eve of the patronal feast, March 24, 1647. When, over a century later, Louis XV's daughter, the Princess Louise-Marie, expressed a desire to follow the Carmelite vocation her personal choice would have been the Compiègne monastery, but her father objected: "Compiègne n'est pas possible," he wrote to her. But she made no difficulty about entering the Carmel at Saint-Denis where her lifelong personification of the Teresian way of life was the edification of all who knew her. Her sustained interest in the sister-monastery at Compiègne was expressed in many ways, not least (having become prioress at Saint-Denis) by directing postulants to the Compiègne community and, when these were too poor to provide a dowry, arranging for one or other of her friends to help out.

Needless to say, the convent's historical links with royalty drew the attention of the revolutionaries. The community which was to suffer at their hands comprised ten choir Sisters, three serving Sisters and one novice together with two secular women, *tourières* as they were called, who took care of any extra-mural business that concerned the Carmel. Victor Pierre provides a brief sketch of each member of the community, based mainly on the written memoir of Sister Marie de l'Incarnation.

The prioress was Madeleine Claudine Lidoine, Mère Thérèse de Saint-Augustin, who had entered the Compiègne community in 1773 at the age of 21, her dowry ensured, thanks to the intervention of the royal prioress of Saint-Denis, by the future queen of France, Marie-Antoinette. She had been elected prioress in 1785 and then re-elected in 1788 at the end of her first period of office. She proved to be the right person in the right place when the storm broke.

Her sub-prioress was Marie-Anne Brideau, Sister Saint Louis, two months younger than her prioress but her senior in profession by three years. She was remembered by the memoirist, Sister Marie, especially for her love for, and animation of, the liturgical life of the community.

Marie Françoise de Croissy, Sister Henriette de Jésus, was a grand-niece of Louis XIV's all-powerful minister Colbert. She had presented herself for admission at Compiègne shortly after reaching the age of sixteen. The prioress of the time thought her too young, but the bishop of Orléans urged her to admit the postulant: "You will see," he said, "that she will be the consolation of the community". She proved to be so worthy of the prediction that in 1779, at the age of thirty-four, she was elected prioress and re-elected in 1782. Her second mandate, renewal of which was precluded by the constitutions, was extended by eighteen months, ostensibly because of the inability of Mgr. d'Argentré to preside at the election of a successor but really, according to the oral tradition, because of his reluctance to see her changed. When her change finally came it was to become novice mistress. "She was a real mother to us," wrote one of her novices in a letter held in the Carmel archives, and many other letters speak affectionately of her.

Anne Thouret, Sister Charlotte de la Résurrection, born 1715, served in all capacities except that of prioress, her final appointment being her favourite one, that of infirmarian.

Marie-Anne Piedcourt, Sister de Jésus Crucifié, was sacristan. "To the end of her long life," wrote her consoeur Marie, "she preserved the humility and spirit of obedience of a novice."

Catherine Charlotte Brard, Sister Euphrasie de l'Immaculée Conception, was a friend of Louis XV's queen, Marie-Leczinska, who liked to refer to her as "my charming philosopher". A Sister once expressed to the ecclesiastical superior of the community, Mgr. Rigaud, her astonishment that Euphrasie had never been elected to a post of responsibility, to which the clergyman gnomically replied, "Sister, there are some souls that achieve salvation only by the path of humility and dependence, and sister Euphrasie is one such". If an element of self-assertiveness in Euphrasie's temperament was concealed in this reply, her virtue was to prove equal to the ordeal in store for her and her companions.

Marie-Antoinette Hanisset, Sister du Coeur de Marie, was "the ever-obliging factotum of the Community".

Gabrielle Trézel, Sister Thérèse de Saint Ignace, was referred to by the other Sisters as "the hidden treasure of the Community" because of her love of silence and her habit of spending every free moment in rapt contemplation in the chapel. Marie relates of her that one day the Prioress had the playful (and perhaps meaningful) idea of holding a competition as to who could maintain complete silence the longest. The Sisters agreed − on condition that Thérèse de Saint Ignace was excluded, since with her in the game there would be no contest.

A touch of drama enters into the story of Rose Chrétien de La Neuville, Sister Julie. Her sense of being called to the religious life dated back to her First Communion day, but she resisted it and (on her own testimony) stifled the urge by accepting a proposal of marriage from a cousin of hers. The death of her husband six years later transformed her into a melancholic recluse, refusing all contact with her family and friends, draping her personal rooms in black, and substituting the reading of secular literature for practices of devotion. An uncle of hers, Canon de La Vaulx, wrote letters to her to draw her out of her pathological depression, but received no answers. He refused to be put off and, after two years, his niece finally agreed to receive him. His gentle and tactful encouragement gradually drew her out of herself, to such an extent that at one point she told him that her urge to enter religion had never left her, and that she felt she would find happiness again if he would make the necessary arrangements for her to enter the Compiègne Carmel. However, when she entered, her introvert ways were not automatically healed. Aged 35, she was very much the eldest of the novices and her companions found her humourless presence an inhibition to their youthful verve. Marie de l'Incarnation records that they addressed a petition to their novice mistress: "Mother dear, we hope that God will permit Sister Julie to lose her desire for the Carmelite way of life, or to be refused by the chapter for admission to vows. We don't know if heaven will grant this, but we are certainly praying for it!" But their prayers were not heard, at least in the sense they intended. Their elder sister was admitted to vows and this act of consecration worked the miracle of transformation which turned her into a humble, gentle, loving and lovable Carmelite, ever prepared to oblige anyone who needed her help.

Anne Pelras, Sister Marie-Henriette de la Providence, had, at the age of sixteen, entered, with two of her sisters, the Nevers convent of the Daughters of Charity, but her attraction for a contemplative life had led her to withdraw and seek entrance at the Compiègne Carmel. Appropriately, at the end of her novitiate she was given the duty of assistant infirmarian, "a charge which," says Marie de l'Incarnation, "she fulfilled to the last with admirable zeal and charity."

In addition to these ten choir Sisters there were, as has been mentioned, three serving Sisters, *converses* as they were styled, or sometimes, more familiarly, "the white-veiled Sisters". These were Antoinette Roussel, Sister du Saint-Esprit, "of a character lively and active despite a chronic and painful ailment"; Marie Dufour, Sister Sainte Marthe, and Juliette Verolot, Sister Saint François. When the time came for Juliette to pronounce her perpetual vows the Prioress felt it her duty to warn her of the trials that loomed on the horizon. "Don't worry, Reverend Mother," said Juliette (as reported by Marie), "if you grant me the happiness of being irrevocably consecrated to God, that is all I want. And He will take care of me."

The one novice, and the youngest member of the community, was Marie Jeanne Meunier, Sister Constance, born May 28, 1766, and therefore only twenty-three at the dawn of the Revolution. She had entered the Compiègne community the day after her twenty-second birthday, but was destined to remain a novice. Her parents tried hard to bring her back to her home, but she remained faithful to her name up to the day she laid her head under the blade of the guillotine. Constance is one of the few members of the Community to appear under her own name in Bernanos' dramatisation and she is brilliantly portrayed at the centre of the drama.

And to close the roll-call there were the two *tourières*,

who were neither professed religious nor novices, but simply
domestics serving the community for external matters, more
by devotion for them than for the pittance they received for
their work. They were Catherine and Thérèse Soiron, sisters;
the elder one, Catherine, at the age of forty-seven, had been
employed at the convent seventeen years, and Thérèse nearly
as long. Both were happily referred to by the nuns as Sister
Catherine and Sister Thérèse; and both were to prove no less
steadfast than the nuns in face of the ordeal to come.

As the various monastic laws succeeded one another, the
Compiègne prioress, Thérèse de Saint-Augustin, tried to keep
the religious life of her community as normal as possible. The
case of Sister Constance gave her much worry, as to whether
she should defy the law and allow the twenty-three year old
novice to pronounce her vows (as Constance so ardently
desired) or yield to the wishes of M. and Mme. Meunier to
have their daughter sent home to them. Normality included
the celebration of familial events, and one such that occurred
at this time was the golden jubilee of religious profession of
Sister Charlotte de la Résurrection who was on the verge of
her eightieth year and suffering from all kinds of infirmities.
But she was loved by the Sisters and, despite the menaces
at their door, they insisted on her wearing her crown of
flowers and carrying her floral wand, and they made sure
that the invited celebrant of the Mass was well briefed as
to her virtues for his panegyric.

The ordonnance applying the Constituents' decree of
February 13, 1792, suppressing religious vows, included,
it will be recalled, the visitation by officials of every
monastery of contemplative religious with the objective
of ascertaining the choice of the members as to whether
they wished to continue their religious life or to return
to secular life. The date chosen for this visitation at the
Compiègne Carmel was August 4, 1790, and the party of
enquirers consisted of five men of whom the chairman was
a certain Citizen Pronnay, a former monk of Cluny who
included a Carmelite nun among his relatives. The first day
was spent in drawing up the inventory of the community's
possessions. The following day the Sisters were summoned
individually before the five men, each being assured by the

chairman that the object of the visitation was to offer the religious the liberty which was their due and to ascertain at that stage whether they accepted the opportunity to return to their own homes. All replied negatively, but were not content simply to decline the offer but added an expression of their claim to the liberty of remaining faithful to their vocation: all echoed the Prioress's wish "to live and die in this holy house". The minutes of the interviews, each signed by the Sister concerned, have been preserved and Victor Pierre quotes one or two of them. Sister Marie Anne Piedcourt, aged 75, interviewed after the Prioress and the Sub-prioress, gave the visitors an early inkling of what they were up against: "I have been a Carmelite fifty-six years," she said, "and I would give anything in the world to have as many years again to consecrate to my Lord!" Sister Brard, she whose tendency to an independent self-assurance had given Mgr. Rigaud some cause for concern, manifested that characteristic in declaring that she was "a religious of her own full and free volition, and was firmly resolved to continue wearing her Carmelite habit even if she had to purchase the happiness of doing so with her blood". Sister Trézel, the community's "hidden treasure", broke her beloved silence to say "simply that she was happy in her vocation and wished to live and die therein".

The whole proceeding had the opposite effect to that intended by the lawmakers. The opportunity for the religious to renounce their vocation became an occasion for a triumphant affirmation of fidelity. Victor Pierre mentions incidentally that in this, the Compiègne community was only typical of all the fifty or so Carmels in France at that time: he quotes a statistic attributed to the historian Hesmivy d'Auribeau (in *Mémoires pour servir l'histoire de la persecution française*, Rome, 1795) that, of some 1900 Carmelite nuns resident on French soil, only five or six took occasion of such interviews to withdraw. After this first visit, which left no doubt that the Compiègne Carmel was "on file", the Sisters were left in relative tranquillity for several months. The rest of 1790 passed without incident as did the whole of 1791. A consolation for them, and for all Carmelites, during that year was the beatification on June

5 of Madame Acarie, foundress in France of the Teresian reform.

But, as we have seen, the Legislative Assembly meant business, and had no time for the exemption clause of the Constituents' decree of February 13, 1790, which allowed women religious to remain in their own convents. On August 17, 1792 (the day before the promulgation of the decree suppressing the *congrégations séculières)* an intended *coup de grâce* was delivered against the contemplative Orders:

> By the first day of October of this year, all houses at present occupied by religious, female as well as male, will be vacated by the said religious, female as well as male, and will be put up for sale by the diligent action of the municipal administrations.

The Compiègne Carmelites were not allowed the full time indicated by this ordonnance. A directive, dated 12 September, was addressed to Madame Lidoine to the effect that all the personnel of the convent were to leave immediately. Sister Marie notes in her memoir that "It was on September 14, feast of the Exaltation of the holy Cross, that we were torn from our beloved solitude". Madame Lidoine (the Sisters had, by common consent, reverted to their secular names and adopted lay dress) had arranged (following what seems to have been the standard procedure) for the community to separate into four groups for which she had found domiciles, all in the one parish of Saint-Antoine. Communication was relatively easy from one group to another and discreet evening reunions for community prayer were possible. The parish priest, Abbé Thibaux, was an "intruder" but he proved sympathetic and helpful, allocating a side chapel for the Carmelites' use, with facilities for their chaplain, the Abbé Courouble, to celebrate Mass there.

It was an uneasily acceptable accommodation to circumstances, but one to which the municipal authorities were not likely to turn a permanently blind eye, even if, as seems the case, they would have liked to. Just a week after the Sisters had taken up their new residences, the Mayor, M. de Cayrol, accompanied by the Town Clerk, paid a visit to the one in the Rue Dampierre where the Prioress had taken shelter with five other members of the Community. De Cayrol's attitude was friendly: "We have no hostile intentions with this visit. We simply wish to ensure tranquillity for you and also for ourselves." He then reminded Madame Lidoine of the decree of August 14 imposing the liberty-equality oath. He invited the Prioress to lead the way for her community by signing a register he presented to her, to signify her adherence to the principle of the oath. In fact the page to which she was invited to add her signature was blank and Madame Lidoine told the Mayor that she would have nothing to do with subterfuge. "But you are worrying needlessly," De Cayrol told her, "It is not a question of swearing the oath here. Your signature simply guarantees that you will do nothing to disturb the public peace but will rather contribute as fully as you can to maintaining it. Do you, in all honesty, see anything in that to trouble your conscience? Come, stop worrying and sign. I have no time to waste." The Prioress, who was aware that clergy of the stature of the Vicar General of Paris, the Abbé Emery, had expressed the view that the liberty-equality oath was compatible with the Christian conscience, and who felt convinced of the Mayor's integrity, but still with misgivings, signed the blank page and was followed in doing so by her companions.

It seemed, however, that subterfuge had played a part in the transaction after all. The signed register, still consultable in the town archives, records that:

On Wednesday, September 19, 1792, the following former Carmelite religious (the names are listed: Citizens Lidoine, Thouret, Piedcourt, Brard, Dufour and Soiron), all citizens of this town, have presented themselves before the authorities for the purpose of swearing the oath prescribed by the law and in consequence, M. Mosnier, the Town Clerk, has read out the words of the oath of fidelity to the nation and of maintaining liberty and equality, or of dying in defence of them. The above named women have, with arm raised, all separately pronounced the words, "I swear" and have signed, all except Marie Dufour, unable to write.

When the Prioress discovered what had happened, her immediate reaction was to wish to make a public denial of the facts as reported, but she was persuaded to temporise in order to avoid what would have been a drastic reaction. In fact, the Sisters were now left untroubled for a year and nine months.

A document quoted by Victor Pierre provides an insight into the evicted nuns' way of life at this time. It is a letter addressed by Madame Lidoine to Madame Hanisset who lived with the group whom the Sub-prioress, Madame Brideau, had accompanied to one of the other improvised residences. Madame Brideau had paid a visit to the Rue Dampierre to consult the Prioress about something, but was unable to make contact with her. We are not told whether the Sub-prioress had expressed displeasure about this, but it was not to her, but to her companion, Madame Hanisset, that the Prioress addressed the following reflections on the incident:

October 1. J.M.J.T. [Jesus. Mary. Joseph. Teresa] If dear Mother Sub-prioress was upset by her disappointed visit yesterday, I was no less so myself. So many obstacles prevented me from seeing her, a daughter whom I cherish tenderly in Our Lord. But then neither the present time nor the circumstances are appropriate for seeking satisfactions. Our daily practice should be to make a perpetual sacrifice of them and concentrate rather on being charitably useful to our neighbour for the love of God whom we must have in view in all things. Charity for others will do duty for all practices of exterior mortification which you should leave aside completely during these times. I approve and bless with all my heart your resolution to be more exact in the practice of our rules, for we have all unavoidably fallen short in our observance during these present times — though surely without displeasing Him whose holy and ever-adorable will has permitted our life to be so disrupted. But let us now return to the practice of recollection, meditation, silence and spiritual reading, as much as possible and according to the timetable we hitherto observed. Several persons quite believe that we do continue to follow our accustomed timetable, and I have been struck by their care to avoid calling at those times, just as some have shown surprise to find us busily occupied at 5.00 a.m., and not at prayer. So we must be faithful in all this, as much for the edification of others as for our own spiritual well-being. Yet there must be no scruple in all this, only do what we can; for our present circumstances certainly entail exceptions which we must honestly admit but not abuse. So, my dear daughter, fidelity with peace of mind is my counsel to you; in the heart of Jesus you will find the tender heart of a mother.

It is a letter, comments Pierre, which manifests the good sense of the Mother Prioress no less than her concern for the fervour of her Sisters.

Other incidents of this period of the contemplatives' uncloistered existence are recorded by Marie de l'Incarnation. One which was to be exploited (but with much artistic licence) by Bernanos because of its inherent dramatic tension concerned an initiative of the Prioress which Marie remembered as follows:

> Madame Lidoine liked to remind us of one of the purposes our holy Mother Teresa had proposed in undertaking the reform. This was that the Carmelites should make expiation, to the point even of sacrificing their lives, for the salvation of France. For this great saint did not think only of her own country, Spain, but also of our France, so often torn by civil and religious strife, with the nation's faith ever in jeopardy. One day our Prioress said to us that, after much meditation, she had had the thought of inviting us to consecrate ourselves as a holocaust of reparation to appease the anger of God, so that the peace which His beloved Son had come to bring to the world, might be restored to Church and State. "It has seemed to me," she said, "that since we have entered holy religion in order to labour for our sanctification, the immolation of ourselves need not be too costly for us." Thereupon our Mother recited an act of consecration and invited each of us to repeat it.

But it was not all as simple as that. Two members of the community, the two eldest surprisingly enough, Madame Piedcourt and Madame Thouret, both aged seventy-seven, were seized with panic, not so much at the thought of losing their lives (we have read Sister Piedcourt's spontaneous response to the offer of her "liberation") as at the prospect of the means whereby they would die.

They could not refrain (continues Sister Marie) from saying to their superior that the very thought of the guillotine made them shudder and filled them with revulsion. "Do you think, dear Mother," they began, "that ..." and their emotions stifled the rest of the sentence. "Dear Sisters," responded Madame Lidoine, "I do not know what fate awaits us, and although I am confident that God will give us all the grace of fortitude to make Him the sacrifice of our lives, I would not have you think there is any obligation on you to join with us in this offering, or that I shall be in the least way disedified if you dissociate yourselves from the act."

At this, the two aged Sisters withdrew, but already that same evening they returned to our Mother and, on their knees, implored her pardon for the weakness they had shown, blaming themselves in severe terms for having, on the threshold of eternity though they already were by reason of their age, shamefully manifested such cowardice. Humbly they begged, as a great favour, to be allowed to unite with the Community in making the act of consecration.

This solemn communitarian act was to sustain the resolution of the sixteen during the short time of life which remained to them. It was the key, says Victor Pierre, to the secret of their unshakeable solidarity, the explanation of their will to remain united in their resolve, whatever prospect of violence loomed before their innocent spirits. And, truly enough, grace transmuted in them a heroic acceptance of a humiliating death into a joyful longing for it as a supreme manifestation of their love of God and of their fellow-beings.

But the moment was not yet come. A further period of uneasy tranquillity ensued for the Carmelites and, since anti-religious activity was intensifying all around them, the explanation for their apparent exemption must be sought in De Cayrol's contrived report that they had sworn the liberty-equality oath. The new central government which, assuming the title of the Convention, had taken over from the Legislative Assembly on September 21, 1792, had sent, as its executive agent to the Oise *département* (which included Compiègne) one Collot d'Herbois, an ex-actor whose splendid voice won him the sobriquet "the Trumpet of the Revolution" and who eventually figured prominently in the overthrow of Robespierre. On arrival in his *département* Collot promptly commandeered the medieval royal palace at Chantilly for a prison to which he began to assign all whom he deemed suspect of anti-revolutionary sentiments. From August to October 1793, seventy-three persons were incarcerated, not excluding a group of twenty-six nuns from nearby Senlis, but the scattered Carmelites of Compiègne (a few kilometres to the north) seemed to have been lost sight of.

But the degree of zeal thus far shown by Collot d'Herbois apparently did not satisfy the authorities in Paris. On January 17, 1794, he was replaced by André Dumont, a strong man, one of whose remembered boasts was that he had only to put in an appearance in any town for the citizenry to be seized with fear and trembling. Three days after his arrival in the Oise he wrote to his masters in the capital:

> Citizen colleagues, the clerical vermin now senses its approaching extermination. It has attempted to react but has only weakened itself further. The trickery of these animals has been so completely unmasked that even the country people are helping to clear out the former churches. The pews have been transferred for seating to the hospitals; the stumps of wood which the fanatics call saints are keeping the administrative offices warm; the hideouts called confessionals have been converted into sentry-boxes; the stage-furnishings called altars, where the charlatans put on their act and performed their juggling tricks with goblets, have been thrown out. However, the pulpits, which served for fooling the people, have been kept in place and are used for promulgating decrees and informing the citizens. The churches themselves are used as markets where people can now buy food where, for so many centuries, they had bought poison.

The letter is signed Pioche Dumont, the writer's baptismal feastday, November 30, Saint Andrew, having become, in the new calendar, the feast of the Pickaxe.

But even Pickaxe Dumont's dig-deep mission left the Carmelite mini-diaspora unmolested. In May 1794 the Prioress felt secure enough to send Madame Philippe, Sister Marie de l'Incarnation, to Paris to claim an arrears of stipend. The visit was expected to last a few days but bureaucratic trivialities ensured a tedious and interminable extension. As Marie reported back to her superior, she was "sent from Caiaphas to Pilate and from Pilate to Herod and then again ..."

Madame Lidoine herself had occasion (and felt the liberty) to visit the capital soon afterwards. She had received a pressing request from her widowed mother to visit her; they had not seen each other for many years, and the widow's age made the prospect of their ever doing so again increasingly remote. The old lady's letter concluded edifyingly: "I feel confident that Our Lord does not disapprove of my desire to see you, since I never cease to pray for the fulfilment of His will." Her daughter resisted the appeal for some time: a religious superior carries the burden of leadership by example, and the evangelical counsel of detachment from family ties was practised more literally then than now.

But finally the Prioress, encouraged by the Carmelites' ecclesiastical superior, the Abbé Rigaud, yielded, but with the intention of spending only a week with her mother in the Rue Prêtres Saint-Paul (later named Rue Charlemagne). No doubt, during her stay there, she learned the story of the treatment, the previous February, of her fellow-Carmelites of the Rue de Grenelle, a few streets away on the other side of the Seine. Other incidents of her short visit to the capital served to remind her, if there was any need to do so, that the apparent security of her flock at Compiègne was a fragile thing.

Marie de l'Incarnation had made contact with her Prioress as soon as she had learned of her arrival in Paris. One day they left the house in the Rue Prêtres Saint-Paul, unidentifiable, of course, in their secular dress, and armed with their certificate of *civisme* which they had made sure to obtain before leaving Compiègne. Their business required them to pass through the Rue Saint-Antoine, but they found their way blocked by an excited crowd of people lining the street. Soon a procession appeared, of carts carrying victims to the guillotine which stood in the Place du Trône Renversé (later named the Place de la Nation). Marie has left an account of the incident in her memoir:

When I saw the horse guards approach I said to our Mother that we should retrace our steps, but the spirit of faith with which she was imbued prompted her to answer, "Oh, don't deprive me of the sad consolation of witnessing how saints go to their death." I could not but acquiesce. We were standing quite close to where the carts were to pass. Mother Prioress was entranced at the sight of the serenity reflected on the faces of the victims. Two of these seemed to fix their gaze on us, and I said to our Mother, "Do you see how those two men are looking at us? Their eyes seem to say that we shall soon go the same way." "And what a joy it would be for us," she replied, "if God deigned to grant us that grace!"

Just before Madame Lidoine was due to return to Compiègne, she learned the disquieting news that Mgr. Henri Joseph Claude, the ousted Bishop of Soissons (the diocese which included Compiègne) had formally condemned the liberty-equality oath. The Prioress forthwith returned to her scattered community with an added sense of urgency. Marie remained behind to conclude the business which had brought her to Paris and which still dragged on.

The very day − June 21, 1794 (3 messidor, Year II) − that Madame Lidoine took the carriage for Compiègne, the Revolutionary Committee for Public Security of that town voted the following ordonnance:

Whereas information has been received that the ex-Carmelites residing in the different quarters of this town are assembling together in the evenings; and whereas, since the arrest of the notorious Théot, the self-styled "Mother of God"[1] there have been signs of growing agitation and increased activity on the part of the aforesaid ex-religious and of other fanatics of the town, the Committee, being already in possession of registers attesting that these nuns are still leading a community existence and following the fanatical regime of their

---

[1] Catherine Théot was a simple-minded ex-servant girl apparently convinced that she was a prophetess. She claimed the title "Mother of God" and gained a following among people to whom, in return for a fee, she predicted things they liked to hear. The gratuitous linking of her name here with the Carmelites can only have been intended to discredit them as similar dangerous disturbers of public order.

their former cloister, and that a criminal correspondence may be taking place between them and the fanatics in Paris, giving reason to suspect that meetings are taking place with fanatical intent,

DECREES that a visit be made to each of the houses occupied by the ex-religious, the inspectors being accompanied by an appropriate armed guard.

The result of the visitation was minuted as follows:

Examination of the papers found has proved that the ex-religious, although separated out into different houses were, in contempt of the law, still leading a community life. They continued to observe the rules of the proscribed monastery and their correspondence shows that they were intriguing secretly against the principle of liberty and conducting several conspiratorial relationships ... In view of this it has been decided that the afore-mentioned ex-Carmelites ... be immediately placed under arrest and led to the remand centre.

The "remand centre" was the former convent of the Visitation Sisters on the Rue des Minimes. A community of twenty-one English Benedictine nuns of Cambrai had preceded the Carmelites there eight months before, on October 23, 1793. The law protecting foreign religious establishments from harassment had been ignored on that occasion since an invading force was preparing a siege of Cambrai and the Benedictines, precisely because of their nationality, were deemed a threat to public safety. When the Carmelites reached the Visitation convent, however, they were locked up separately from the Benedictines.

The papers confiscated by the searchers of the Carmelites' dwellings, and forming the grounds for the decision to place the Sisters in custody, are available for consultation, one series (letters of spiritual direction) in the departmental archives of Oise, the other in the national archives at Paris. It was the second series on which the charge of conspiracy was based, and Victor Pierre, who researched them, quotes a number of extracts to illustrate how the hostile minds were able to claim sinister intentions on the part of the writers and of the recipients. One letter addressed to the Prioress (as far back as 1790) was from a nun of another Congregation, inviting the Compiègne community to take part in a "league of prayer for the times of calamity in which we live". Another, addressed also to Mother Thérèse de Saint Augustin (Madame Lidoine), was from a priest friend of her family: it concluded with the words, "In these tempestuous times we must be prepared for martyrdom for, by all appearances, that is how things will end for us. Happy those who will be found worthy to win the crown!" A letter from a Carmelite of Senlis, written in April 1791, included the following: "The bishop, Massien, [an "intruder"] is the greatest source of our fears. We have no intention of ringing our bells for him since we are determined not to acknowledge him. What will result from that we don't know." A particularly damning letter was one dated July 6, 1791, addressed to the Compiègne Prioress by an Ursuline Sister of Paris. Her topic is the installation of the imposed bishop of the capital, Jean-Baptiste Gobel (whose name has already appeared more than once in these pages):

We do not know, Madame, how our Ursuline sisters of Beauvais are comporting themselves with regard to Monsieur Massien, but we can tell you with certitude that here in the capital we are all determined to have nothing at all to do with our intruder bishop. If he visits our convent and seeks entry we shall refuse to open the door. If he insists, with threats, we shall open to him to avoid the scandal which would be caused by any violence, but we shall not show him our chapel. If he wants to see it he will have to go there himself. If he asks to see our registers, acting as if he were a legitimate bishop making a canonical visitation, we shall refuse to show him them. If he absolutely insists we shall show him them, but protesting that we do so, not as acknowledging him to be our lawful bishop, but only to avoid possible violence. We shall tell him that we recognise only Mgr. de Juigné as our bishop. When he departs we shall draw up a procès-verbal of the incident to the effect simply that the gentleman called in order to have himself acknowledged, that he entered our house by force, that, in brief, we do not recognise him as bishop and that everything he did during his visit was a kind of act of violence. Our Mother Superior and the senior Sisters will sign the statement which we shall have witnessed by a notary and kept safe.

These and other documents, including some expressing admiration for the Christian king, Louis XVI, provided inflammatory fuel for the case to be drawn up by the public prosecutor.

So the Carmelites found themselves under arrest at the converted Visitation convent from June 22 to July 12, 1794. Three days after their confinement there, the revolutionary committee of Compiègne addressed the following letter to the Committee of Public Safety and General Security at Paris:

Equality. Liberty.
This 7 messidor year II of the French Republic, one and indivisible.
Citizen Representatives,
Ever in pursuit of traitors, our attention is unceasingly directed to the perfidious people who dare to contravene liberty or form plans to destroy it. The ex-Carmelites of this town have long been an object of our suspicions that, although lodged in separate houses, they still lead a community life subject to the rules of their former convent. Nor were our suspicions groundless. Having conducted thorough searches at their places of residence we have found correspondence of the most criminal kind. These persons not only impede the development of a good public spirit by receiving persons for enrolment in a so-called confraternity of the scapular, but they further form vows to resist the revolution and to destroy the Republic and restore the tyranny. You will judge for yourselves from the thirty-one documents we append. Having read these papers we have, without hesitation, placed the ex-religious under arrest.

The names of the Sisters are added, in three groups corresponding to the places of residence, and the letter concludes:

Since the charges under which these individuals are held come within the competence of the Revolutionary Tribunal, we await your authorisation, under article II of the law of 22 prairial last, for the transfer of the prisoners to Paris. But if another procedure is preferred be pleased to give us your instructions accordingly.
You may count, Citizen Representatives, on our zeal and vigilance. We shall know, at every moment, how to unmask

the criminals under whatever guise they present themselves. Fraternal greetings.

Have signed: Rogée, Ducrey, Leclerc, Baillet, Bourgeois, Valansart, Trézel

Have countersigned: Regnard (Secretary), Desmarest (ex-president).

Meanwhile, the concern that dominated Madeleine Claudine Lidoine's thoughts at this time was not the prospect of death portended by this sudden surge of aggression against herself and her community but the news she had learned in Paris that her bishop had issued a formal condemnation of the liberty-equality oath. She had learned there also, without doubt, about the firm refusal of the Rue de Grenelle Carmelites to swear that oath. A thought that had often troubled her conscience — that the relative tranquillity which her Sisters had been accorded since their eviction was due to their reported acceptance of the oath — now returned with shock force as a conviction. What price the solemn act of offering their lives in sacrifice, which she had invited her Sisters to make, if their deaths were to be shadowed by an act of infidelity?

We know from Marie de l'Incarnation's memoir what steps the Prioress was moved to take as a result of such thoughts. She successfully submitted a request for the mayor of Compiègne to visit the detention centre where she and the Sisters were held. To him she declared the wish of the Community to make a formal retraction of the oath they were reputed to have taken. His attempt to dissuade them, on the grounds of the threat this would mean to their lives, was met by the assurance that they preferred death to the oath. Marie claims to have seen the register containing the minutes of this act (and to have kissed the appended signatures of her sisters) though Victor Pierre notes that the register concerned has disappeared.

The denouement now developed at an accelerated pace. The reply to the Compiègne revolutionary committee's message of 7 messidor to the authorities in Paris was received a fortnight later. It read as follows:

Liberty. Equality.
NATIONAL CONVENTION.
Committee of General Safety and Security.
This 22 messidor, Year II of the French Republic, one and indivisible.

We have read the letter of the 7th of this month, addressed to us by the revolutionary committee of Compiègne, to which were appended three packets, one of which contained twenty documents, including an engraving representing Capet, found in the domicile of one Lidoine, ex-Carmelite residing at Compiègne. The second packet contained nine documents found at the dwelling of one Brard, and the third, two documents found with one de La Valle — all of these ex-Carmelites at present at Compiègne.[2]

Considering that all these documents show that the above-named persons were able to indulge in private discussions alien to the principles of the Revolution and supportive of the crimes of the tyranny, and that the following persons [the names are listed here], according to the letter of the revolutionary committee, are guilty of, or charged with, complicity in the same offences, DECREES that the above-named persons shall be handed over to the Revolutionary Tribunal to be judged according to the law; and that the documents referred to be sent to the Clerk of the Revolutionary Tribunal.

The revolutionary committee of Compiègne is charged to arrange the transfer of the persons named to the Conciergerie.

By the People's Representatives, members of the Committee for General Security.

(Signed) Amar, Vadier, Jagot, Elie La Coste, Louis (du Bas-Rhin).

This instruction was received on July 12 and the next day, at 2.00 p.m. precisely, the Mayor of Compiègne, accompanied by the local chief constable, a squad of eight guards, and also two straw-lined carts, arrived at the entrance of the Visitation convent. The Carmelites were doing their laundry at the time, but they were ordered to leave everything where it was (they would not need clean

---

[2] Not so: Madame de La Valle was the proprietor of the house in the Rue des Cordeliers which had accepted the second group under the direction of the Sub-prioress, Madame Brideau.

linen where they were going, the Mayor told Sister Henriette de Jesus who protested indignantly at the absurd irruption) and to get into the carts, their hands handcuffed in the manner of the time, that is with cords.

The slow journey took just twenty-four hours and the two cart loads of contemplative nuns arrived at the entrance to the Conciergerie prison at 3.00 p.m. the next day, a little surprised to find a crowd of spectators, some hostile, some sympathetic, awaiting them. One of the sympathisers, a Madame Fouchet, later told Marie de l'Incarnation that all the Sisters except one managed, despite their bound wrists, to get down from the carts. The exception was the 79-year old Madame Thouret, who was unable to stir her benumbed body from the place on the cart where she had remained immobile throughout the journey. The two carters lost patience as they waited for her to move and finally they bundled her off on to the pavement where she lay still, blood pouring from her face. Some of the horrified bystanders cried out to the men, "You blackguards! You've killed her!" But as they picked her up she turned to the carters with the words, "No, you haven't killed me, and I thank you for that, since otherwise you would have deprived me of the martyrdom that awaits me. I bear you no grudge." Too pat to be true? But we are talking about a Carmelite nun who had spent a long life in the practice of contemplative prayer and who was at that moment pulsating with the Spirit's gift of fortitude.

The archived statistics leave us in no doubt that at the time of the Carmelites' consignment there, the Conciergerie was a veritable slaughterhouse. Two tribunals had been set up for the judging of the prisoners (the rooms were called respectively the Liberty Court and the Equality court), with the state prosecutor Fouquier-Tinville moving from one to the other in alternation with his deputy. The day before the arrival of the nuns, Sunday, July 13, 34 men (including 8 priests) and 6 women had been condemned and executed. The next day, the anniversary of the storming of the Bastille, the trials were suspended, but on the 15th 30 death sentences were pronounced and carried out, on the 16th 36 — making for the three days a total of 106, comprising 76 laymen, 17 women and 13 priests. It was a bloodcurdling situation in which the nuns found themselves, but July 16th, precisely, was the feast of their Patroness, Our Lady of Mount Carmel, and their thoughts were serenely fixed at this time on her who is invoked also under the title of Queen of Martyrs.

At least they had not long to wait to consummate their offering. They were arraigned the following day, July 17. The prosecutor opened his indictment with a reference to their persistence in living a community life:

> Although separated by their places of residence, they nevertheless held meetings and counter-revolutionary discussions.

The evidence that this plotting took place, declared Fouquier-Tinville, was the collection of articles found in the prisoners' possession — letters, the portrait of Capet, sacred heart badges, well-known to be the emblems of the rebels of the Vendée: a paper inscribed with a hymn to the Sacred Heart was produced to corroborate the charge.

> This counter-revolutionary hymn was, without any doubt, that with which the Vendée priests roused the victims of their criminality to murder their brothers.

And, inevitably, the question of the oath was raised. The minutes show no awareness on the part of the prosecutor of the formal act of retraction which had taken place, but it is evident that the Sisters were held to have refused the oath. And that particular accusation was heard by Madame Lidoine and her companions with profound joy. All else in the indictment was false, but that one was true a million times over, and, if the prosecutor but knew, his words flooded his victims' souls with a great wash of relief.

The official archives lack documentary evidence of what happened after the close of the prosecution case. Two other sources exist, one the memoir of Marie de l'Incarnation, the other a chapter in a work by Mgr. Jauffret (Vicar General of the diocese of Lyons when Cardinal Fesch, Napoleon's uncle, was archbishop, and later himself bishop of the diocese of Metz) *Mémoires pour servir l'histoire de la Religion la fin du XVIIIme siécle*. The close correspondence between the two sources encourages confidence in their witness.

Extracts from Marie's account show that, with all their willing acceptance of the treatment they had received, the Sisters did not acquiesce in any distortion of the truth. The presiding magistrate, Toussaint Gabriel Scellier, in his summing-up added a gratuitous accusation that arms had been stored in the monastery "to await the return of the emigrants":

> Mother Prioress drew a crucifix from her breast and said, "There, Citizen, that is the only weapon we have ever held in our house and none of you will succeed in proving that we have ever had others!"

Another of Scellier's remarks was intended to provide evidence of royalist sympathies:

> "You were accustomed to expose the Sacrament under a canopy resembling a royal mantle." The Prioress replied:
> "The canopy had long been part of our altar furnishing. It was no different from any other such altar adornment. It had absolutely nothing to do with any supposed conspiracy that we are accused of. I cannot believe that this claim is intended seriously."

Scellier pressed the point: "But this altar furnishing manifested, did it not, some attachment to royalty, and specifically for the fallen monarch and his family?"

> Mother Prioress (continues Marie) could have ignored, by refusing to answer, a remark that seemed to her ridiculous, even if it was intended as a trap. But she was a woman who could no more disguise her sentiments for the Bourbon dynasty than she could deny her belief in God, and she replied, with a foolhardy frankness and sincerity: "If that is a crime, we are all guilty of it, and you will never be able to deprive us of our sympathy for Louis XVI and his august family! Your laws cannot forbid that sympathy nor extend their power over the affections of the heart. God alone is the judge of those."

The proceedings terminated with the pronouncement of the verdict that all the Community were guilty of

having held meetings for the purpose of counter-revolutionary plotting, of having maintained correspondence of a fanatical nature and of having harboured writings destructive of liberty as well as emblems supportive of the Vendée rebels.

Both Marie de l'Incarnation and Mgr. Jauffret report at this point an unexpected intervention by the thirty-four year old Anne Pelras, Sister Marie Henriette. She seized on the word "fanatical" in the verdict, and although (says Marie) she knew very well what it signified, she assumed an air of seeking enlightenment. Her serenity unshaken by the death-sentence just pronounced, she asked the judge, "Would you please, Citizen, explain to us what you mean by the word 'fanatical'?" Scellier, not at all pleased by the failure of his solemn pronouncement to impress, ignored the question "but directed a flood of insults" at Marie Henriette.

> But our Sister, in no way disconcerted, said to him in a dignified and firm tone of voice, "Citizen, it is your duty to take account of a question addressed to you by a condemned person. I demand that you tell us what you mean by the word "fanatical". This time Scellier gave an answer: "I mean your attachment to childish beliefs, your foolish religious practices." Our Sister Marie Henriette thanked him and then turned to Mother Prioress and her other companions with the words, "Dear Mother, dear Sisters, you have just heard our accuser declare that we have been condemned for our attachment to our holy religion. We have all wished to hear such a declaration and we have done so. Undying thanks be rendered to Him who traced for us the route to Calvary! What a happiness it will be for us to die for our God!"

Among the fellow-prisoners of the Sisters at the Conciergerie was a merchant named Denis Blot, detained for his adherence to the old religion. His case did not come before the tribunal before the collapse, on July 27, of the Robespierre regime, and a month after that date he was discharged (his order of release is in the police archives in Paris). Our memoirist, Sister Marie, met him at Orléans in October 1795 and he was her principal eye-witness source for the imprisonment and trial of the Carmelites, to whose prayers, he told Marie, he attributed his own escape from death. Marie's account quotes this witness verbatim for the final moments of her sisters' imprisonment.

Blot told her that he wept as he saw the Sisters return from the tribunal chamber, "their faces reflecting their union with God". One of them said to him, "Why are you weeping? Are we not now at the end of our sufferings? You should pray rather that the good Lord and the blessed Virgin may deign to assist us in these final moments." The witness added the picturesque detail that the Sub-prioress, Madame Brideau, requested, and obtained, a cup of chocolate each for the Sisters who had had no nourishment all day. Then came the repellent ritual of the tying of the victims' hands behind their backs and the uncovering of their necks. Artists who have painted the scene of the Compiègne nuns' execution have shown them wearing their brown habits and white mantles, but Victor Pierre provides a lengthy note showing that this was by artistic licence and that it can only have been in secular dress that the Carmelites went to the scaffold.

A total of forty victims had been condemned to death that day and a trio of carts were lined up in the prison yard. The Carmelites were all allocated the same one. As they climbed into it as best they could they intoned the *Salve Regina*. The procession left the yard towards the Rue Saint-Barthélemy and moved slowly forward by the Place Baudoyer, the Rue Saint-Antoine, the Place de La Bastille, on to the road leading to the Place du Trône Renversé. The people lining the streets as the procession passed showed their usual hostile attitude according to one commentator by the name of Delille but, according to Marie de l'Incarnation (who claims to have been told by witnesses in the crowd) they maintained a mournful silence as the tumbrils passed by, one of them self-evidently conveying a community of religious Sisters chanting religious hymns. The people recognised the *Te Deum*, and were moved by the ecstatic fervour with which was sung the verse *Te martyrum candidatus laudat exercitus*! – To Thee the white-robed army of the martyrs gives praise! One witness even told Marie that someone near her exclaimed, "Oh, the saintly souls! I wager they'll go straight to heaven!" and that another responded to this, "Oh yes, surely, else a heaven there is not!"

Finally the square was reached where the guillotine stood silhouetted against the evening sky. The Sisters got down from their cart and gathered around their Prioress. Unlike their less fortunate companions in the other carts, who confronted the ordeal with only their individual courage to sustain them, the Carmelites stood together and made the sacrifice of their lives a sublime community act. Let us, for the final scene, quote the eloquent words of Victor Pierre, whose critical study has been our guide throughout:

The Carmelites exchanged no farewells. There was no need for such, since death would part them only for a few moments. In unison they recited their formula of vows, then together intoned the *Veni Creator Spiritus*. After that, the youngest of them, Constance Meunier, she who had perforce remained a novice since 1789, knelt before the Prioress and received from her the words of blessing. Then, as she would have done at the convent, she requested a last permission, the permission to die. She then stood up, climbed the steps of the scaffold and presented herself before the executioner. The rest followed one by one, their singing growing fainter as the voices diminished in number. Finally it was the turn of the Mother Prioress who, assured, like the mother of the Machabees, of the fidelity of her children, serenely mounted the steps. The witnesses say that in the presence of this imposing, unhurried, ceremonious spectacle, the executioners, the guards, and the crowd, showed no sign of impatience. The drums remained silent at each fall of the blade, and the spectators refrained from raising their hands and their voices in customary applause.

PART III

DROWNINGS AND
DEPORTATIONS

9

THE CALOTINS' DRINK

Later historians have discredited the thesis once held and propounded as axiomatic by some Catholic apologists that one facet of the Revolution represented an intervention in history of Satan, aimed at the destruction, once for all, of the Church. But it is not self-evident what adjective more appropriate than "diabolical" can be used to qualify the ingenuity with which Jean Baptiste Carrier went about his tasks when named the "people's representative in mission" for the area of Nantes, the inland port on France's greatest river, the Loire.

Carrier, born March 16, 1756, at Yolet in the *département* of Cantal, had, by the age of twenty-nine, reached the office of *procureur* (a magistrate whose role, under the Ancien Régime, was to protect the interests of petitioners at law) in Aurillac, the principal city of Cantal. He had declared himself an enthusiastic supporter of the Revolution from the start. At Aurillac he had given cause for concern to colleagues and petitioners because of the contradictory and unpredictable elements in his character: one day he was morose and taciturn, absorbed in his own thoughts and violently impatient of interruptions; the next, excited and vociferous to a degree that made people suspect mental imbalance. His addiction to alchohol was notorious, but his competence and capacity for hard work when sober won him an election as representative of Cantal to the Convention governing body.

He made his mark there sufficiently to be sent in the summer of 1793 to suppress a move among the provincial Girondists to displace the central government . He reported from Rennes on September 11, a few weeks after his appointment:

> The people are waiting impatiently for the rounding-up and punishment of the traitors. They won't have to wait long. My arrival is expected in all the towns and villages around here, but I cannot leave Rennes itself until I have completely stifled any hope of a federalist uprising and counter-revolutionary move. I have already taken all necessary measures for the security of the people in several townships, but even so, the state of Brittany can only be regarded as disquieting ... However, you may rest assured of my firm resolve to crush all conspirators. I shall not leave Brittany until I have delivered all concerned to the vengeance of the nation, or else until the soil is cleansed by a wholesale flight which I shall be unable to prevent.

A week later, in another despatch from Rennes to Paris, dated September 15, a concluding remark suggests that he already had his eye on the larger city of Nantes as a more fitting centre for his purging operations:

> It is time for the Covention to know that only a few towns around here are on the true revolutionary track, that the sans-culotte mentality exists only in a few places which have the right idea. All others are openly against the Revolution. And the city which more than any other should draw your gaze and provoke your concern is Nantes.

The hint was taken in Paris and on October 5 of that year, Carrier was able to write to J.B. Noel Bouchotte, the minister for war:

> I am to leave for Nantes where treachery has been allowed to organise itself and the counter-revolution is making the most menacing progress. You can count on me to do the necessary un-organising and to ensure the triumph of *sans-culotterie!*

And his first impressions on reaching Nantes are partially expressed in a letter to the same correspondent:

> I arrived in Nantes yesterday and my first reaction was a strong desire to shatter the administrative set-up and get rid

of the federalist clubs – in a word, to dance a right merry carmagnole![1]

By this last phrase, of course, Carrier meant reducing everyone around him to a state of craven fear. "Everything in his bearing," says the Sorbonne historian, Henri Wallon, "and everything in his language manifested a man who thought fit to trample on all decencies in order to show that he was above the law. Much of this was native to his character, but there was an element of contrived theatricality in his despotic behaviour. Even officials of the municipality who came to see him on business were received with insulting and gross language. The slightest sign of disagreement brought a threat of the guillotine."

Remarks attributed to him at this time include: "What kind of a revolutionary committee have we got here? Five hundred heads should have fallen and I don't see one!" and "We'll get things as we want them if we have to turn France into a cemetery in the process!"

Both of these remarks were made in the context of a city where the number of prisons had been increased out of all proportion to the population and where all of them were overcrowded with people most of whom were there on suspicion of anti-revolutionary sentiments. Six prisons existed for men, three for women and children. A recent estimate (in Tulard, Fayard and Fierro, cf. bibliography) puts the total number of their inmates at 6000. The process of trial and execution by guillotine had reached the stage of being unable to keep up with the continuous accumulation of prisoners, and Carrier's initial solution to the log-jam was recourse to firing-squads. In a letter to the Committee

---

[1] The *Carmagnole* was a revolutionary song, composed while Louis XVI and his family were in custody in the Temple – twelve stanzas of contempt for the King and his wife, Marie-Antoinette, with a double refrain repeated alternately:

Chantons notre victoire,	Dansons la carmagnole
Vive le son (bis)	Vive le son (bis)
Chantons notre victoire,	Dansons la carmagnole,
Vive le son du canon!	Vive le son du canon!

for Public Safety, dated October 20, 1793, (i.e. a couple of weeks after his arrival at Nantes) he wrote:

> I have arranged today for the shooting of all the more flagrantly guilty prisoners, anyone found with incriminating evidence of rebellion. We shall win through, but we shall need to instil fear by exemplary procedures.

At his trial later (for the Thermidorean vengeance made sure to include him in its sweep) Carrier admitted to having killed by fusillade an average of between 150 and 200 a day, though he claimed that in doing so he was only interpreting the wishes of the central government. "I informed the Convention," he said (as reported at the time in the *Bulletin du Tribunal Révolutionnaire*) "that we were shooting the brigands in their hundreds; they praised me for that and gave orders for my letter to be reproduced in the *Bulletin*".

Carrier was assisted in his task of reducing the mass of prisoners by a squad of forty cut-throats recruited by Jean-Jacques Goullin, a prominent member of the Nantes revolutionary committee. These had chosen for themselves the title of *La Compagnie Marat* and their commitment to their task was declared in the form of an oath, placing themselves under the "patronage" of the dead Marat, and swearing death to all royalists, fanatics and others who hindered the onward progress of the Revolution. The local people referred to these feared and hated prowlers as "the Marats". The Academician, G. Lenôtre, in his work *Les Noyades de Nantes* (to which I am indebted for most of the documentary citations in this chapter) lists their names and singles out some of them for special mention regarding the notoriety they gained in the public mind by their activities.

But apart from Goullin and his squad there was a group of more intimate henchmen of Carrier, who liked to think of themselves as his "general staff". These were Guillaume Lamberty, a coach-builder on whom Carrier conferred the title of Adjutant General; Robert Fouquet, a storekeeper who was named as Lamberty's aide-de-camp and Theodore Lavaux, given the title of deputy aide-de-camp. Two young men, surnamed Robin and Lalouet, made up the team Carrier needed to carry out the operations which were already taking shape in his mind and which have ensured him a lasting remembrance in the annals of human cruelty.

We know that he had early begun to form these plans from remarks that he dropped casually during his early days at Nantes, remarks which were duly noted at the time and recalled against him later. Addressing, at Ancenis, a town on the Loire thirty miles upstream from Nantes, a gathering of people who were demonstrating against the shortage of food and other commodities, he said:

> You are as idiotic as the people at Nantes. You live with abundance all around you and you are short of everything! Don't you know that the wealth of these fat businessmen belongs to you? And haven't you got a river here?

And at Nantes itself, complaining about the slowness of the tribunal proceedings, he said:

> You're a fine heap of so-called judges, a real bunch of wimps! You need a hundred proofs, a hundred witnesses to guillotine one man! Throw the so-and-so lot into the water and get things moving!

But the judges were not unduly impressed by Carrier's gutter rhetoric and Wallon remarks "in fairness to them" that they were in fact "a relatively humane tribunal who, prior to Carrier's arrival, had condemned only 59 prisoners to death and acquitted 331".

So Carrier decided to take things into his own hands. And his first victims — the guinea-pigs of what he was to call "a procedure of a new kind" — were a hundred or so Breton priests arrested for the refusal of any oath. They had been held at the Capuchin friary only since early August, but had spent previous months in other places of confinement. According to M.A. Lallié in *Histoire de la persécution des prêtres noyés,* quoted by G. Lenôtre, the fifteen oldest of the group were in a state of extreme physical weakness; another fifty-four were over sixty years of age. All had been despoiled of any possessions of value. Another authority on the subject (again quoted by Lenôtre), the Abbé Briand in *Notices sur les confesseurs de la foi dans le diocèse de Nantes pendant la Révolution*, notes that although all of the group had refused the oaths, "they had in no way shown themselves hostile to the new order of things". There were even some among them who had cooperated, to a certain extent, with the reforms, and Briand instances the case of the Abbé Julien Landeau, parish priest of Saint Lyphard, who was so esteemed by the local people that he was elected mayor of the township, and his curate was appointed his secretary. He filled the role for a few months, but when he was called upon by the authorities to prove his suitability for the office by swearing the oath, he resigned and now found himself among the harmless band at the Petits Capucins. (But he has a still more important claim to history's attention: he survived the ordeal awaiting him and the others, and his account of what happened is a primary source.)

As Lenôtre remarks, the prisoners were a docile group, resigned to their lot, giving no trouble to their custodians — but presenting to the Nantes town council the inconvenience of having to be fed. It was true that the daily allocation of twenty-five sous per head allowed for only one meal a day, but even this represented a steady drain on municipal funds. And, after all, the half-starved men of God represented only a fraction of the six thousand mouths to be fed in the Nantes prisons.

Carrier became aware of the situation a mere three or four days after arriving at Nantes as the people's representative. On October 10 he gave instructions that the particular "bouches inutiles" ("useless mouths") at the Petits Capucins be transferred to one of the ships anchored in the river. The priests drafted an appeal against this gratuitous addition to their sufferings and the town council delayed the implementation of the order. But on October 25 the instruction was renewed, this time in more specific terms, naming the fishing-vessel *La Gloire* as the new place of confinement.

The transfer took place three days later — on foot, since the grounds of the friary sloped down to the quay where *La Gloire* was waiting. One by one, carrying their few belongings in hastily improvised packages, the aged helped by the stronger, the pathetic band made their way down to the swaying vessel, mounted the gangway and disappeared from sight. A sad anonymity surrounds the group in general but a few names have been traced and handed down, among them an 80-year old Capuchin, Père Kermoran, another octogenarian, the Abbé Lemercier, the 79-year old Abbé Fleurian, who was a parish priest of Nantes itself, a Franciscan Recollect, Père Pouessel, aged 71, Canon Le Normant, aged 62, who was a native of Nantes and a graduate of the Sorbonne, and another Capuchin, Père Le Grand, aged 68. But among them were younger men also, no less firm in their refusal to swear even the liberty-equality oath, like the curates François Foulon, aged 31, and Alexis-Julien Lucas, of about the same age, who had served an apprenticeship as a printer in order to evade, but without success, the attentions of informers while still continuing his ministry. A. Barraud, in *Le Clergé Vendéen*, mentions the detail that one of the priests, the 43-year old Abbé de Meyrac, a Nantais also, led the way singing at the top of his voice one of Grignon de Montfort's hymns to the Blessed Virgin, "In you I put my trust, O Virgin blest!" And not forgetting, of course, the parish priest of Saint Lyphard, Julien Landeau, already mentioned.

But if the hundred *réfractaires* were soon out of sight, they were very far from being out of mind, so far as Jean Baptiste Carrier was concerned. A few days after the embarkation two men presented themselves at one of the hangars flanking the river and requisitioned, "in the name of the law", a large cargo barge of the kind used to transport goods downstream to the point where ocean-going vessels had to station, unable to negotiate the river further. The two men were Carrier's "adjutant general", Lamberty, and his aide-de-camp Fouquet, and the "law" they had quoted to the terrified warehouseman was a threat from their master.

In the name of the same law the two men paid a visit, a day or two later, to a certain boat-builder and refitter by the name of Baudet, and required of him a squad of his carpenters with orders to cut portholes into the sides of the requisitioned barge, with temporary releasable covers.

It was the strangest commission the boat-builder had ever been given, but he was reassured when Lamberty explained, with the steady gaze of a seasoned liar, that the intention was to steer the barge to a point on a tributary of the Loire and sink it there to block a threatened approach of rebel vessels. A team of four men were duly assigned (their names were published later).

When the mastermind of the project, Carrier, returned to Nantes on November 5 from a visit to Angers, Lamberty and Fouquet were able to report that all was ready for the "operation", but they requested an order, in writing, to proceed — for even they were conscious of the enormity of what they were about to do. The paper handed to them by Carrier was subsequently printed and included in the dossier to the post-thermidorean commission of enquiry into Carrier's activities at Nantes. It is quoted by Lenôtre:

> Authorisation is hereby given to the Citizens Fouquet and Lamberty to pass everywhere they need to with a barge load of brigands, without hindrance or interference of anyone whomsoever. CARRIER.

As Lenôtre comments, it was a fairly non-committal instruction, one that was less specific than the two front men would have wished; but they thought it prudent not to argue the point.

On the night of November 16, the two men, escorted by a squad of Marats, made their way to *La Gloire*. At about the same time, the landlady of a quayside tavern, a Madame Victoire Pichot, who missed nothing that happened untoward within the view from her vantage-point, noted (she testified later) a cargo-barge slide down into the river from the workshop of the boat-builder Baudet and move in the direction of the schooner *La Gloire*. This and other details of what precisely happened are based on the statements made by witnesses to the commission (of twenty-one members) investigating Carrier's crimes at Nantes. G. Lenôtre reconstructs the event, citing these depositions and other documentary sources (all precisely indicated) for almost every detail, while admitting that the secrecy with which the nocturnal operation was carried out leaves many details obscure. Such a detail, for example, would be how, when Lamberty and his men boarded the fishing vessel, they confronted the captain of *La Gloire* and his crew who were under orders of the same Carrier to supervise the priest-prisoners. Lenôtre surmises that Lamberty showed the captain the note he had received the previous day from Carrier and invented the supplementary detail that he was charged to remove the prisoners with a view to their deportation to the colonies. And it was with such an assurance that the prisoners themselves were only too ready to be moved from the stinking hold of the ship on to the waiting barge. Life even in the notorious convict colony of French Guyana must be more bearable than the burial alive they had endured during the past three weeks.

While the stumbling transfer of the hapless ministers of Christ was taking place, Carrier was participating, as guest of honour, in the inauguration of a new social centre for the local revolutionary party, the requisitioned parish church of Sainte-Croix. An eight-page account of the proceedings was published later and it is cited by Carrier's biographer, A. M. Lallié. The "people's representative" (or "proconsul", a term sometimes used for these officials and one seemingly preferred by Carrier) made the principal speech and, suiting his exordium to the nature of the new premises, remarked that "all the ills that plague the human race derive from the throne and the altar". It was history, he claimed, that provoked the national vengeance against the priests, and he drew a colourful picture of the scandalous life of luxury of "the vendors of Masses", "despicable lackeys of kings" well able to "set up shop and swell the numbers of their customers".

As Lenôtre comments, the orator had chosen his theme well. The news of the horrific enterprise that was under way even as he spoke would break the following day and his harangue was designed to forestall any revulsion of popular feeling that might occur. Moreover, the bursts of applause that punctuated his speech could later be claimed, if needed, as his warrant for dealing with "the miscreants whose incarceration was depriving good citizens of their food".

Meanwhile the transfer of the priest-prisoners was taking place, a slow process, since they were brought up on deck two by two, searched, and bound together by the wrists, then assisted by the Marats into the waiting barge – the whole operation carried out with a show of courtesy and of regret at the inconvenience caused in the course of duty.

Then Lamberty and Fouquet, with their escort, got down into a tug-boat which had been attached to the prow of the barge. The mooring ropes were unfastened and the barge, guided by the men in the tug-boat drifted downstream. It was half an hour past midnight and a full moon illuminated a scene which belonged to darkness. There was an anxious moment for the leaders of the undertaking when they drew near a floating pontoon supporting cannons, and a cry split the silence, "Qui vive?" – "Who goes there?" (The incident was reported to the Committee of Twenty-one by the officer in charge of the sentinel station, by name P.F.J. Vailly.) Lamberty called out that he was escorting a cargo of prisoners and demanded free passage. But Vailly shouted back that his orders were to let no vessels pass his cannons. Lamberty had the boat moved to the pontoon and produced Carrier's note, and the operation was allowed to continue. But Vailly continued also to observe the proceedings. Not a sound, he noted, came from the barge as it continued on its way, passing the village of Trentemoult on the left bank of the Loire and the township of Chantenay on the right, until the river opened out into an estuary half a mile wide. This, Carrier had decreed, was where the "accident" was to take place.

The tug-boat was unhooked from the barge and rowed round to the side of the vessel where the Marats, armed with the sledge hammers they had brought with them, dislodged, one after the other, the covers of the Baudet portholes, half below the surface of the water. From inside the barge the silence of the night was now broken by murmurs rising to a crescendo of cries for help. The task of corporate murder done, the tug-boat was pulled away from the barge so that its occupants would not be sucked into the submersion. Then the isolated vessel drifted on, sinking gradually until finally it disappeared below the calm surface. The sentry officer,

Vailly, reporting later to the committee of enquiry, recalled the moment in these words:

> By favour of the nocturnal silence I was able to hear loud cries issue from the barge which I had allowed, a little before, to pass my post. I realised straight away that they were the cries of men trapped inside who were being disposed of in this horrific way.

But the instinct for self-preservation played its part even here. Already, before the vessel sank, a few of the victims, who had spent the time of the drift downstream working to unfasten the cord manacles, had struggled out of the trap and were desperately trying to swim away to safety. But Lamberty's men rowed after them and, with hammers and oars, made sure, as they thought, that the bid for survival failed: dead men, as the perennial wisdom has it, tell no tales. In fact, as we already know, the Abbé Julien Landeau had succeeded in escaping the maelstrom and the coups de grace, and G. Lenôtre devotes a full chapter to his remarkable survival.

His escape had gone unnoticed by the men in the tug-boat, and Lamberty was so satisfied with the success of his enterprise that he had the idea of offering, a few days later, a celebratory dinner to all who had participated. And his choice of venue for the celebration was the schooner *La Gloire*, cleaned up and embellished for the occasion. Carrier readily accepted the invitation to be the guest of honour and the total number of invitees amounted to no more than twenty. Only one of these had not taken part in the drowning of the priests — an official of the military transport department called Sandrock. The reason for the addition of Sandrock's name to the guest-list is not clear — perhaps he was a particularly close friend of Lamberty — but it was his subsequent deposition to the Committee of Twenty-one which provided the details of what went on at the party.

A local caterer had been charged to ensure a good supply of food and drink (no matter that the housewives of Nantes were hard put to to buy the wherewith to keep their families from going hungry), and as the wine flowed the conversation and laughter grew, with each diner's exaggerated reminiscences of his personal exploits on the night of 16-17 November. Came the speech-making and Lamberty, the complacent host, gave a moment by moment account of what he called "the great bathing-party". "His sallies were greeted with vociferous applause," wrote Sandrock in his deposition, "the applauders not wishing to be themselves the victims of a future bathing expedition. As for myself, I shuddered with horror as he spoke."

Then it was the turn of the guest of honour who began by paying his bad men and true the compliment of letting them hear what he had written, but not yet despatched, to his Paris superiors. The letter he produced from his pocket was subsequently published in the journal *Les Nouvelles Politiques* of 27 brumaire, an III (November 17, 1794). Lenôtre cites a brief passage from it:

> An event of an unusual kind has apparently made a reduction in the number of priests. Ninety of those whom we had designated as refractory had been confined in a boat on the Loire. I have learned, and the information is quite certain, that all perished in the river.

It was an evasive formulation, comments Lenôtre, interpretable as the report of an accident. The diners saw the advantage of this from their personal point of view and were loud in their appreciation of the proconsul's astuteness. And, having thus put his listeners' minds at ease, Carrier entered into the spirit of the gathering with sallies of humour aimed at demonstrating that his underling Lamberty had not a monopoly of the comic vein. Referring back to his report to Paris he remarked that it was understood that the presence of the priests in the barge was in view of their deportation, and that the priests had been assured of this as their transfer was made from *La Gloire*. Well, said Carrier with a snigger, it was a kind of deportation, wasn't it? – only a vertical one! (Laughter and applause). He concluded with a toast: "To the Loire, that truly revolutionary river, that generous provider of drink to the calotins!"

After his speech the festivities continued, with young Robin a lively master of ceremonies. The party finally broke up and the celebrators made their unsteady way home, feeling secure that their secret was safe. The caterer's bill for 364 livres was archived later, still unpaid a year after the party.

The happenings of the night of November 16-17, 1793, are known to history as *La première noyade de Nantes* – the first mass-drowning at Nantes. For there were more to follow, the second a mere three weeks later, on the night of December 9-10, and the victims of this again were priests. A contingent of *réfractaires* had been transferred from Angers on December 6th, and had been locked up in the vast quayside warehouse called the Entrepôt. For Carrier the solution to the problem of having to waste public money feeding fifty-three additional "useless mouths" was now automatic. The arrangements were entrusted again to the same team under the direction of Lamberty who, however, chose a different carpenter, one Affilé, for the preparation of the barge. The first *noyade* had not had quite the expected result: there had been all that unforeseen extra trouble despatching the few victims who had struggled out of the boat. The new carpenter was instructed to ensure that his method would render escape impossible and he and his workmen proved suitably efficient and the second drowning took place as planned.

Carrier's report of the event to Paris was read in the Assembly and, the fiction of an accident no longer even claiming the pretence of a belief, the report was loudly applauded. And the proconsul, having been officially encouraged, began to think of applying his "procedure of a new kind" to the problem of the other "anti-revolutionary" activists and suspects crowding the Nantes prisons. Just a week after the second *noyade*, a third one despatched a bargeload of 129 inmates of the Bouffay prison; Lenôtre lists the names of all of these, the first to do so, having personally discovered the document concerned in his researches at the National Archives of Paris. Thenceforward Carrier was not to be stopped. A recent estimate, that of the *Histoire et dictionnaire de la Révolution Française*, 1987, puts at 3,500 the total number of his victims despatched in this way. According to Henri Wallon, quoting valid attestations, women prisoners were not excluded from the holocaust, and if these happened to have their children with them, these were not spared. Wallon adds the macabre detail that the river became contaminated by the corpses and the town council issued an instruction forbidding the use of its water for any purpose or the selling of fish recently taken from it.

The guillotine standing in the Place de Grève at Paris ended the life of Carrier at about five o'clock on the afternoon of Tuesday, December 16, 1794. He had shown no remorse or regret throughout the two and a half weeks of his trial, during which he had been obliged to conduct his own defence, since the lawyers nominated for the task by the tribunal had all, one after the other, refused the brief.

10

THE CONVICT SHIPS

Mention has been made earlier of the Legislative Assembly's decree of May 27, 1792, the vetoing of which by Louis XVI precipitated the events which culminated in his arrest and eventual execution. This decree introduced the penalty of deportation for "refractory" clergy, specifically imposing the sentence of immediate exile on any priest denounced as "anti-revolutionary" by twenty "active" citizens of his locality. Deemed after three months to be insufficiently productive of results, this decree was superseded by another of August 26, imposing the same sentence ("the dry guillotine" as it was cynically termed) on any non-juring clergyman denounced by any six citizens from anywhere in the whole *département* in which the targeted priest resided. Pierre Henry- Larivière, a prominent member of the Legislative, speaking in the debate that led up to the new decree, had said to the Assembly: "The most beautiful spectacle you can offer the people is the departure of the *réfractaires*." And another, Jean-François Delacroix, more vehemently: "Let us give our attention to the Army, let us take measures for the economic well-being of the country, but before all else, before all else, let us get rid of the priests!"

According to the terms of the new decree, the non-jurors (described as "one of the first sources of danger for the fatherland, a threat to interior peace at a time when the French people need to be united in the all-out struggle against the foreign foe") would be given a week in which to pronounce the liberty-equality oath, failing which they must leave the country within the fortnight. Every such parish clergyman, says the text as given in Volume IV of

177

J.B. Duvergier's *Collection complète des lois, décrets et ordonnances* . . . "will present himself before his municipal authority to state to which foreign country he intends to go, whereupon he will receive a passport detailing his statement with his signature, and indicating the route he is to take and the time-limit within which he must be out of the country". Any who had failed to obey this order within the fortnight were to be deported to French Guyana. An exception was made of those who were 60 or over or who had a medical certificate declaring them to be too ill to make the journey. All these were to be assembled in a central place of detention and supervised by the local authority.

Precisely a week to the day after the promulgation of this decree occurred the massacres in Paris, setting a pattern imitated in many places in the provinces. A number of priests, refusing the alternative of the liberty-equality oath, yielded to the conditions of the August 26 decree, obtained their passports and made for the frontiers, disguised among the crowds of civilians who voluntarily sought the security of foreign lands. An estimated total of 29000 émigrés had left France before the end of the year and, of these, the figure of 25 per cent is given (in the 1987 *Histoire et Dictionnaire de la Révolution française* cf. bibl.) for the clergy.

But the departure of 7000 who thus opted for what was termed "voluntary deportation" left some 50000 *réfractaires* within the country, many of them excluded from the requirements of the August 26 decree, but most continuing to serve, secretly and in constant peril of their lives, the faithful who refused the ministrations of the jurors.

The government showed surprisingly little hurry about addressing this problem, and not least because it was a bigger problem than it wanted, with an enemy without posing an even greater threat than the supposed enemy within. Claude Fauchet, constitutional bishop of Caen and a colourful member of the Assembly twitted the minister of finance, Pierre Joseph Cambon, "To deport 50000 priests we shall need a hundred ships. Does Citizen Cambon, so solicitous as he is of the financial security of the country, wish to impose this additional drain on the Treasury?"

But representations from the *départements* were soon

reaching Paris with ever-increasing persistence: the prisons were filling up in the provinces with delated clergy, but the local authorities had not bargained with having these on their hands indefinitely. The Legislative had brought in the August law, when was the Convention going to see to its implementation? The complaints went unheeded for over six months, save for occasional bland and non-committal assurances from the ministries of the Interior and the Marine. But on March 27, 1793, the new Minister of the Interior, Dominique Joseph Garat, sent the following circular to the departmental administrations (the document is held in the National Archives):

> Citizen Administrators, I hereby give notice that within three weeks a transport vessel will leave the port of Bordeaux for Cayenne. If you have any priests due for deportation to Guyana, under the terms of the law of August 26, you may have them conveyed to this port under escort of the national gendarmerie.

Garat was an inept minister, more suited to philosophical discussion than to the practicalities of government, and this brief document was worthy of him. An open invitation to all and sundry *départements* to send their *réfractaires* to the one port for deportation on the one vessel was an obvious recipe for confusion worse confounded. More, Garat certainly knew that since the Convention's declaration of war against Britain two months earlier (on February 1) the British fleet had established a blockade along the Atlantic coast negativing any prospect of a French ship's leaving Bordeaux, or any other port, for Guyana, or any other destination. But as far as Garat was concerned, that would be Bordeaux's problem - Bordeaux's and the priests' who were going to be carted along the roads of France and left to their fate at the port.

The inevitable happened. The convergence began on April 16 with the arrival of priests from the Dordogne *département* (contiguous to Bordeaux's *département*, the Gironde). By April 27 over a thousand priests had been conveyed to Bordeaux where they had been temporarily lodged in the town's prisons, ordinary and improvised. The Bordeaux council sent a vigorous protest to Paris and refused to accept any more prisoners, moving new arrivals downstream to the subsidiary port of Blaye. By the time (May 20) Garat issued a directive to all the *départements* to suspend operations, a total of 1,494 priests were crammed into the eight prisons of Bordeaux and the two of Blaye. Neither town council had been given notice to make preparations for a mass deportation and, inevitably, the material conditions in the crowded prisons were appalling. Unexpectedly, however, the supervision was reasonably tolerant; the Convention's "representative in mission" was an ex-priest, Claude Alexandre Ysabeau, and he had enough fellow-feeling for his former confreres to try to ease their lot.

But the whole situation represented a breakdown in the creaking machinery of government and neither the authorities nor the people were disposed to tolerate the encumbrance indefinitely. The deadlock continued, though the problem (and the exasperated provincial authorities were assured of this) remained at the forefront of the agenda of the Assembly's sessions in the capital. The talk, however, went on for several months (Jacques Hérissay allocates several pages to a discussion, with citations, of the debates, researched by him in the National Archives) and the net result was a new decree, promulgated on October 21st, which did nothing to ease the log-jam but, if anything, aggravated it: the place of exile was to be no longer Guyana but the north west of Africa, and henceforth *no* priests were to be exempted from the deportation order. France was to be purged of the entire "sacerdotal stench" (a term of Danton's who wanted the refractories dumped *en masse* somewhere on the coast of Italy "the fatherland of fanaticism").

It took another three months for any semblance of a practical move to be made. On the "6 pluviose, Year II" (January 25, 1794) an instruction went out to the *départements* from Paris naming a new port of embarkation to which the refractory priests were to be sent. This was Rochefort on the river Charente, a naval base created only a century before by Louis XIV's minister Colbert, and it is the drawn-out agony of the 840 clerics consigned there on which our attention can focus as the best-documented example of "deportation" as a weapon in the de-Christianisers' armoury.

There is an abundance of source-material, of the nature, on the one hand, of memoirs by priests who experienced but survived the ordeal and, on the other, of studies based on research of the mass of material in the national and departmental archives. Of the former at least half a dozen published accounts are listed in the bibliographies, but of these one stands out in particular for the objectivity of its approach and for the detail of the information it contains, information which subsequent research has served only to corroborate. In his preface the author, Abbé Pierre Grégoire Labiche de Reignefort apologises for assuming the "unbecoming role" of narrating the sufferings which he had personally shared with so many others. It would have been better, he says, if someone other than one of those who had "defended the good cause" had been available to undertake the sad task with the same exactitude. He continues:

> I shall not exaggerate. I would deem it a sin to do so. I shall not even say all that could be said, not with the intention of hiding anything, but because there are some facts which never came to my knowledge and others which I have forgotten. And anyway the sense of what I had suffered is no longer as intense as it was when I first gained my liberty. I shall likewise avoid bitterness in my reflections and animosity in the details I shall give. I am not vindictive by nature and I am conscious, in any case, of what my religious belief prescribes in that regard ...

In the following pages the references to, and citations from, Reignefort's memoir are based on his second edition, published in 1801 which, says the author himself, "is much superior to the first" (published in 1796) because he had in the meantime found opportunities to check his memories with other clergy survivors and to "rectify a number of incidents previously narrated inexactly". The critical account we have used as a control of Reignefort's memoir is a 450-page work by Jacques Hérissay, entitled simply, *Les Pontons de Rochefort 1792-1795*, published in 1925 and described by another writer on the subject, Canon L. Poivert, as "a masterly study by a scrupulous and well-documented historian". In fact, Hérissay's pages are almost all furnished with footnotes indicating the sources, archival and other, for his very detailed information. His book is dedicated to the memory of another scholar of the subject, Canon P. Lemonnier, who had generously made available to Hérissay his massive collection of notes taken in the Paris and other archives but who had died before Hérissay's work was published.

The separate journeys have been charted in some detail, with the naming of the towns through which the convoys passed from the various starting-points. Thus, for example, a first detachment left Moulins on November 21 and reached Angoulême 170 miles away, via Limoges, on December 9. Among the twenty-seven priests was a Jesuit ("ex-Jesuit") named Joseph Imbert who had been named by Pope Pius VI Vicar Apostolic of Moulins. He had composed new words for Rouget de Lisle's patriotic hymn, *La Marseillaise* which was being sung everywhere at the time. Père Imbert's *Chant de Départ*, as he called it, had for its theme a mission for the expelled priests in a foreign land - for it was understood that the journey to the port was in certain view of deportation. It had four stanzas (reproduced in full by L.M. Dubois in *Rochefort et les Pontons de l'Ile d'Aix*) of which the first is as follows:

Allons, enfants de l'Evangile,
Loin de ces climats dangereux,
Chercher en Afrique un asile
Ou l'on puisse être vertueux.
Allons gaiment chercher des hommes,
Aux lieux où règne le lion;
Ils ont une religion
Et je n'en vois plus où nous sommes.
  Courage, chers amis, bravons les passions!
  Courons (*bis*) porter la foi chez d'autres nations![1]

---

[1] Come, Sons of the Gospel, let us seek, far from these dangerous climes, a shelter in Africa where the practice of virtue is allowed. Let us rejoice to find humanity there where the lion has his kingdom: for there is a religion there, and I see none where we are. Courage, then, dear friends! Let us defy the passions of our foes to bring the faith to other lands!

Hérrisay records, with a light touch, that the villages through which the convoy passed were astonished to hear the condemned deportees strike up a full-throated rendering of what sounded very much like *La Marseillaise*!

But seven priests failed to survive this journey and their corpses were left to the local people to bury. Canon Deschamps died on the evening of arrival at Angoulême, and the Abbé Bougarel had to be left behind, in a state of collapse, when the rest restarted the journey on December 12; he died on the 30th.

The second Moulins convoy had a nightmarish experience at the previous main stopping place, Limoges, where they were forced to join a mock-religious procession about to begin when they arrived. It featured a donkey carrying, back to front, a lout wearing Mass vestments and carrying a chalice; a coffin draped in black with an inscription in silver lettering: "Royalty, Feudalism, Fanaticism" and accompanied by pretended monks singing the introit to the Requiem Mass; and, bringing up the rear of the procession, a hog, draped in a cope and with a tiara fixed to its head bearing the inscription, "Ego sum Papa". The procession drew up at the Place de la Fraternité where the town's guillotine stood. There the prisoners en route for Rochefort were made to stand in a row below the platform to witness the guillotining of a young cleric, a deacon by the name of Rempnoux, found guilty of possessing an anti-revolutionary song. And (so the published account goes) the executioner accompanied the routine gesture of showing the severed head to the crowds with the words: "All the scoundrels you see here deserve the same fate as this fellow! Which one shall I begin with?" To which someone in the crowd found enough breath to say, "It's up to you!" But the executioner had had his moment of sadistic pleasantry and the priests were led back to their carts to resume their journey.

But not all the towns through which the convoys passed were unfriendly, and Reignefort is at pains to give the names of the towns where his own group received marks of sympathy.

The first arrivals at Rochefort were lodged in the Saint Maurice prison, and when that filled up, successive groups were consigned to a vacated religious house — coincidentally a former Capuchin friary, as at Nantes. When accommodation was used up in the town, later arrivals were put either on a superannuated warship, the *Bonhomme-Richard*, anchored upstream from Rochefort and serving as an isolation hospital for prisoners suffering from contagious diseases, or on another, *Le Borée*, anchored in midstream of the Charente. The maritime records of Rochefort show that typhus sufferers were on board both vessels before the arrival of the priests and it is not clear whether the town council's decision to lodge the later arrivals there was prompted by spite at having been encumbered with so many *réfractaires* or by a sheer lack of other accommodation. The records show, anyway, that thirty-three of the priests died there.

The confinement, whether in the town or on the two hospital ships was intended to be only temporary, the pretence of a supposed deportation to Africa having to be sustained. But, for the first arrivals, the detention lasted three months, up to March of 1794, and the memoirs provide details of the ordeal, many of their statements verified (or not nullified) by consultation on the part of Hérrisay and others, in the departmental archives. The Abbé de Reignefort was among those assigned to the former Friary, and he recalls the cold of the winter season, the starvation diet of meagre rations of bread and vegetables, and the nights passed with only the floor or a wooden bench to sleep on.

A solemn inventory was made of the priests' possessions by three officials, wearing the tricolour sash, and during this the breviaries and other books of prayer were confiscated, while occasion was taken also to make fun of other objects of piety found among the possessions. Valuables (watches, assignats and small change, snuff-boxes . . .) were listed, with the assurance that these were to be retained for safe-keeping until the transfer to the deportation ships, when they would be returned to their respective owners; but the objects were never seen again.

It is characteristic of Reignefort's account that he takes whatever opportunity his retentive memory affords him to relieve the poignant narrative with an interesting anecdote, sometimes flavoured even with humour. One such occurs during his account of this legalised pillage at the friary prison and it is worth telling in his own words:

> Before leaving the room from where we were to go to be searched, I took the precaution of hiding my books of piety. But I did not think I needed to worry about books of general interest which I had brought with me to nourish my mind. Among these was a copy of the *Colloquies* of Erasmus, the elegant latinity of which I loved to read. The officials questioning me made as if to confiscate this. I pointed out that it was only a work of Erasmus, and I opened it at the title page and indicated the prominent words: *COLLOQUIA ERASMI*. It was a mistake. A book written in Latin needed nothing else to make it suspect; it had to be a work of religious devotion! "But no, gentlemen!" I protested, "This is no more than a copy of Erasmus's *Colloquies!*" And the reply: "What do we care about your Erasmus! Was he good patriot?" "Alas," I said, "that I do not know. All I know is that he was a Dutchman who died over two hundred years ago. The point is that this work is very well written, it has become a classic. It has nothing to do with religion." My protests were in vain. My book was not the *Hymne des Marseillais* nor a copy of *Le Pere Duchesne*[2] and I had to sacrifice my poor Erasmus. Worse still, I also lost a small pocket atlas which surely meant nothing to them, unless they saw the maps as signs of anti-revolutionary thinking. Either that or else they simply intended to deprive us of anything that could help us to forget our sufferings for a while.
>
> What I did manage, however, to hide from them was a religious object which was of quite another order of importance than the two pastime books. This was my box of holy oils, which proved to be of much help on the ships, enabling a great number of my confreres to have the consolation of receiving the sacrament of the dying.

At last came the order to begin the embarkation. Two slave-trading vessels had been assigned by the Marine Ministry, the *Deux Associés*, with a crew and guards amounting to 110 in all, under the command of Jean Baptiste Laly, and the *Washington* with a complement of 120 captained by

---

[2] Defined by the *Petit Larousse* as a political newsheet published by Hébert during the Revolution and characterised by the violence of its tone and ideas.

Louis Gibert. Both vessels were anchored in the roadstead of the Ile d'Aix, a fortified island a few miles off the mainland coast from the mouth of the Charente. It was a traditional halting-place for ships leaving Rochefort, a place for making final preparations for the ocean voyage and waiting for the favourable winds for setting sail. The two slave vessels, contrary to the expectations of the priests and religious crowded on to them, were to remain permanently anchored there, come favourable winds or no, stationary convict ships for 822 priests and 7 Brothers of the Christian Schools, who had hampered the de-Christianising process and of whom no more than 285 survived.

The transfer began on April 11, 1794, all the clergy imprisoned at the Capuchins or the Saint Maurice, and those who had been assigned to the *Borée* hospital ship, being embarked on the *Deux Associés*. Embarkation on the *Washington* began only a month or so later when new arrivals at Rochefort had filled the places vacated by the prisoners assigned to the *Deux Associés*. The Abbé de Reignefort was, of course, among these latter and it is their fortunes we shall follow, with his help, here. J.B. Laly was only twenty-eight years old at the time of his appointment as captain of the *Deux Associés* but his fierce patriotism had earned him the promotion. When his captives, most of them weak and infirm from their long confinement, and many of them aged, had accomplished the painful task of boarding the ship, Laly assembled them to hear him read the following list of regulations (the document is not given by Reignefort; it was discovered in the Rochefort maritime archives by P. Lemonnier who made it available to Jacques Hérissay):

I. The deportees are not to proceed beyond the main-mast, under pain of eight days in irons and deprivation of wine during that period.

II. They will remain in the gangways in numbers fixed by the commandant, and if they depart from these without his order, they will be put in irons and deprived of wine for a period decided.

III. They will clean their quarters and empty their slop-buckets every day, and if they make any objection to this they will be punished by a week in irons with deprivation of wine.

IV. If any sign of plotting is seen, the culprits will be shot there and then.

V. When the officer-in-charge gives the order to go below they will take up the places assigned to them by the captain of the vessel. If they show any reluctance to do this they will receive the penalty indicated in Article I, and if they repeat the offence they will be put in irons and deprived of wine throughout the whole voyage.

VI. Any crew member, whether officer, mariner, volunteer or apprentice, who communicates with the deportees will be punished with the rigour of the law.

Although the Abbé de Reignefort does not reproduce the document, his reminiscences show that it was no list of idle threats. True, the application of Article IV occurred only once, and that a mere few weeks after the embarkation, when the 33-year old Abbé Antoine Roulhac of Limoges was overheard saying to another young priest, "They have no need to be afraid of a revolt. There are four hundred of us to their hundred and twenty, and if we wanted to revolt, even a hundred of us, like you and me, would suffice to have taken over the boat already." As Reignefort comments, it was imprudent talk, but the very opposite of an incitement to revolt, but Roulhac was promptly taken up on deck, tied to the main-mast and, in the presence of some of his comrades lined up for the purpose, was shot by firing squad and his body thrown into the sea.

This was an isolated case, but the order for anyone to be put in irons, that is, consigned to the hold of the vessel with feet so chained as to limit movement to slow painful steps, was an everyday occurrence, and for supposed offences not even specified in the list. Reignefort gives instances of this: a priest who begged a piece of fruit from one of the sailors was given fifteen days in irons; another who ventured to point out weevils in his biscuit was sentenced to spend the night in irons, and not only he but also the four companions who were eating with him. A few of the prisoners requested Laly's authorisation to present a petition to the Rochefort town authorities and were more than surprised when the captain gave his consent. But when the letter was drawn up and presented for his counter signature, he became furious and immediately sentenced all the petitioners "aux fers". The sentence was given so many times, in fact, that the supply of chains ran out and other offenders were given longer periods of confinement in the hold to make up the loss of due punishment.

Insults on the part of captain and crew were also everyday fare. "I see you're praying to Jesus," one of them remarked, noticing the lips of one of the priests, "well, you can save your breath, he isn't going to get you out of here!" And on one occasion Laly shouted at a group of priests huddled together, and no doubt praying also but without betraying it, for fear of "the irons", "Hey, you scoundrels, why aren't you laughing? Didn't your Jesus tell you that you should be happy when you have to suffer something?"

But the worst moment of the day was when the order was given at dusk to go down to the underdeck for the night. Bunks had been stacked, one above the other, along the sides of the area, and hammocks slung from the low ceiling; that left the floor for whoever failed to obtain a bunk or a hammock. Thus was a cubic space which might at a pinch have accommodated a hundred men for a night's rest, made to hold four hundred. Reignefort dwells at some length on the literal lack of breathing-space this entailed: those stretched on the floor had the bunks and hammocks over their heads; those in the bunks spent the sleepless nights a few inches below the bunk above them; those in the hammocks knew that they must not raise their heads in the darkness if they wished to avoid bruising them.

To this agony of long sleepless nights was added the ordeal of the mealtimes, food ill-cooked and disgusting rather than appetising, eaten always standing and crowded together on deck. The days were spent, for the greater part, in forced idleness, with no books, as Reignefort says, to nourish the mind. The younger men were sometimes called upon to help the crew with scrubbing the deck and other chores and they were only too glad to co-operate. But whatever the attention to the maintenance of the ship itself, the hygienic conditions of the prisoners' quarters deteriorated and Reignefort hints at, but generally leaves his readers to surmise, the consequences of so many men living in such conditions, with rudimentary sanitary arrangements. He is, however, explicit, and even insistent, about the problem of lice and the impossibility of getting rid of them despite repeated washings of linen in sea-water hauled in buckets up the side of the ship.

But the memoirist places at the head of the prisoners' sufferings the impossibility of offering Mass or even of reciting the breviary, all copies of which had been confiscated. Nor could they even group together for community prayer. We must suppose that the personal meditation and unobtrusive vocal prayers of each must have been intense to sustain them in such a test of their faith. In the midst of the sombre story recounted in the Abbé de Reignefort's narrative there occurs, like a sunburst breaking through storm clouds, a reference to "a kind of code of regulations or resolutions which we adopted on board the *Deux Associés* and which shows that in the midst of our sufferings and our want of all material comfort and spiritual resources, our souls were not deprived of all sense of the perfection to which a Christian must aspire". Our author reproduces the nine resolutions in an appendix to his memoir, and since the single motive for this book is to honour the memory of the Revolution's martyrs the reader, it is hoped, will permit a translation here of the full document. A much more authorised judge than the present writer, Professor André Latreille, has written of it: "When men are able, in the midst of their sufferings, to rise to such heights, history must stoop low in homage, for the impartiality of history consists, not in refusing either admiration or blame, but in simply recognising heroism or cowardice for what it is, wherever it is encountered."

RESOLUTIONS TAKEN BY THE PRIEST PRISONERS ON BOARD THE *DEUX ASSOCIÉS* DURING THE EARLIER PART OF THEIR DETENTION.

I

They will not surrender to useless worries about their release but will strive to put the time of their detention to good use by meditating on the years gone by and making holy resolutions for the future. Thus will they find spiritual liberty in their physical captivity.

They will deem a failure in resignation to God's will the least murmurs, the slightest signs of impatience and, above all, an excessive eagerness to seek news of better things, for all such distractions can only hinder the continual state of recollection in which they should live, and that submission to God's will which should exclude all inquietude as to the future.

II

If God permits that they regain, wholly or in part, the liberty for which nature yearns, they will refrain from an excessive demonstration of joy when they hear the news. In preserving a tranquil spirit they will show that they have borne without complaint the cross that had been laid upon them and that they were prepared to bear it longer still with the courage of true Chrstians who never allow themselves to be cast down by adversity.

III

If there be question of their possessions being given back to them, they will avoid any sign of avidity in reclaiming them. They will simply, and with an exact concern for truth, make whatever declaration will be asked of them. They will then accept without complaint what is returned to them, being accustomed, as they should be, to hold cheap the goods of this world and to be satisfied with little, after the example of the prophets.

IV

They will refrain from satisfying the curiosity of people they may meet, answering nothing to useless questions that may be put to them about their experience. They will show only that they have borne their sufferings with patience, but will avoid describing any of these in detail, or showing any resentment against those who have inflicted such sufferings.[3]

V

They will conduct themselves with the utmost moderation and most exact sobriety in the hostelries they may enter, carefully avoiding, especially before strangers, making comparisons

---

[3]In a footnote, Reignefort appeals to what he has written in his preface in vindication of his apparent personal departure from this article IV.

between the meals they are served there and those they were given in captivity, or seeming to relish unduly the new food. Over eagerness for a good table is an occasion of scandal for the faithful, who expect to find in the ministers of Jesus Christ imitators of His penitential life.

VI

Once arrived back in their families they shall avoid excessive haste in relating their sufferings; they will speak of them only to their relatives and friends and with much prudence and moderation even to those. They will never speak of them in public as, for example, from the pulpit, and will not yield to any pressure in this regard. Both at home and when visiting others, they will be frugal in the matter of meals and will behave with modesty and sobriety when invited out.

VII

They will observe the strictest and most absolute silence concerning the defects of their confreres and any failings these may have been drawn into by their trying situation. They will maintain the same charity regarding all whose religious opinions may differ from their own. They will avoid any sign of bitterness or animosity and keep any disagreements to themselves, seeking only to bring others into the way of truth by their benevolence and moderation.

VIII

They shall manifest no regret for the loss of any of their possessions, nor concern to get them back, nor resentment towards any who may have held on to them. But they will accept without complain anything the State may grant them for their subsistence, being always content with the bare necessities whether in the matter of clothing or of food.

IX

They will, as from this moment, form but one heart and one mind, not excepting anyone, and not keeping their distance from any one of their brethren, under any pretext whatever. They will not become involved in the new politics, but will be content simply to pray for the well-being of their country and to prepare themselves for a new life if God permits them to return to their homes. There they will seek to become a source of edification, models of virtue for their people by their avoidance of worldliness, their assiduity in prayer, and their love of recollection and meditation. In conclusion, they will re-read these resolutions from time to time in order to become imbued with their content and to strengthen their practice of the sentiments that have inspired them. *Quicumque hanc regulam secuti fuerint, pax Dei super illos et misericordia.* [Whoever shall have observed this code of behaviour, the peace and mercy of God be upon them.]

As the heading to the list indicates, these resolutions were taken at an early stage of the incarceration in the convict ships and it is noticeable that there is a certain optimism in them about the prospects of an eventual release for the prisoners and even a return to their homes and former missions. But in the event the fulfilment of such hopes was limited to a minority of those concerned. The period of confinement lasted, in fact, only a year, slightly less, but the conditions were such that during that short time illness ended the lives of two-thirds of the total of prisoners on the two ships.

What was to become an epidemic first manifested itself in May, eleven deaths occurring during that month (Hérissay lists the names of those concerned, ten priests and one of the Brothers of the Christian Schools). In June the mortality rate accelerated. On the *Deux Associés* the captain, Laly, ensured that his log-book recorded all the names and this is the source of the details. On June 1 (but, needless to say, the dates are given according to the Republican Calendar) one death, on the 6th one death, on the 9th one death (this was the valiant Père Imbert who had set his dream of an African missionary apostolate to the stirring music of the *Hymne des Marseillais*), on the 10th two deaths, on the 11th one, on the 13th one, on the 16th five, on the 17th two, on the 19th three, on the 21st three and so on - the total for the month of June, twenty-five.

In an attempt to stem the epidemic two long-boats were sent out to anchor alongside the convict ships and serve as floating hospitals. But each could take no more than fifty patients and no special preparations had been made for caring for the sick. The concern was less to cure those already infected than to prevent them from infecting others on the *pontons*.

Hérissay comments that, from the accounts left by one or two witnesses who, against all the odds, survived, "there is conjured up a dantesque vision about the treatment given in the hospital boats, evoking the torments of hell".

As vacancies occurred on the hospital boats more sick were transferred from the convict ships but, even so, the diseases continued to spread there. Hérissay gives the names of prisoners not yet infected who devoted themselves with sublime charity and lack of concern for themselves, to the care, such as they were able to give, of their stricken companions.

In July ninety-seven of the captives succumbed, 88 on the *Deux Associés* and 9 on the *Washington*. Day after day the corpses were moved in the ships' lifeboats, become deathboats, to the Ile d'Aix, accompanied by confreres detailed as the burial party (Hérrisay names the ten clergy concerned) who dug the graves and, as reverently as the two chivvying guards would allow them, lowered the bodies and shovelled back the earth, the guards refusing their requests to be allowed to place improvised crosses to mark the spots. (The bones of the two hundred or so victims finally buried on the Ile d'Aix were discovered almost a century later (1879-80) during excavations for new fortifications, and the Mayor of the time, an Admiral Mandet, had them gathered and placed in the crypt of the parish church.)

The Rochefort authorities, fearing the occurrence of an epidemic in the town, sent two naval surgeons, Beraud and Laforest, to inspect the ships. As a result of their report orders were given for another ship, the *Indien*, to be sent alongside the *Deux Associés* for the sick to be transferred, so that the contaminated ship could be cleaned and disinfected. At the same time an order was given for the two "floating hospitals" to convey their patients to the Ile Citoyenne (formerly the Ile Madame, but recently given the more democratic name), a couple of miles distant, and for the sick to be put on land there in marquees erected to receive them. The first group were transferred there from the 18th to the 20th of August, a total of eighty-three, of whom thirty-six died within hours of the transfer (owing, according to the report of the medical officer appointed as superintendent of the improvised hospital, "to the lack of precautions with which the transfer was effected"). Burials henceforth took place on the Ile Citoyenne. A total of 254 victims died and were interred there during the period from August 18 to October 31.

Meanwhile - and weeks before! - the terrorist government had collapsed but, as Hérissay remarks, Rochefort is a long way from Paris and the fate of a crowd of deported *réfractaires* was far from the immediate agenda of the men who had ousted Robespierre, the Thermidorians, as the historians call them. In any case, the epidemic on the convict ships and the Ile Citoyenne was too far advanced for any government decree to arrest it, even if any intervention had been wished.

It may be said, however (and Reignefort says it, with emphasis) that conditions on the Ile Citoyenne were immeasurably better than those that had been endured on the ships. True, the medical treatment in the marquee hospital fell below the accepted standards even of that time. A young deacon of Poitiers, by the name of Arnadudeau, nursing the sick there, narrowly escaped being sent back to his ship to spend an indefinite period "aux fers" for having, one day, been so exasperated as to say to the medical officer in charge of his tent: "Sir, do you come here to insult suffering human beings or to bring healing to the sick?" But the contrast between life on board the *Deux Associés* and that on the island moves our memoirist to almost idyllic language. "I still recall with emotion," he says, "the delightful sensations I experienced when I first set foot on the little island. I seemed to be entering an earthly paradise." He speaks of his sense of "rebirth" on gazing at the green grass, the hedges and the trees. "I spotted a butterfly. It was a boon and my happiness in contemplating it was immense." Still greater was his joy on seeing and hearing "linnets, swallows and wagtails". The fever, he says, which had qualified him for transfer to the island diminished in a few days and he experienced a sense of concern that he was improving too quickly and might be sent back to the ships! And better, even, than the quasi-bucolic surroundings, the supervision was much less stringent: the nursing clerics and the convalescent patients were able, even, to meet in groups for prayer ...

But the new existence was due to be of short duration. October brought rain and high winds with impossible ground conditions and freezingly cold nights, and the order was given to abandon the island and return to the ships. But the Ile Citoyenne had seen the death and burial of 254 of the sick who had been transferred there, and the total personnel now to be returned to the vessels numbered only 274. It was decided to place the remaining 55 sick on the *Indien*, the 86 convalescent on the *Deux Associés* and the 133 well (other than those detailed for nursing duties) on the *Washington*. When the re-embarkation was complete, and as soon as the weather conditions permitted, the three vessels were moved back to the mouth of the Charente and then upstream to cast anchor off Port-des-Barques, another minor harbour downstream from Rochefort.

The reduction in numbers already ensured a more tolerable existence for all, whether sick, convalescent or fit but, in addition, a new attitude was noticeable in the officers and crew of the vessels. News of the July "palace revolution" in Paris was now everyday talk amongst these, and stories reaching them, true or exaggerated, of the reprisals being meted out to the terror-mongers, were giving them food for thought. Captain Laly, in particular, was a U-turn personified. He had a sobering experience during a visit he made to the mainland in an effort to pre-empt hostility towards himself and his colleagues and crews. Making his way to a public meeting in a church in the Port-des-Barques, he was instantly recognised and ejected with shouts of, "Get out, priest-killer!" and his attempt to reach the pulpit to plead his self-justification was blocked by citizens holding knives at a menacing angle.

Laly's "conversion" is worth dwelling on a little since it tells us more about the spirit of the priests and brothers he had so ruthlessly maltreated. The captain proposed to his fellow- officers that a certificate from the prisoners clearing them of tyrannical behaviour would be of great value in the event of any future charges that might be made. The saintly men could be counted upon to go along with this: were they not believers in a gospel which enjoined forgiveness of enemies? They were not wholly disappointed in their expectations, but neither did they find themselves dealing with simpletons. The formal request they submitted to their captives was studied by a representative committee of these and their reply, as reported by Hérissay, stated that they were very far from wishing harm to those who had harmed them, but that they could not "attest manifest untruths" and that, in any case, "the proposed certificates would count for nothing, since the signatories would be known to have been still in captivity and not at liberty to agree or to refuse to sign". But the petitioners renewed their request with craven appeals to Christian mercy and finally prevailed on the committee to draft vaguely worded certificates such as the one delivered to Laly himself and quoted by Hérissay:

> We, the undersigned, attest that, despite the severity of the treatment we have received aboard the *Deux Associés*, we like to think that Captain Laly acted as he did only because he was forced to by the imperative circumstances of the time. And with even greater conviction we believe that from the time he was able to deal with us more leniently he has taken pleasure in doing so.

The certificate eventually saved Laly's life, but not his position. In April 1795, according to document 245 of the dossier concerned, held in the Port of Rochefort archives and quoted by Hérissay, he was ignominiously, and without pension, dismissed the marine service, judged unworthy of employment by the State.

But to return to the three ships anchored off Port-des-Barques, the halt there, from the day of arrival in November 1794, lasted just over two months into early February. It was a particularly harsh winter that year, as it happened, but the numbing cold was bearable with the warmth of better prospects glowing now more brightly in the heart. Letters could be received and sent (but the incoming ones were inspected and withheld if they contained news of the changes in the political situation — the prisoners being still officially unaware of the events of July). Money sent from relatives and friends was duly delivered and the recipients were able to use it to buy food and other necessities from hawkers allowed on board.

At last, on 8 Pluviose (January 27) came the thaw and with it new orders for a move upstream from Port-des-Barques, the destination this time being the town of Saintes, about thirty miles beyond Rochefort. Small transport vessels were requisitioned for the purpose and the prisoners were disembarked at Tonnay-Charente, the rest of the journey to be made in carts. The transit had been a slow and painful one for men so reduced in health and physical strength, but journey's end was happy beyond their most sanguine hopes. The town council had been asked well in advance to accept this contingent of clergy detainees and three weeks before the anticipated arrival posters had been published appealing to the citizens to co-operate. Hérissay quotes a passage from one of these posters held in the Saintes municipal archives. The document is dated "23 Nivose, an III" (January 12, 1795) and the extract reads as follows:

> ...Let our citizens not fear that this appeal may be a snare for their good faith, giving occasion for the kind of reproaches that may have been levelled at them under the frightful regime of the Terror. That calamitous time has gone for ever. The municipal authority now counts on the generous patriotism of its citizens for this benevolent activity, demanded by considerations of simple humanity and by the sense of duty of republicans whose hallmark is the practice of virtue ...

Labiche de Reignefort is at one with all other sources in praising the way the citizens of Saintes responded to this appeal of their municipal authorities. Their old bishop, Pierre Louis de La Rochefoucauld, done to death in the Carmes prison three years before, would, we might say, have been proud of them. This is what Reignefort says about the arrival of the prisoners in the town:

> Here at last the scene changes. The time has come to breathe freely again, to set in contrast to this long and mournful recital of horrors endured, the most touching representation of humanity and generosity shown by the people of Saintes ... From the moment of our entry within their city's boundary we began to experience the humane and sensitive quality of its

inhabitants. They were lined up along the streets to welcome us as we passed, their eyes glistening with tears, their features expressing a blending of joy, compassion and kindliness. For the first time for many months I realised just then that I had not become so hardened as I had thought, that I still had a heart. Tears which our jailers had never been able to draw from me now began to flow freely ... We were lodged in the magnificent former convent of the Congregation of Our Lady, and no sooner had we set foot therein than the townsfolk, of all ages and conditions, followed us in, bringing all kinds of material help, linen, clothes, furniture, money and food. It was a contest of generosity and charity such as was surely never seen anywhere. It seemed to me as if we were back at the birth of Christianity ...

Almost simultaneously with the arrival at Saintes, the Convention in Paris issued a decree on February 21, 1795, enacting the separation of Church and State, with freedom of worship. Clergy under arrest anywhere were no longer to be treated as rebels; their liberation became a matter of course. Reignefort concludes his memoir with an adapted quotation from Pascal: "I can heed people who are prepared to die violently for the truth of what they believe." And the memoirist, with a nice blend of humility and pride, adds the comment: "Might it not be said, by anyone who has read this account, that this maxim, as profound as it is luminous, can be applied to us?"

POSTLUDE: THE ROLL OF HONOUR

The Roman Catholic Church has, from time immemorial, honoured its martyrs with a special veneration, and it was inevitable that those of its members who, during the French Revolution, bore witness with their lives to the faith that was in them, would emerge as prime candidates for beatification. The surprising thing is that the move towards bringing this about came later than might have been expected. At any rate, when the Sisters of the restored Carmel at Compiègne took the initiative of celebrating with a triduum of prayer on July 15, 16 and 17, 1894, the first centenary of the guillotine-deaths of their sixteen predecessors and notified the hierarchy of their intentions, the recorded reaction of the Bishop of Rodez, Cardinal Bourret, was to express astonishment that no action had yet been taken towards beatification, and to offer his support for any such action. It was the word of encouragement hoped for, not only by the Compiègne community but by all the Carmels re-established in France, thanks largely to the efforts of Mother Camille de Soyecourt.

The speed with which the cause for beatification then advanced served only to demonstrate that the delay in initiating it had been unnecessarily protracted. For the beatification of a martyr the Church requires only incontrovertible proof that a proposed candidate died as a result (immediate or even only consequent) of hostile treatment, and secondly that the motive for the hostile action was hatred for the Catholic faith (and not, for example for political, or even partially political, reasons). The proponents of the cause of the Compiègne Carmelites seemed likely to have no difficulty in satisfying both of these requirements.

199

Cardinal Richard, as Archbishop of Paris where the executions took place, opened the diocesan process of enquiry on February 23, 1896 and, not quite seven years later, on December 16, 1902, the Pope, Leo XIII, approved the introduction of the cause into the court of Rome – the stage of examination of the evidence presented by the diocesan tribunal. The process for this was inaugurated on June 22, 1903, and closed six months later, January 27, 1904. Pope Pius X, himself a future canonised saint, who had succeeded Leo in 1903, signed the decree dated May 27, 1906, according the title of Blessed, with the honours attached thereto, to the following "Venerable servants of God": Mother Thérèse of St. Augustine (Marie Lidoine) and her companions, Sisters St. Louis (Marie Anne Brideau), Jesus Crucified (Marie Piedcourt), Charlotte of the Resurrection (Anne Thouret), Euphrasia of the Immaculate Conception (Catherine Brard), Henrietta of Jesus (Marie de Croissy), Thérèse of the Heart of Mary (Marie Hanisset), Thérèse of St. Ignatius (Marie Trézelle), Julie of Jesus (Rose Chrétien de la Neuville), Marie Henrietta of Providence (Annette Pelras), Marie of the Holy Spirit (Antoinette Roussel), St. Martha (Marie Dufour), St. Francis (Juliette Verolot), Constance (Marie Meunier), Catherine Soiron and Thérèse Soiron.

Writers on the subject have sometimes said, and not without justification, that the cause for the beatification of a martyr makes easier progress than one for a person whose holiness of life has been the motive for proposing a cause. For one thing, it is less difficult to establish the circumstances of a martyrdom than to prove that a person has practised "to a heroic degree" the theological virtues of faith, hope and charity, and the cardinal virtues of prudence, justice, fortitude and temperance. As Pope Benedict XIV wrote in his classic work *De Servorum Dei Beatificatione et Beatorum Canonizatione*, which established the norms of procedure followed from the year of its completed publication, 1738, down to very recent times, the freely accepted death of a martyr constitutes and embraces all heroism. For this reason, also, the requirement of miracles has usually been dispensed with in the case of martyrs (never for others).

But this does not mean that a martyr's cause goes through

automatically, and the case of the four Daughters of Charity guillotined at Cambrai, who were the next of our group of martyrs to be beatified, illustrates this (but typically), as a perusal of the published *Acta Apostolicae Sedis* makes clear. The cause reached the court of Rome prior to February 21, 1911, since on that date the Cardinals met to establish whether the diocesan processes had been duly and correctly conducted. An affirmative answer having been given to this, the next meeting took place on January 30, 1917 (it is, of course, reasonable to suppose that the incidence of the first World War contributed to this extensive gap). This was the first of two preparatory meetings (the "Antepreparatoria") to discuss the reality of the fact and motives of the mar-tyrdom. The second such meeting (the "Preparatoria") was held almost two years later, on October 29, 1918. Another eight months passed and then a decree dated July 6, 1919 declared that the fact and the motives of the martyrdom of the four Daughters of Charity had been proved and that the cause could now proceed to its final stage. This was reached with Pope Benedict XV's formal decree of June 13, 1920, bearing the "seal of the Fisherman's ring" and countersigned by the Secretary of State, Cardinal Gasparri, and declaring Blessed: Marie Madeleine Fontaine, Marie Françoise Lanel, Marie Thérèse Fantou and Jeanne Gérard.

The cause for the beatification of the thirty-two nuns guillotined at Orange had been introduced at Rome four years before this, on June 14, 1916, but the meeting of the Cardinals for the vote on the validity of the process took place only on December 14, 1920. The Antepreparatoria was held on December 18, 1923 and the Preparatoria just a year later, on December 23, 1924. The decree "de tuto" (that the cause could "safely" proceed to its final stage) was promulgated on May 1, 1925, and the decree of Beatification, granted by Pope Pius XI, and dated May 10, 1925, named the thirty-two new "Blesseds" in the following order: a representative of each of the four congregations honoured by this glorious event: a Sacramentine, Sister Iphigenia of St. Matthew (Suzanne Gabrielle de Gaillard), an Ursuline, Sister Elizabeth Thérèse of the Heart of Jesus (Thérèse Consolin), the one Benedictine, Sister Maria Roas (Suzanne Agathe

Deloye) and one of the two Cistercians, Sister Mary of
St. Henry (Marguerite Eléonore de Justamond). Then came
the names, according to the respective Communities, of
their Companions "Sociae") as follows: 12 Sacramentines,
Sisters Saint Pelagia (Rosalie-Clotilde Bès), Théotiste Marie
(Elisabeth Pelissier), Saint Martin (Marie-Claire Blanc), Rose
of Saint Xavier (Madeleine Thérèse Talieu), Martha of the
Good Angel (Marie Cluse), Madeleine of the Mother of
God (Elisabeth Verchière), Annunciation (Henriette Faurie),
Saint Alexis (Anne Minutte), Amata of Jesus (Marie-Rose de
Gordon), Mary of Jesus (Marie-Thérèse Charransol), Saint
Joachim (Marie Anne Béguin-Royal) and Saint Augustine
(Marguerite Bonnet); 15 Ursulines, Sisters Mary of the Angels
(Marie Madeleine de Rocher), Madeleine of the Blessed Sac-
rament (Dorothée Madeleine de Justamond), Catherine of
Jesus (Marie Madeleine de Justamond), Saint Francis (Marie
Anne Depeyre), Saint Sophia (Marguerite d'Albarède), Agnes
of Saint Louis (Sylvie Agnèse de Romillon), Saint Bernard
(Jeanne Marie de Romillon), Saint Basil (Anne Cartier), Saint
Melanie (Marie Madeleine de Guilhermier), Saint Sophia
(Marie Marguerite de Ripert d'Alauzier), Saint Gervase
(Marie Anastasie de Roquard), Saint Francis (Marie Anne
Lambert), Saint Michael (Marie Anne Doux), Saint Andrew
(Marie Rose Laye) and Saint Rosalie (Marie Claire du Bac);
and the one other Cistercian, Sister of the Heart of Mary
(Madeleine Françoise de Justamond).

Interestingly, but not surprisingly, the first group to give
their lives for conscience's sake, the victims of the September
massacres, were the last to reach the honours of beatification.
The sheer number of candidates proposed for this category
sufficiently explains the lengthier period of study of the
cause. In fact, a total of 213 names were submitted in the
first place, comprising 110 victims of the Carmes massacre,
77 of Saint-Firmin, 23 of the Abbaye and 3 of La Force.
That the examination was individually searching may be
deduced from the fact that, at the penultimate stage of
the procedure, 22 of these candidates were "put back
pending further information", which meant in practice
that they were dropped from the cause. Already in 1910
(on June 21) a meeting of the theologians was held to

initiate a study of the writings of the many theologians and scholars among the September 1792 victims. The cause does not appear again in the *Acta* until December 9, 1919, when the validity of process was examined and approved by the Cardinals. The Antepreparatoria took place on October 23, 1923 and the Preparatoria on November 17, 1925. An additional meeting was held on October 1, 1926, and it was at this that the decision was taken to postpone the 22 victims whose cases were in doubt. The papal decree of beatification, granted by Pope Pius XI, was dated October 17, 1926.

The names of the 191 new "Beati" are listed in the decree in four groups corresponding to the four prisons that were the scenes of the massacres. The names are given in full, and after each the details of the title held and ministry engaged in. To save space here I group them, alphabetically, according to their title and ministry, giving only initials with surnames and indicating the prisons concerned with the letters (C) for the Carmes, (F) for the Saint-Firmin, (A) for the Abbaye and (L) for La Force:

BISHOPS: JM Du Lau (C), FJ La Rochefoucauld (C), PL La Rochefoucauld (C).

VICARS GENERAL: JAH.Boucharenc de Chaumeils (C), AA.Chapt de Rastignac (A), G.Desprez de Roche (C), A.de Foucauld de Pontbriand (C), ACO.du Bouzet (A), FL.Méallet de Fargues (C), JHC.Pazery de Thorame (C), PF.Pazery de Thorame (C).

CANONS: P.Brisse (F), A.Grasset de Saint-Sauveur (C), L.Longuet (C), JT.Pazery de Thorame (C), JL.Guyard de Saint Clair (A), FU.Salin de Niart (C), JP Simon (A).

PARISH PRIESTS: V.Abraham (C), JBC.Aubert (C), P.Bonse (F), JB.Bottex (L), JC.Caron (F), N.Colin (F), TR.Dubuisson (C), P.Fougères (F), N.Gaudreau (F), J.Goizet (C), JM.Gros (F), J.de La Lande (F), M.Leber (F), R.Le Bis (C), JJ.Lejardinier Deslandes (C), JT.Leroy (F), MFA.Loublier (F), GC.Maignien (C), CL.Marmotant de Savigny (F), L.Mauduit (C), RN.Poret (C), JR.Queneau (C), ML.Royer (A), JL.Schmid (F).

CURATES: A.Angar (C), LFA.Barret (C), LR.Benoist (A), LRN.Benoist (A), JA.Capeau (A), BA.de Caupenne (F),

J.Dufour (F), DC.Duval (F), HH.Ermes (C), C.Fontaine (A), GJ.Giroust (F), GA.Guilleminet (C), MF.de La Gardette (L), P.Landry (C), L.Le Danois (A), J.Le Laisant (F), JP.Le Laisant (F), JJ.Le Meunier (C), FC.Londiveau (C), JP.Marchand (C), HJ.Millet (F), FJ.Monnier (F), TJ.Monsaint (A), MF.Mouffle (F), JB.Nativelle (C), R.Nativelle (C), FJ.Pey (A), P.Ploquin (C), DL.André des Pommerayes, YJP.Rey de Kervisic (F), JHLM.Samson (C), JAB.Seguin (C), PJM.Vitalis (A).

SEMINARY STAFF: PP.Balzac (F), MAS.Binard (F), N.Bize (F), P.Briquet (F), C.Carnus (F), F.Dardan (C), LJ.François (F), EM.Gillet (F), YA.Guillon de Keranrun (F), PF.Henocq (F), LJM.Lanier (F), PF.Leclerq (F), JC.Legrand (F), JA.Menuret (C), M.Nézel (C), JL.Oviefve (F), NC.Roussel (F), PJ de Turmenyes (F), RJ.Urvoy (F).

CHAPLAINS: JP.Bangue (C), N.Clairet (C), C.Colin (C), J.Falcoz (F), GJ.Fautrel (F), JL.Gaultier (C), G.Girault (C), JB.Jannin (C), J.Lacan (C), GLS.Lanchon (F), M.Laurent (A), JJ.de Lavèze-Bellay (F), O.Lefebvre (C), JF.de Lubersac (C), AMA.Nogier (C), JM.Philippot (F), JL.Rabé (F), P.Saint-James (F), PLJ.Verrier (C).

OTHER DIOCESAN PRIESTS OR SEMINARISTS: AA. Alricy (F), J.Bécavin (C), JF.Bousquet (C), C.Chaudet (C), MV.Deruelle (C), F.Dumasrambaud de Calandelle (C), PJ.Garrigues (F), PL.Gervais (A), JF.Hédouin (F), S.Huré (A), LB. Hurtrel (A), PL.Joret (F), J.Lemaître (F), CSR.Mayneaud de Bizefranc (F), J.Poulain Delaunay (C), JJ.Rateau (A), EFD de Ravinel (C), PRM. Regnet (F), A.Robert de Lézardières (C) CV.Véret (F).

CONGREGATIONS: *Benedictines*: L.Barreau de La Touche (C), AA.Chevreux (C), RJ.Massey (C). *Canons Regular*: JCM.Bernard du Cornillet (F), JF.Bonnel de Pradal (F), C.Ponse (F). *Christian Doctrine*: C.Bochot (F), E.Félix (F). *De La Salle Brothers*: GLN.Leclercq (C), *Eudists*: FL.Hébert (C), F.Lefranc (C), PC.Pottier (F).*Foreign Missions*: U.Lefebvre (C). Franciscans: JF.Burté (C), JJ.Morel (C). *Jesuits*: RM.Andrieux (F), F.Balmain (C), JFM.Benoît-Vourlat, CJ.Beraud du Prou (C), JJ.Bonnaud (C), C.Cayx-Dumas (C), J.Charton de Millou (C), GA.Delfaut (C), J.Friteyre-Durvé (C), CF.Gagnières des

Granges (C), PM.Guérin du Rocher (F), RF.Guérin du Rocher (F), E.Herque du Roule (F), AACM.Lanfant (A), CAR.Laporte (C), MN.La Villecrohain (C), CF.Le Gue (C), H.Le Livec de Trésurin (L), VJ.Le Rousseau de Rosencoat (C), T.Loup-Bonnotte (C), JA.Seconds (F), F.Vareilhe-Duteil (C), NM.Verron (F). *Minims*: CL.Hurtrel (A). *Sulpicians*: LAM.Boubert (C), BF.de Cucsac (C), TN.Dubray (C), JG.Galais (C), P.Gauguin (C), PM.Guérin (C), JEP.Hourrier (C), HA.Luzeau de La Mulonnière (C), JBM.Pontus (C), PN.Psalmon (C), C.Rousseau (C), JA.Savine (C), JBM.Tessier (C). *Vincentians*: JH.Gruyer (F).
LAYMEN: S.Desbrielles (F), JP.Duval (F), LF.Rigot (F), CRM.Valfons de La Calmette (C), JAJ.de Villette (F).

The case of the deportees is different. Their story is still one of beatification hoped for, not one of beatification achieved. But the hope has been there from the immediate aftermath of their sacrifice. According to L. Poivert, already in 1794 Pope Pius VI urged the Vicar General of Dijon, visiting Rome, to assemble the information concerning the victims of the Rochefort deportation. Tentative measures to preserve the memory of the heroes were made successively by the Bishops of Rochefort's diocese, La Rochelle. The difficulties which obstructed a smooth passage for a diocesan process, in view of a submission to Rome, centred around the sheer number of the possible candidates – over five hundred! However, the hope was never abandoned and as recently as November 15, 1990, the present Bishop of La Rochelle and Saintes, Mgr. Jacques David, addressed a letter to the bishops of dioceses represented among the victims and to Superiors General of religious congregations likewise represented, informing them of "the very important" work accomplished by the newly-appointed Vice-Postulator, the Abbé Yves Blomme, in assembling a dossier in view of the cause for beatification of a (provisional) representative list of 101 of the deportees. The list is indeed representative, including as it does, diocesan priests of twenty-two dioceses, and priests and brothers of fifteen religious congregations. What better way to conclude our story of the Revolution's martyrs than to express the hope that the heroic men of Rochefort may, in the not too distant future, have their witness honoured as only the authority of the Church they loved can honour it.

CODA

But the souls of the just are in God's hands
and no torment, in death itself,
has power to reach them.
Dead?
Fools think so;
think their end loss, their leaving us, annihilation;
but all is well with them.
The world sees nothing but the pains they endure;
they themselves have eyes only for what is immortal;
so light their suffering,
so great the gain they win!
God, all the while, did but test them,
and testing them found them worthy of him.
His gold, tried in the crucible,
his burnt-sacrifice graciously accepted,
they do but wait for the time of their deliverance;
then they will shine out,
these just souls,
unconquerable as the sparks that break out,
now here, now there, among the stubble.
Theirs to sit in judgement on nations,
to subdue whole peoples,
under a Lord whose reign shall last for ever.
Trust him if thou wilt,
true thou shalt find him;
faith waits for him calmly and lovingly;
who claims his gift,
who shall attain peace,
if not they, his chosen servants?

Book of Wisdom, 3, 1 - 9

BIBLIOGRAPHY

(Note: All titles were published in Paris unless otherwise stated)

Anon. Les Filles de la Charité de Saint Vincent de Paul (Letouzey & Ane, 1923)

AULARD, A. La Révolution Française et les Congrégations (Cornely 1903)

BARRUEL, A. Histoire du Clergé pendant la Révolution Française, 2nd édition (London, 1794)

BATTERSBY, W.J. Brother Solomon, Martyr of the French Revolution (Burns, Oates, London 1960)

BOULOISEAU, M. The Jacobin Republic 1792-1794 (Cambridge University Press, Cambridge 1983)

CHASSAGNON, H. Le Frère Salomon (Procure Générale 1905)

COBBAN, A. A History of Modern France, Vol. 1: 1715-1799, 3rd ed. (Penguin 1963)

DANIEL-ROPS, H. L'Eglise des Révolutions (Fayard 1960)

DELARC, A. L'Eglise de Paris pendant la Révolution Française 1789-1801, Tome II (Desclée, De Brouwer, n.d.)

DURAND, Y. Le Diocése de Nantes (Beauchesne 1985)

FUNCK-BRENTANO, F. La Révolution Française (Flammarion 1935)

GOUBERT, J. La Terreur en Provence: Les Trente-deux Bienheureuses Martyres d'Orange (éd. du Dauphin 1952)

GRENTE, J. Les Martyrs de Septembre 1792 à Paris. 3rd édition (Téqui 1926)

GUILHEM, M. Nicolas Leclercq, Martyr de la Révolution Française Mediaspaul 1990)

GUILHERMY, E. de. Ménologie de la Compagnie de Jésus: Assistance de France. (Schneider 1892)

GUILLON, N.S. Collection générale des Brefs et Instructions de notre Très-Saint Père, le Pape Pie VI, relatifs à la Révolution Française, Tome I (Le Clere 1798)

HALES, E.E.Y. Revolution and Papacy 1769-1846 (Eyre & Spottiswoode, London 1960)

HERISSAY, J. Les Pontons de Rochefort 1792-1795 (Perrin 1925)

LABICHE DE REIGNEFORT, L. Relation très détaillée de ce qu'ont souffert ... les prêtres et autres ecclésiastiques ... détenus en 1794 et 1795 pour refus de serment, à bord des vaisseaux Les Deux Associés et le Washington dans la rade de l'Ile d'Aix, ou aux environs.(Le Clere 1801)

LA GORCE, P. de. Histoire Religieuse de la Révolution Française, Tomes 1,2,3. 3rd édition. (Plon 1919)

LATREILLE, A. L'Eglise Catholique et la Révolution Française. Nouvelle éd. (Cerf 1970)

LECLERCQ, H. Les Martyrs, Tomes XI & XII. (Oudin 1911, 1912)

LEFLON, J. La Crise Révolutionnaire 1789-1846. (Bloud & Gay 1949)

LEMASSON, A. Les Actes des Prêtres Insermentés de l'Archidiocèse de Rennes. (L'Archevêché de Rennes 1927)

LENOTRE, G. Mémoires et Souvenirs sur la Révolution et l'Empire publiés avec des documents inédits: Les Massacres de Septembre. 5th édition. (Perrin 1907) Les Noyades de Nantes. (Perrin 1914)

MADELIN, L. La Révolution. 7th édition. (Hachette 1920)

MANSEAU, A. Les Prêtres et les Religieux Déportés, Tomes I & 2 (Desclée, De Brouwer, n. d.)

MERITAN, J. Les Trente-deux Martyres d'Orange (Bonne Presse du Midi, Vaison-la-Romaine, 1925)

MOURRET, F. L'Eglise et la Révolution (1775-1823) (Bloud & Gay, 1929)

PIERRARD, P. L'Eglise et la Révolution 1789-1889 (Ed. Nouvelle Cité, 1988)

PIERRE, V. Les Seize Carmèlites de Compiègne (Lecoffre, 1905)

PLONGERON, B. Conscience Religieuse en Révolution (Picard, 1969)

POIVERT, L. Les Martyrs des Pontons (Bonne Presse, 1928)

PREVOST, M. & D'AMAT, R. Dictionnaire de Biographie Française (Letouzey et Ane, 1956)

RICHEMONT, Vte de. Correspondance secrète de l'Abbé de Salamon, Charge d'affaires du Saint-Siège pendant la Rèvolution, avec le Cardinal Zelada (1791-1792). (Plon, Nourrit, 1898)

RIGAULT, G. Histoire Générale de l'Institut des Frères des Ecoles Chrétiennes. Tome III La Révolution Française. (Plon, 1940)

SOREL, A. Le Couvent des Carmes et le Séminaire de Saint-Sulpice pendant la Terreur (Didier, 1863)

TEIL de, R. Les Massacres du 2 Septembre 1792 à la Prison des Carmes à Paris. Reproduction du Manuscrit de l'Abbé de Lapize de La Pannonie (Desclee, De Brouwer, 1913)

THIERS, L.A. Histoire de la Révolution Française, Tome II (Fourne, Jouvet, 1866)

TULARD, J., FAYARD, J.-F., FIERRO, A. Histoire et diction-naire de la Révolution Française 1789-1799 (Laffont, 1987)

VAYSSE, A. Les Trente-Deux Religieuses de Bolléne (Vallier, Grenoble, 1906)

VISMES H de. Camille de Soyecourt, Carmélite au grand coeur (Albin Michel, 1958)

VOVELLE, M. The fall of the French monarchy 1787-1792 (Cambridge University Press, Cambridge 1984)

WALLON, H. Les Réprésentants du Peuple en Mission. Tome 1 (Hachette, 1889)

WALTER G. Les Massacres de Septembre. Etude critique. (Payot, 1932)

WELSCHINGER, H. Les Martyrs de Septembre. 3me edition. (Lecoffre, 1927)

WORONOFF, D., The Thermidorean Regime and the Directory 1794–1799 (Cambridge University Press, Cambridge 1984)

Index

Advice to Religious Virgins Consecrated to Jesus Christ 89
Affilé 175
Amiens, Bishop of 6
Andrieux, René Marie 35
Arnadudeau, Deacon 194
Aulard A
– *La Révolution Française et les Congrégations* 105
Auribeau, Hesmivy d' 141
Bailly, J S 3
Barbot, Canon Berthelet de (Vicar General of Mende) 58
– account of initiation of massacres 60
– on tribunal at the Carmes 63–64
– requests to celebrate mass denied 59
Barnave, Joseph 7
Barraud, A
– *Le Clergé Vendéen* 169
Barruel, Augustine 57; 58
– *Histoire du Clergé pendant la Révolution Française* 57
Bas, Le (Friend of Robespierrre) 81
Baudet 169; 170

Baumgarten, Odile 116
– death by firing squad 117
Beauvais, Bishop of 62
Bechet (Vicar General of Paris) 86
Becket, Thomas á 21
Benedict XIV, Pope
– *De Servorum Dei Beatificatione et Beatorum Canonizatione* 200
Benedict XV, Pope 201
Bergeron, Madame 90
Bernanos, Georges
– *Dialogues des Carmélites* 135
Berton, Canon 32
Bes, Rosalie 131
Bibliothèque de la Compagnie de Jésus 29
Biochaye, Sister Louise Thérèse 92
Blot, Denis 158–159
Boisgelin, Archbishop 14; 15
Boizard, Citizen 112
Bordeaux, Bishop of 15
Bossuet 18
Bottex, Jean Baptiste 75
Boullangier, Père 35
– on the Saint Firmin massacre 69–71
Bouloiseau, Marc

– on the number of executions during the Terror 79
Bourbe Prison 90
Bourret, Cardinal (Bishop of Rodez) 199
Bouzet, Canon de 48
Brard, Catherine Charlotte 137–138; 141
Bretonne, Restif de la 1
Briand, Abbé
– *Notices sur les confesseurs de la foi dans le dioceses de Nantes pendant la Révolution* 167f
Brideau, Marie-Anne 137
– request for a cup of chocolate 159
Brunswick, Duke of 25; 39
– ultimatum to French Nation 25
cahiers de doléances 2; 12; 14
Calmet, Augustine 18
Calmette, Charles Régis Mathieu de La (Count de Valfons) 55, 57
Cambon, Pierre Joseph 178
Camus, Armand-Gaston 14; 16
Capeau, Jean André 48
Carcel 41
Cardinal Lemoine College 36
Carrier, Jean Baptiste 1643–1644 169; 171; 173
– arranges for the second barge 175
– authorisation for barge 170
– death by guillotine 176
– letter to Bouchotte 164
– & the party on *La Gloire* 174
– transfer of 'bouches inutiles' 168
Carvoisin, Joséphine de 87
Caubrière, J (Cambrai Public Prosecutor) 114

Cayrol, M de (Mayor) 142
– visit to Rue Dampierre 142–143
Ceyrat, Joachim 41
– & arrest of Istève 53
– sends deputy to Carmelite Abbey 62
Charles Borromeo, Saint 30
Chevreux, Abbot Ambroise Augustin 36
Chrétienne, Sister 92
Chute de la Monarchie 1787–1792 23
Civil Constitution of the Clergy 12–13; 16; 17; 18; 19; 24; 30; 32
– *Exposition of Civil Constitution of the Clergy* 15; 19
– Oath of Loyalty 16; 18
Clement XI, Pope 14
Clement XIV, Pope 29
– suppression of Jesuits 29
Clermont, Bishop of 12
Clermont-Tonnerre, Stanislas 3
Clorivière, Père Picot de 29; 90
Compiègne, Carmelite Convent of 135; 199
– detained in Visitation convent 150f
– directive to leave convent 142
– execution 160
– found guilty of plotting 158
– received gifts from Kings & Queens 135f
– transfer to Conciergerie Prison 155
Constituent National Assembly
– (1789) 3; 4; 7; 8;
– (1790) 9; 10; 11; 15; 16; 17; 19
– (1791) 23
Constitution (1791)

– *article 10* 5
– *article 11* 6
Contacheaux, Sister 111
Convent of the English Nuns
    104
Couthon (friend of
    Robespierre) 81
– friend of Maignet 120
Coz, Claude Le 107
Croissy, Marie Françoise de
    137
Daniel-Rops, Henri 29
Danton, Georges Jacques 77
– death of 78
– plan to exile refractories 180
Daubanel 64–65
Daughters of Charity 107
David, Louis (painter) 79; 81
Delacroix, Jean-François 177
Delarc, O J M
– *L'Eglise de Paris pendant la
    Révolution Française* 56
Depeyre, Sister Marie Anne
    126
Deportation of Refractories
    180–198
– deaths onboard ship 193ff
– Moulin convoys 182–183
Deux Associés (boat) 185; 186
– deaths on board 193ff
– resolutions taken by the
    priest prisoners 189–192
Dieu de Boisgelin, Jean de
    (Archbishop of Aix) 8
Dougazon 51
Dreux-Brézé, Marquis de 2
Dulau, Archbishop of Arles 50
– murder of 61–62
– seizure in garden 61
– singled out for ill-treatment
    59
Duleau, Antoinette 108
Dumonchel, Abbé (Rector of

Paris University) 18
Dumont, André 147
Duponchel, Jacques Philippe
    110
Duvergier J B 178
– *Collection complète des lois,
    décrets et ordonnances* 178
d'Eglantine, Fabre 79
Effroy, Charles Joseph 110
Emery, Jacques André
    (Superior General, Society
    of Saint Sulpice) 20
– on the Liberty-Equality oath
    49
d'Eprémesnil, Jean Jacques
    Duval 11
L'Espirit des Lois 5
Expilly, Abbé 18;
Fabre, Sister Jeanne 111
Fantou, Sister Thérèse
    Madeleine 111
– interrogation 113
Fare, Madame de La 125
Fare, Mgr La (Bishop of
    Nancy) 9–10;
Fauchet, Claude
    (Constitutional Bishop of
    Caen) 178
Faurie, Sister Henriette 134
Fauvety, Jean 120; 121
Fernex, 120; 122–123
Flaust, Abbé Jacques 75
– escaped death by
    pronouncing liberty-
    equality oath 75
Fleurian, Abbé 169
Fonrosa, 120; 122
Fontaine, Sister Madelaine 110
– interrogation 113
– reaction to Arras ordinance
    111
– reaction to summons to
    Cambrai 114

— sentenced to death &
    execution 115–116
Force, La (official prison) 74;
    202
— death of five priests 75
Fort, Gertrud Von
— *Song at the Scaffold, 1931*
    135
Foulon, François 169
Fouquet, Robert 166; 169; 170
— transfers prisoners to the
    barge 172
Fouquier-Tinville, Antoine
    Quentin 101; 155
— on 'evidence' against
    Compiegne sisters 156
— verdict on Rue Cassette nuns
    101–103
François, Vincentian Louis
    Joseph (Superior of Saint
    Firmin Seminary) 35; 71
Garat, Dominique Joseph 179;
    180
Gardette, Michel François de
    La 75
— letter to family after arrest
    75–76
Gaudin, Jacques 106
— decree for the suppression of
    religious congregations
    106–107
Gérard, Sister Jeanne 111
— questioned after her arrest
    112
Gerle, Dom Christopher 10;
    11
Gervais, Pierre Louis 48
Gibert, Louis 186
Girondins 77
Gobel, Jean Baptiste (Bishop
    of Lydda) 19; 151
— appearance before National
    Convention 80

Godard, Abbé (Vicar General
    of Toulouse) 45
Gonsolin, Sister Thérèse 126
— execution 127
— trial of 133
Gorce, Pierre de La 6; 9; 12
— on Talleyrand & oath 19
Goubert, Dr Joseph 120
Goullin, Jean-Jacques 166
— & La Compagnie Marat 166
Gouttes, Abbé 18
Grand, Père Le 169
Greer, Donald 79
— *Incidence of the Terror: A
    Statistical Interpretation*
    79
Grégoire, Abbé Henri Baptiste
    5 18; 19;
— refusal to abjure his
    functions as a Catholic
    priest 80
Grente 55
— on arrest & questioning of
    Count Valfons 55
Gros, Abbé 69
— death of 72
Guillemenet, Abbé Jean
    Antoine 55
Hales E E Y 17
Hanisset, Sister Marie-
    Antoinette 138
Hanot, Sister Thérèse 118
Hébert, Père 32
Henry-Larivière, Pierre 177
Henriot, Monsieur 70
Henry II 21
Herbois, Collot d' 146
Hérissay, Jacques
— *Les Pontons de Rochefort
    1792–1795* 181ff
Hue, Charles Mathieu 66
— questioning of Laurent 68
Imbert, Père Joseph 182; 192

Indien (boat) 195
Istève, Jean Baptiste (Brother Abraham) 53
Jallet, Abbé 18
Jardin des Plantes (Ward & 'section') 35; 36
— prison at Saint Firmin 35; 202
Jauffret, Mgr (Vicar General of Lyons)
— *Mémoires pour servir l'histoire de la Religion la fin du XVIIIme siécle* 156
Josse, Raymond 92
Juigne, Mgr de (Archbishop of Paris) 4
Justamond, Sister Dorothée Madeleine de 126
Kermoran, Père 169
Lallié, M A
— *Histoire de la persécution des prêtres noyés* 167
Laly, Jean Baptiste 185; 186; 187; 188
— 'conversion' 195–196
— records names of those who signed the resolutions 192
Lamballe, Princess de 76
Lamberty, Guillaume 166; 169; 170; 171; 175
— host of the party on *La Gloire* 174
— sinks the barge 172–173
— transfer prisoners to barge 172
Landeau, Abbé Julien 168
Lanel, Sister Marie 111
— interrogation 112–113
Latreille, André 2
— on massacres at Orange 134
Launay, De 86
Laurent, Abbé Claude Ignace 66;

— questioning & arrest 67–69
Lavaux. Theodore 166
Lazowsky, Claude 33–35; 59
— search at Rue Mouffetard 86; 87
Lebon, Guislain François Joseph 108
— on penalty to be given to Louis XVI 109
— order to escort Daughters of Charity to Cambrai 114
Leclercq, Dom Henri 15
— on arrest of Camille de Soyecourt 87
— on inventory signed by Sr Fontaine 110
Leclercq, Nicholas (Brother Solomon) 53; 54
— on the Irish college 56
Leflon, Jean 15; 17
Legendre 25
Legislative Assembly 23–24; 106
— declaration of war on Austrian Emperor 24
— decree of May 27, 1792 177
— decree of August 17th, 1792 142
— decree of August 26th, 1792 177; 179
— disbandment of royal bodyguard 25
— *Liberty-Equality Oath* 26
Legris-Duval 86
Lemercier, Abbé 169
Lenôtre, G
— *Les Massacres de Septembre* 58
— *Leds Noyades de Nantes* 166; 170; 171; 174; 175
Leopold II (Austria) 24
Lidoine, Madeleine Claudine

(Prioress at Compiègne) 136
- directive to leave Compiègne 142
- execution 160
- on the prospect of death 145–146
- & Sister Constance 140
- sympathy for Louis XVI 157
- visit to Paris 148
Livec, Hyacinthe Le 75; 76
Louis XVI 1; 3; 17
- & *Civil Constitution of the Clergy* 14–15; 24
- death 78f
- flight & arrest 22
- imprisonment in the Temple 25
- refusal to sign decree of May 27, 1792 25
- stipend to du Rocher 36
- trial for conspiracy 77
- vetoes decree of May 27, 1792 177
Lucas, Alexis-Julien 169
Luçon, Bishop of 12
Luxembourg (Ward) 29; 30
- Luxembourg section 35; 40
Maignet, Etienne Christophe 120; 123
Maillane, Durand de 12
Maillard, Stanislas 47; 49; 51
Manuel, Louis Pierre 38
- *Essais historiques, critiques, littéraires & philosophiques (1783)* 38
- refused to vote for execution of Louis XVI 38
Marat, Jean Paul 77
- death of 78
Maire Antoine Marie 92
Marie-Antoinette, Queen 24; 36; 76; 136

Marolles, Claude 22
Martineau 12
Maury, Abbé (later Cardinal)
- letter to Bottex 75
Massey, Dom 62
Mathiez, Albert 16; 17
Méhée (recording clerk of Paris Commune) 42
- account of transfer from Mairie to Abbeye 43–44
Méritan, Canon Julius 120;
- on the executions at Orange 124
Meunier, Marie Jeanne 139
Meyrac, Abbé de 169
Mézières, Mrg Béthisy de (Bishop of Uzès) 11
Michaeu, Sister Rose 111
Mirabeau, Honoré-Gabriel 2; 7
Molleville, Bertrand de 75
Montagnards 77
Montesquieu 5
Montesquiou-Fezensac, François de 10
Montmorin, Count 15
Morris, Gouverneur (American Ambassador to Paris) 23
Mortimer-Ternaux
- *Histoire de la Terreur* 74
Mury, André 112
- repeats charge against Daughters of Charity 114
National Convention (September 1792) 77; 146; 179
- abolition of Gregorian calendar 79
- abolition of monarchy & proclamation of a republic 77
- & new liturgy by David 79
Neuville, Rose Chrétien de La 138–139

Noailles, Duke de 3
Noble, Charles 130
Normant, Canon Le 169
Olier, Jean-Jacques 29
Orange, 'Peoples Commission' 120ff
– execution of the nuns at 'cirque' 129; 201
– incarceration of nuns at 'La Cure' 127
– indictments against the nuns 128 – 129; 131 – 134
Pancemont, Mayneaud de 29
Pannonie, Abbé Pierre François Vidal de Lapize de La 57
– eyewitness account of the massacres at the Carmelite Monastery 57; 59
– how he came to be saved 64
Pascal 18
Pater, Citizen 112
Paujade, Sister Jacquette 118
Pelras, Sister Anne 139
– questions Scellier on meaning of 'fanatical' 158
Philip IV 1
Philippe, Françoise Geneviève 135
Pichot, Madame Victoire 170
Piedcourt, Sister Marie-Anne 137; 141
Pierrard, Pierre
– *Géographie des Serments* 20
Pierre, Victor 135
– descriptions of the members of the Compiegne Convent 136 – 142
– on the responses of Compiegne sisters 141
– on the way of life of the Compiegne nuns following the suppression of the convent 144 – 145
Pius VI, Pope 14; 15; 182
– verdict on *Civil Constitution* 20 – 21
Pius XI, Pope 203
– Beatification of 'Orange' nuns 201
Plass, Canon Françios Xavier
– *La Clergé Français réfugié en Angleterre* 57
Poissonnière (section & ward)
– initiate proposal to put to death all those held in prisons in Paris 40
Pottier, Pierre Claude (Assistant General of the Eudist Congregation) 72
– retraction of his oath 73
Pouessel, Père 169
Poulet, Dom 109
Priere, Louis 40
Pronnay, Citizen 140
Quiévrain (defeat) 25
Ragot 120; 123
Reignefort, Abbé Pierre Grégoire Labiche de 181; 184; 186 – 190
Rempnoux, Deacon 183
Revolutionary Tribunal 78
– & Rue Cassette nuns 90
Robespierre Maxmilian 3; 5; 6; 194
– arrest of 78
– dismissal of 'Liberty' service at Notre Dame 80
– & Legislative Assembly 23
– & Montagnards 77
– & service to 'supreme being' (June 8, 1794) 81
Rochefoucauld, La (family) 11; 12
Rochefoucauld, François

Joseph La (Bishop of
   Beauvais) 31
— will of 31 – 32
Rochefoucauld, Pierre Louis
   de La (Bishop of Saintes)
   31; 197
Rochefort
— authorities summon doctors
   193
— *Bonhomme-Richard* (boat
   prison) 184
— *Le Borée* (boat prison) 184
— Capuchin Friary (prison) 184
— Saint Maurice Prison 183
Rocher, Pierre Guerin du 36
Rocquard, Mother Superior
   Marie Anastasie 125
Royer, Marc-Louis, Curé of
   Saint Jean-en Grève 45;
   46; 47
— first to accept death for his
   conscience 48;
Rose, Abbé 32
Roulhac, Abbé Antoine 187
Rousseau Jean Jacques 1; 5; 18
Roux, Abbé 30
Rue Cassette nuns 90 – 104
— gain safety at Convent of the
   English Nuns 104
Rutan, Marguerite 117
— execution 118
Sacramentines at Bollène 124;
   125
Saint-Firmin (seminary turned
   Prison) 66; 202
Sainte Geneviève (section &
   ward) 88
Saint Germain des Prés
   (religious hous turned
   prison) 36
— home to scholars 36
Saint-James, Abbé Pierre de 36
Saint-Just (friend of

Robespierre) 81
Saint Nicolas du Chardonnet
   (seminary) 35
Sainte Pélagie (women's
   prison) 87
Saint Sulpice (seminary) 29; 33
Salamon, Mgr de 37 – 38;
— account of confinement &
   slaughter at Abbaye 42;
   44 – 45; 47; 51
— & the statutes of the Liberty-
   Equality oath 50
— *Memoires* 51
Salins, Abbé de 61
Sandrock 173
— account of party on *La
   Gloire* 173 – 174
Scellier, Toussaint Gabriel 157
Sicard, Abbé Roch Ambroise
   42; 43; 44
Sieyès, Abbé 3
Simon, Louis Benoît 48 – 49
Social Contract, The 1
Soiron, Sisters Catherine &
   Thérèse 140
Sorel, Alexandre
— *Couvent des Carmes, Les* 53
— grounds for arrest of
   Leclercq & Istève 53
Soyecourt, Camille de 86; 199
— interrogation 88
— lodges complaint against
   confiscation of papers 87
— release 89
States General 17;
— *May 5, 1789* 1; 2
Talleyrand-Périgord, Charles
   Maurice de (Bishop of
   Autun) 7; 19
— & 1791 Consecrations 22
Terror, Reign of (March 10,
   1793 – July 27, 1794) 78
Third Estate 1; 19

Thouret, Sister Anne 137
– ill-treatment at the
    Conciergerie 155
Tisserand, Sister Anne
    Catherine 118
Torné, Pierre Anastase (Bishop
    of Cher) 107
Tournai (defeat) 25
Treilhard, Jean Baptiste 8 – 9;
    10; 12; 16
Trézel, Sister Gabrielle 138
Vaillot, Marie Anne 116
– death by firing squad 117
Vailly, P F J 172
Vienne, Bishop of 15
Villette, Jean Antoine Joseph
    de 66
Violette, Jean Paul 62
Viot (State Prosecutor at

Orange) 128
Vitasse, Sister Angélique
– account of interrogation
    90 – 100
Voltaire 18
Vovelle, Michel 23
Wallon, Henri
– on Jean Baptise Carrier 165
Walter, Gérard 42; 64
– on the payment given to
    those who carried out the
    massacre 51 – 52
– on Saint Firmin massacre 71
– on tribunal at the Carmes 62
Washington (boat)
– deaths on boad 193ff
What is the Third Estate?... 3
Ysabeau, Claude Alexandre
    180